THE EAST END

As the fashionable riverside restaurants multiply, the prosperous young move into Wapping and Spitalfields, and the shining office blocks of the new Docklands spread south towards the Millennium Dome, the words 'East End' begin to have a different ring. For centuries the East End has been synonymous with poverty and sweated labour, with Cockney solidarity and popular protest. The poverty is still there but now, once again, east London is beginning to reshape itself.

Alan Palmer takes us back through four centuries of life in this great melting-pot which was once the very centre of Empire trade. People as well as goods have flowed in and out of it, from the Huguenot weavers of the seventeenth century to the Indians, Pakistanis and Bangladeshis of today. Its story is one of extremes – of small deprived streets and grand Hawksmoor churches, of great social campaigners like George Lansbury and out-and-out criminals like the Krays. This fascinating book, with an introduction by London's great chronicler Peter Ackroyd, captures the spirit of the East End and its people, of those who have left their mark on it and those whose lives were marked by it for ever.

Alan Palmer grew up on the fringes of east London and remembers it in the 1930s and 1940s. He was a schoolmaster in north London for nearly twenty years. He has written more than thirty books including *The Decline and Fall of the Ottoman Empire, Dictionary of the British Empire and Commonwealth* and *Victory 1918*. He was elected a Fellow of the Royal Society of Literature in 1980.

THE EAST END

Four Centuries of London Life

With an introduction by
PETER ACKROYD

ALAN PALMER

JOHN MURRAY
Albemarle Street, London

Text © Alan Palmer 1989, 2000
Introduction © Peter Ackroyd 2000

First published in 1989

Reissued in paperback as a revised edition in 2000
by John Murray (Publishers) Ltd,
50 Albemarle Street, London W1X 4BD

A catalogue record for this book is available from the British Library

ISBN 0-7195-5666 X

Typeset in Photina

Printed and bound in Great Britain by The University Press, Cambridge

Contents

CONTENTS

Illustrations

(between pages 108 and 109)

The author and publisher wish to thank the following for permission to reproduce illustrations: London Borough of Tower Hamlets Local History Library 6, 7, 8, 9, 10, 13, 16, 17, 22, 23, 25; Hulton Picture Library 3, 4, 5, 11, 12, 18, 19, 20, 28, 29; London Borough of Newham, Local Studies Library 21; The Museum of London 15, 26, 27, 30; Greater London Photograph Library 1, 14; Miss Margaret MacDonald 2.

THE EAST END

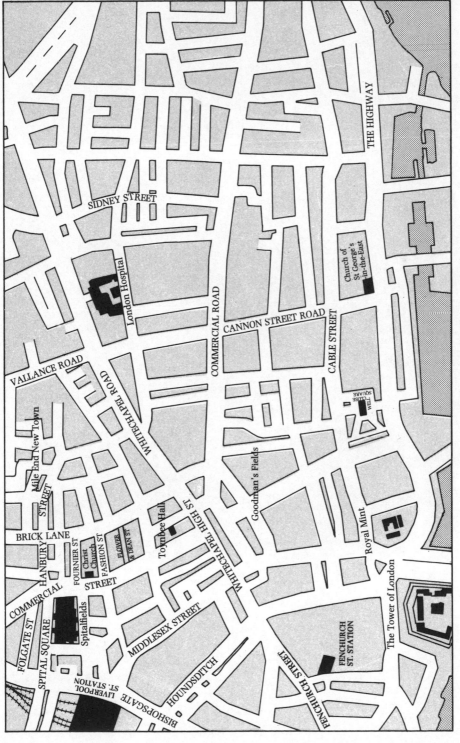

THE HEART OF THE EAST END

Introduction

THE East End of London has been separated from the rest of the city for far longer than the conventional historical division: it lies upon a strip of gravel separate from those others called the Flood Plain gravels which emerged at the time of the last glacial eruption. Whether this longevity has played any part in creating the unique atmosphere of east London is open to question, perhaps, but the symbolic importance of west and east cannot be discounted in any attempt to understand the particular associations and connections with which the East End has been burdened over the centuries. The Roman burials of London, some of them in the very precincts of what is now the East End, are characteristically laid out with their heads to the west – suggesting in the process that the western quadrant of the heavens embodies more glory or more harmony.

Certainly from the earliest periods of London history the eastern side – defined differently, of course, as the city grew – has enjoyed a less enviable reputation than that of the west. Archaeological evidence suggests that the invading Saxons of the fifth and sixth centuries settled to the west of the river Walbrook, while the now demoralised or at least defeated Romano-British citizens dwelled upon the east bank. The records of early medieval London suggest the same patterns of habitation, and from the thirteenth century the eastern end was regarded as the site for the poorer or less fashionable quarters of the city. This development was anticipated and reinforced by the building of Westminster in the eleventh century, whereby the courtly and diplomatic functions of London were consolidated in the more wealthy and fashionable regions of the west.

The city then moved steadily and ineluctably forward in that direction. When Nash developed Regent Street he divided west from east in a smaller but no less decisive manner. The Strand has received more tributes than Mare Street in Hackney, while the reputations of Kensington or Chelsea have not suffered the same depredations as those of Bethnal Green or Shoreditch. There was also a further anomaly which, in this excellent study, Alan Palmer fully describes. He explains how the early domination of the Church in the manors of Hackney and of Stepney meant that the suburbs of London were unable to spread in that direction, so impeding the development of the city in its eastern portion. These ancient estates were also responsible for an additional restriction – copyholders were unable to lease their land for more than thirty-one years, on pain of forfeiture. As a result land was relatively inexpensive, but this restriction also led to short-term speculation and cheaply produced housing. The straggling and confused state of the East End, as both Stow and Defoe noted, was permitted precisely because there was no sense or understanding of long-term development. Houses and shops and work-shops were run up by individuals with an eye only on short-term profit, which in itself accounts for the 'piecemeal' appearance of the area in the centuries before the Blitz of 1940. There was another consequence. The planning of squares and estates in the western areas could continue on the secure basis of long-term leases – that is essentially the reason for the grand homogeneity of many prosperous areas – but the possibility of planning and building for the long term also meant, crucially, that the poor could systematically be excluded. In the East End, in contrast, it was inevitable and perhaps necessary that as many cheap plots as possible should be exploited in the pursuit of quantity rather than quality.

So from the earliest times the East End has been associated with the great blight of London poverty. It became the home of industrial workers employed in the 'stink industries' which grew up around the purlieus of the Lea, just as at a later date it was to be the abode and refuge of those thousands of dock labourers who were employed – if at all – on short time. The 'sweated' industries of the cloth-workers and the silk-workers seemed to have their natural home in the East End, while on the poverty map of Charles Booth the areas of Shadwell, Limehouse and White-chapel contained the highest proportion of that blue shading which denoted 'Very poor, casual. Chronic want.'

Just as the East End has characteristically been the home of manual labourers so too, in trading terms, it has represented wholesale rather than retail. The same pattern of deprivation has continued well into the twentieth century, where the decline in manufacturing has not been bal-anced by any increase in what we have come to know as the 'service' sector. The conditions in some of the housing estates in the East End bor-oughs are worse than anything elsewhere in London, and as bad as any-thing in England. Other statistics, culled from other ages, might be introduced here to suggest the practical effects and consequences of this endemic poverty: in the nineteenth century there were far more cases of fever and consumption mortally affecting the older part of the population than in any other region of the capital while, in the twentieth century, it has been reported that there are three hundred per cent more examples of nervous breakdown.

Yet in many respects, as Mr Palmer suggests at the end of his fascinat-ing and exhaustive account, the East End also remains 'a microcosm of London's past'. It may surprise many to be informed, or reminded, that the great glory of London theatre began in Shoreditch with the erection of two playhouses known as The Curtain and The Theatre. It is surmised that Shakespeare performed in both establishments and they in turn were the forerunners of the tea-gardens, penny gaffs and music-halls which rendered the East End as famous in song and drama as it was notorious in social surveys and public prints. There has in fact always been a cheerfulness and a gaiety associated with the citizens of these areas. Whether they are true 'Cockneys' is of course open to territorial doubt, but the verve and energy of East Enders were as evident in the music-hall songs of Wilton's in Wellclose Square or the 'Brit' in Hoxton High Street as they are now in the dialogue or confrontations of the television series *EastEnders*.

The region is also representative of a general London spirit in the sense that it has been the home, or haven, of religious dissent and of political radicalism. The mantle of Wesley and his crusade covers the areas of Spitalfields and Wapping, in particular, but the East End has always been marked out by those groups of radical artisans espousing millennarian (and generally 'levelling') beliefs. The Ancient Deists of Hoxton, who believed with William Blake that they might converse with angels, were joined by Ranters, Muggletonians, Anabaptists, Fifth Monarchy men and Quakers – all of them devotees of a peculiarly vivid spirituality that springs from the very conditions of the eastern region. In the seventeenth and eighteenth centuries religious dissent was accompanied by a sense of grievance and exclusion so strong that it also acted as a form of political dissent. Members of the London Corresponding Society and, at a later date, the Chartists met in the 'mug houses' and public houses of the east in order to toast their revolutionary causes.

There is in fact an especial atmosphere in the area which seems to encourage an anti-authoritarian spirit. Mr Palmer notes the presence of anarchist groups among nineteenth-century Russian and German immigrants, while the whole political ethic of the East End was in the first decades of the twentieth century dominated by the 'municipal socialism' of that great East End hero, George Lansbury. There is also a fine tradition of trade unionism in this most deprived of areas – the Bryant and May 'matchgirls' strike of 1888 and the dockers' strike for a 'tanner' in the succeeding year provide a splendid example of solidarity and communality in the face of bad or venal management. But the struggles for recognition and decency did not end at that point. When Sylvia Pankhurst set up her headquarters for the suffragettes in the Old Ford Road she declared that 'I regard the rousing of the East End as of utmost importance . . . The creation of a women's movement in that great abyss of poverty would be a call to the rise of similar movements in all parts of the country.' Here the East End becomes a beacon of dissent and perhaps even of insurrection. And why should it not be so? That area which has suffered most from the social and political conditions of a thousand years is the one most likely to engender rebels and dissenters within its very centre.

The East End is a 'microcosm' of London, also, since many generations of immigrants have steadily and permanently altered its nature. The history of London is the history of its immigrants, since so large and so voracious a city requires a continual supply of new skills and new trades – indeed, new people – to maintain its energy and sustain its momentum. It is said that in other cities and towns in England it requires a residence of many years before a new arrival is accepted; in London the process takes as many months. Anyone living in the East End immediately becomes, almost by osmosis, an East Ender. This may not necessarily be a consequence of the supposed 'openness' and 'hospitality' beloved of Cockney enthusiasts – it has to be recalled that Mosley recruited some of his most vociferous supporters from the East End, and that racial attacks were once common in the area – but, rather that, to suffer the conditions of the East End is to join a long line of suffering. Mr Palmer charts the flow-lines of immigration from Europe and from the Indian subcontinent. Huguenot weavers were followed by Jews, who were in turn succeeded by émigrés from Bangladesh. By one of those curious features of London's topography – what may almost be called a topographical imperative – these bands of immigrants have over the centuries settled and worked in the same place. A chapel can become a synagogue, and then a mosque, the same edifice guarding in turn the same backrooms and the same 'sweat shops' where eighteenth-century weavers once plied their looms and where now Bangladeshi women piece together saris and dresses.

Yet this concentration of foreign workers has in turn helped to create the identity of the East End as somehow an alien and mysterious territory. The location of Chinese immigrants in the area of Pennyfields, by Limehouse, offers a significant and striking case of altered perceptions. There were not very many of them, and they were not noticeably less well behaved than any other group of Londoners, but the image of 'Chinatown' with its lascars and its opium dens swiftly became associated with the identity of the East End. This influx of apparently mysterious people also served to reinforce the other territorial myth of the area – because it lay in the east, it became associated in the general consciousness with the blight of the greater East, the empires of Russia and Turkey. 'The Eastern Question' was one of the insoluble dilemmas of the nineteenth century and, by a strange osmosis, the East End became associated with that menace.

The threat came also in the shape of sickness and death; the smoke and the smell of the wind from the east were thought to be harbingers of disease, while the incidence of cholera and other fatal contagions was

abnormally high in the poorer districts of these deprived neighbour-
hoods. 'All smell is disease,' Ernest Chadwick once declared, and it was
apparent to many Londoners that the peculiar noisomeness of the trades
and factories situated in the east threatened a more general fatality. The
problem then could only be compounded; as soon as the inhabitants of
the east grew affluent, they moved out. The clerks of the nineteenth
century, for example, took advantage of the burgeoning transport system
to migrate to more salubrious areas some miles away. The result was that
only the poor remained, their numbers growing larger as their fate
became more desperate. That in turn established a sense of separation
and of grievance which has not even now been dissipated. East Enders
were known to be fiercely loyal and protective of their areas – even before
the worst days of the Blitz, evacuated women and children returned to
their homes in Poplar and in Limehouse, in Hackney and in Bow – but
this loyalty was in part an act of desperation.

So the East End, in a phrase, became the harbour of the poor. Out of
that poverty sprang reports of evil and immorality, of savagery and
unnamed vice. It was in the middle of the nineteenth century that this
salacious and somewhat inaccurate image of the East End first began to
be disseminated. There are some who blame it upon De Quincey who, in
his account of the Ratcliffe Highway murders of 1812, entitled 'On
Murder, Considered as One of the Fine Arts', apostrophised the area as
one of the 'most chaotic' and 'a most dangerous quarter', a 'perilous
region' replete with 'manifold ruffianism'. The impression was taken up
by writers as diverse as Dickens and Wilde, Pierce Egan and Arthur
Conan Doyle, but the defining sensation which forever marked the East
End was of course the series of murders ascribed to 'Jack the Ripper'. Mr
Palmer makes it clear that, contrary to popular belief, the habits and conditions of the region had been thoroughly examined and publicised long
before those notorious murders but there is no doubt that the scale of the
sudden and brutal killings effectively marked out the area as one of
incomparable violence and depravity. The fact that the killer was never
captured, and that there has as a result been endless fascinated speculation about his (or her) identity, only seemed to confirm the impression
that the bloodshed was almost created by the mean streets themselves –
that the East End was the true 'Ripper'.

And so in the late nineteenth and early twentieth century an out-
pouring of books emphasised the horror and darkness which were to be
found there – *The Bitter Cry of Outcast London*, *The People of the Abyss*,
Ragged London, and so forth. Yet if the darkness of the East End has been
continually advanced as the true nature of its condition then, in Mr
Palmer's phrase, it is only acting once more as a 'microcosm of London's
past'. London has always been a dark city because it has been built upon

the imperatives of commerce and of trade; for two thousand years it has been established upon the power of money, and the East End itself has been both a casualty and a victim of that process. It has attracted the poor, and the unemployed, and the immigrant, before crushing them in its wake, leaving a dark stain which can be seen everywhere in the east. On the same page as Charles Booth's description of nineteenth-century Whitechapel there are two separate pictures – one is of the tables of the poor, 'fairly black' with swarms of flies, while the other depicts the streets outside where, at the level of the hip, 'is a broad dirty mark, showing where the men and lads are in the constant habit of standing'. These are the true shadows of the East End – the shadow of disease and the shadow of torpor, together with the shadows of the outcast and the dispossessed. Now the great churches of Hawksmoor are challenged by the glittering towers of Docklands. This is perhaps a moment of transition, when the darkness of the area will be abolished and the shadowy surface of the Thames renewed, but those who have known and loved the East End in all its aspects may be assured that its history is too strong and too potent ever to be removed. This book is an essential part of a continual process of retrieval and understanding.

PETER ACKROYD
London, 1999

Preface

EVERYONE knows the East End, at least as a generalised concept. A popular television series, together with media coverage of the building boom in Docklands, keeps it firmly in the public eye; and over the last hundred years no part of London has remained so consistently newsworthy. But the whole area between the City and metropolitan Essex is rich in a history which is of national significance rather than merely of local curiosity. My principal aim in writing this book has been to sketch in the details of much of this colourful past, while relating what was happening in the East End to the rise and fall of London as an imperial city.

Although everyone may think that they know the East End, to pinpoint it on a map is harder. When Jack London, the American novelist, came to England in 1902 he complained that 'Thomas Cook and Son, path-finders and trail-clearers, living sign-posts to all the World, ... knew not the way to the East End'; and when at last he took a hansom there, the cabby put him down at Stepney station 'as the one familiar spot he had ever heard of in all that wilderness'. Today's American visitor would fare better: driverless coaches from a red and blue train-set carry tourists down to the southern tip of the Isle of Dogs in fourteen minutes, eight times every hour; and, from the raised tracks of the Docklands Light Railway (DLR), the changing scene of Stepney, Limehouse and Poplar opens up like a fairground peepshow. Or so it seems. But the East End is something greater than a panoramic view from a DLR carriage window. Well north of the tracks, there are still alleys as shabby as in Jack London's time; and many East Enders prefer to seek fresh air for their lungs in Victoria Park rather than from the vast building sites along the Thames. Confusion over the precise borders of the East End is as great as ever: newspapers have, before now, annexed to it Barkingside, Romford and Upminster, which is like extending the West End to Heathrow or to Ruislip. This book, however, confines the East End within traditional limits – the old Inner London Boroughs of Hackney and Tower Hamlets, together with the western fringe areas of Hoxton and Shoreditch and the dockland overflow into West Ham and East Ham during the nineteenth and twentieth centuries.

Perhaps I may claim to be an East Ender by proxy. I was born and spent my childhood in Ilford, a few miles across the old Essex border. But I used often to travel up to Liverpool Street, Aldgate and Fenchurch

Street; a 101 bus ride from Manor Park down to the Woolwich Ferry
was a great delight, surpassed only by a river trip. The East End of the
1930s comes vividly to mind: the smell compounded of breweries, railway
smoke, sweet factories and soap works; the sound of trams and ships'
sirens; the sight of brightly coloured funnels and mastheads, a towering
backcloth behind cobbled streets of terraced houses. I remember looking
down from the top deck of a tram on Fascist rowdies as they jostled
their way up Mile End Road; and I sense once again the excitement of
wondering how the *Mauretania* would edge her way unscathed into King
George V Dock on that August evening just before the Second World
War. Like so many thousands of other Londoners, I remember, too, a
Saturday afternoon thirteen months later, shortly before my fourteenth
birthday. I was returning with my father from Barking Park and, at the
bus-stop outside Ilford station, we watched massed formations of Heinkels
and Dorniers heading up river, as ominously impressive as in a ceremonial
fly-past.

Around us, in my boyhood, were many relatives and friends who had
moved out from east London; a few continued to work there. My mother's
father had come to London from Devon to a desk job at the British &
Foreign Wharf in 1872; he was still there half a century later. After his
retirement he took me to visit the Wharf in 1934 and I recall clearly the
unloading of casks of wine from a ship newly in from Bordeaux. My
grandfather had tales of the great Dock Strike and the building of Tower
Bridge. His brother, born before the Crimean War and outlasting Hitler's,
worked in Wapping while the traditional excursion to Fairlop Fair was
still a great occasion each summer; he was already a regular worshipper
at St Anne's, Limehouse, when Blomfield gave the church its late Victorian face-lift. From my father, too, I learnt much about the East End,
for he taught for many years at evening classes, and I remember going
with him to social events in Stepney in those last two winters of peace.

During 1987–8, and again in recent months, I have revisited many
parts of the East End, sometimes as puzzled as Rip van Winkle by what I
have found – that Aldgate subway rabbit warren, for example, from
which I have yet to emerge at the exit I had intended. On contemplating
those rapidly changing acres of Docklands and Spitalfields, I decided not
to seek guidance by briefings from interested parties but to go around
alone, for the most part by bus or on foot, looking and listening. Everyone
to whom I talked was friendly and communicative. Subsequently I supplemented what I had heard and seen with a perusal of the local press.

Anyone reading this book will soon see the heavy debt which I owe
to the numerous specialist studies and articles cited in 'Notes on Sources'.
In particular it has been my good fortune to have had the opportunity
of reading the back numbers of three excellent periodicals: *East London*

Papers; *East London Record*; and *The London Journal*. William Fishman's fascinating and evocative *East End 1888* appeared after my book had gone to the printers; but, like everyone interested in late Victorian and Edwardian London, I have profited much from the vivid narrative and erudition of Professor Fishman's earlier writings.

It is a pleasure to acknowledge gratefully the patient help I received in preparing the original edition of this book from the staff of the local history section at Tower Hamlets Central Library, Bancroft Road, particularly Mr Chris Lloyd. I would also like to thank, for their kind assistance in many different ways, Mr M. Bloch at the Newham Local Studies Library in Water Lane, Stratford, and the staffs of the Museum of London, the Public Record Office at Kew, the London Library, the Hulton Picture Library, and the Bodleian Library, Oxford, particularly Mrs Helen Rogers. At John Murray Ltd I have profited from the good counsel of Duncan McAra, Roger Hudson and their successors, and I am indebted to Dorothy Moir for designing the original book and jacket. Finally, I am extremely grateful to Mr Peter Ackroyd for the interesting and evocative Introduction he has written for the second edition of *The East End*.

I finished revising this book on the third anniversary of the funeral of my dear wife, Veronica, who had spent her childhood in a Forest Gate vicarage and received her schooling at the Ursuline Convent in Upton Lane. She compiled the original index, which I shall extend for this edition. Veronica's memories of east London were of great help when, in 1988, we discussed the book as I wrote it, chapter by chapter, and I sorely miss her comments and assistance. Although we moved out to Oxfordshire thirty years ago, Veronica always saw herself as a Londoner, delighting in familiar sights and sounds whenever we went 'up to town'. Like me, she would I am sure have welcomed the imminent return to London of corporate self-government, with its promise of cohesion and a renewed sense of purpose for a metropolis which remains, potentially, as fine and fair a city as any in the world.

ALAN PALMER
Woodstock, Oxfordshire
April 1999

1

Cream and Good Cherries

F ROM the overhead walkway of Tower Bridge the view westwards is impressive. Along the north shore world-familiar landmarks – the Tower itself, the Custom House and old Billingsgate – brood beside the Upper Pool. A tidal current laps HMS *Belfast*, the Royal Navy's largest cruiser, moored permanently in midstream. Half a mile up river London Bridge cuts the arc of the Thames in three-spanned elegance, a press of traffic nudging its way from the City to the Borough over concrete cantilevers. To the south skeletal brickwork among arched roads and railway viaducts threatens to create a regenerate suburb in historic Southwark. To the north stands the Monument, a 202-foot column of Portland stone to 'preserve the memory' of the Great Fire. 'Horrid to be so monstrous a way up in the air, so far above London and its spires,' Boswell complained in 1762 after climbing to its balcony. But that was another London, its skyline refined by the genius of Wren. In today's City the finance houses shoot up three times as high as the Monument; both column and spires are dwarfed by the clustered towers of capitalism around them.

Look eastwards from the walkway and the panorama is, as yet, less compelling on the eye. On the left bank of the river the severely modern Tower Hotel seems to prop up the World Trade Centre like a book-end; small boats sidle towards the lock of St Katharine's yachting marina while, behind them, waterside Wapping has a mock-warehouse residential frontage, backed by the brick fortress of News International. The Thames flows on towards the sea, with the Lower Pool swinging southwards into Limehouse Reach and then around the peninsula facing Greenwich to the mouth of the River Lea and the pivotal gates of the flood-control barrier between Silvertown and Woolwich, seven miles by water from Tower Bridge. This sweep of river is visible from the walkway, even on a hazy day; so, too, on the right bank is the wooded hump of Shooters Hill and the high ground along the old route to Dover. But north of the Thames the land has long been featureless: mud-flats drained of sludge and dyked against the floods of a high tide. Now empty docks shine as oblongs of artificial lake, between embanked roads and railways; a few quayside cranes, once grouped like a line of gibbets, point skywards in isolation, mere museum-pieces dwarfed by the Canada Square Tower, the 800-foot monolith that dominates the Isle of Dogs. Among this architectural bric-à-brac the casual eye discerns the slim spire of St Paul's, Shadwell, and the hollow lantern of a Hawksmoor church, still solidly serene. But it is hard to focus on particular buildings: yesterday's packing-case flats spatter the bend of the river; tomorrow's Metropolitan Water City falls into shape, a fast-changing concrete outline, spectral and speculative.

Half a century ago the panorama, away from the riverside itself, was dominated by a mass of tiled roofs, bluish grey or black, with pert, reddish clusters of chimneys half-hidden by a parapet of stonework continuous along a terrace. Here and there an austere housing barracks would throw into shadow the narrow courtways creeping between two-up-two-down homes in these back-to-back streets. But that was the scene before it was changed by the bombing and rocket onslaught in the Second World War. Even today gaps in the streets remain visible from a distance, as though the ground was pock-marked; and often, around Stepney Green or in Poplar, it is possible to trace in these empty spaces a line of house foundations. For archaeologists of the recent past these are the tragic artefacts of a war which imposed slum clearance brutally on the working class.

Purists contend that the heart of east London lies, not along the waterfront of the Lower Pool, but around Spitalfields, almost a mile north of the river. From these hugger-mugger alleys, on the fringe of the City, the silkweaving industry spread northwards and eastwards, attracting wave after wave of immigrants to a craft which promised a prosperity rarely attained by those who were apprenticed to its skills. Spitalfields does indeed remain quintessentially East End in character, even if City development trespasses across Bishopsgate. From Spital Square down to Whitechapel drab streets are boisterous with the competitive repartee of small trading, as market-stalls attract eagle-eyed bargain hunters from Britain and overseas. It is here that tourists thrill to a peculiar intimacy which cherishes a folk myth of murder. The visitor feels close to the East End of sinister legend; imaginative perception senses the dank miasma of a pea-souper, with trams pinioned in the murk, a muted trumpeting from river craft, and the muffled monotony of fog signals detonated along the railway tracks.

But this gas-lit nursery of crime and mayhem belongs to relatively modern times, when Whitechapel and Bethnal Green were the poorest quarters of an imperial metropolis. There was an 'east end' to London long before mid-Victorian concern over sweated labour and the more noxious aspects of an industrial revolution thrust the area into a collective identity which merited the use of initial capital letters.

No government would be so rash as to give the East End local administrative unity, not least because no one can draw its boundaries with definitive precision on a map. But inevitably the districts between Aldgate, Shoreditch and the River Lea have at times been associated with each other in convenient cohesion. When in 1965 Bethnal Green, Poplar and Stepney united to form the London Borough of Tower Hamlets, they were reviving after a lapse of half a century a name rich with past associations. Originally it had a military connotation, for under Mary Tudor, Elizabeth I and James I the men of the villages east of the City were required to fulfil militia duties when called out by the Lieutenant-Governor of the Tower of London. But there remains some confusion over what districts were liable to render this service; in 1720 the great antiquary John Strype – rector of Leyton for an improbable sixty-eight years – listed as many as twenty-one Tower Hamlets, over an area far larger than the modern London Borough, from prosperous Hackney village in the north down to riverside settlements as far east as Blackwall and the Middlesex county boundary along the Lea. Strype's list covers the East End at its fullest extent, until in the present century it overspilt into metropolitan Essex.

In one sense, however, the name Tower Hamlets distorts history. No doubt to the Tudors and early Stuarts it seemed as if the palace-fortress built beyond London's walls by Norman kings to awe a conquered people continued to overshadow the lives of their subjects, just as the great keep of the Bastille stood guard over Paris. Yet, apart from the militia duties imposed in the sixteenth century, the Tower of London made little mark on the day-to-day existence of the folk who lived east of the City. For them, throughout the Middle Ages and the earliest years of Reformation, the dominant influence was not some secular authority but their greatest landowner, the Church.

Half a mile inland from the Thames, at the top curve of Limehouse Reach, is a bluff of slightly higher ground where there rises, quiet and secluded in its graveyard, the Perpendicular tower of St Dunstan & All Saints, Stepney. Historically no building has a better claim to be the heart of the East End, for this church – basically fifteenth-century, with a facelift in the 1870s – stands on the site of the earliest Christian settlement above the marshlands east of London. Today's worshippers may still see, on the east wall behind the altar, a carving of the crucifixion, Saxon in origin and going back a thousand years, to the time when it is said that the formidable Dunstan of Glastonbury, in his brief months as Bishop of London, replaced the wooden fabric of All the Saints, Stebeunhithe, with good solid stonework. For four centuries this building, which incorporated Dunstan's name in its dedication after he was canonised in 1029, was mother church for all Middlesex between the River Lea and the Tower, a huge ecclesiastical district divided by the beginning of the twentieth century into no less than sixty-six parishes. Most of this land had a further link with Dunstan and his successors, for from Saxon times until the 1550s the Bishops of London were Lords of the Manor of Stepney, with their principal hall a hunting lodge in Bethnal Green to the north of the lane to Old Ford. The woodland around the hall brought good profits to the See of London from the Domesday survey down to the early years of Henry VIII; aldermen and sheriffs were entertained at Bethnal Green with ordered magnificence by a succession of Church dignitaries; and there was stag-hunting on the higher ground from Hackney to the Lea. The bishops, however, recognised their social responsibilities, making certain, for example, that the leper hospital in the wasteland of Mile End was efficiently run. Like other seignorial landlords in southern England, by the early fifteenth century they had sold or leased out to farmers many of the broad, open fields characteristic of their estate. The Dean and Chapter of St Paul's Cathedral acquired some 15 acres around Shadwell, much of it marshland when it was granted to them by a thirteenth-century bishop. But while that sound Protestant, Bishop Nicholas Ridley, felt obliged to surrender to the Crown what remained of the episcopal demesne in Stepney, the Dean and Chapter held on to their property tenaciously, right into the twentieth century. Today the London Chest Hospital stands on the site of the bishops' hall, in a road off Bishop's Way and named after Edmund Bonner, the last manorial prelate.

Evocative street-names also recall vanished abbeys, priories and convents around the fringe of Stepney Manor. Several clustered close to the eastern wall of the City, such as the Minoresses of the Abbey of St Clare, whose nunnery at Aldgate gave its name, in corrupted form, to the Minories. No trace remains of the largest and most prosperous of the abbeys, Holy Trinity Priory, Aldgate, which owned a manor in Bromley, but Spital Square and Spital Yard cover the precincts of an Augustinian house established while Richard I was crusading in the Holy Land and dedicated to St Mary. By 1235 this hospital of Augustinian canons was so well known that the house was refounded as the Priory of St Mary Spital, its surrounding meadows called Spitalfields long after the last canons surrendered their property to Henry VIII.

Another hospital for the poor survived the dissolution of the monasteries largely because for centuries it had enjoyed royal protection as a dowry of the queens of England; St Katharine-by-the-Tower was set up by the wife of King Stephen on 13 acres to the east of the forbidding fortress, its lands and tenants acquiring special trading privileges and remaining outside the jurisdiction of either the City or the Bishop of London. Some 500 yards to the north and only slightly farther south-east of the 'Poor Clares' was the abbey of St Mary Graces, founded by Edward III in 1350; briefly it was known as 'Eastminster', as if to challenge the primacy of London's famous royal abbey, three miles downstream. But, while Westminster was a Benedictine house, the monks of St Mary Graces were Cistercians, and their main achievement was to use their agricultural skills to drain the alluvial deposits on lands of the abbey's manor in Poplar, seeking to turn them into rich pasture. Some of the Church lands were held by more distant religious houses – even the Augustinian abbey of St Osyth, sixty miles away on the Essex coast – and that mighty crusading military order, the Knights Templar, had a manor in Hackney and mills on the River Lea.

Closer at hand, the Cistercians across the Lea at Stratford Langthorne were pioneers at flood prevention in the marshes of West Ham and assumed responsibility for the Bow causeway, built on the orders of Henry I's queen after she had been accidentally 'well washed in the waters' of Old Ford on a journey to the great Benedictine nunnery at Barking, of which she became Abbess. South of Bow Bridge, at Bromley St Leonard, was a Benedictine convent, less prosperous than Barking although owning two water-mills along the Lea and, like several other religious houses, benefiting from the fisheries and osier beds of the river. Saint Leonard's was once a peaceful retreat house for royalty but there is little quiet in today's Priory Road and St Leonard's Street, which run parallel to the Blackwall Tunnel approach route; only street-names and a corner clump of churchyard rescue from oblivion the nunnery where Chaucer's Madame Eglantyne acquired her French, 'after the scole of Stratford atte Bowe'.

To linger in this way over a phantom past is tempting but unin-

structive; the predominance of Church land in what was to become
the East End has a historical significance more important than any
romanticised association of place-names. For the intrusion of monastic
property so close to the City cramped the development of suburbs, post-
poning the eastward spread of London until after the Crown dissolved
the monasteries and accepted the surrender by Bishop Ridley of the
diocesan manors. The villages in south-eastern Middlesex during the
later Middle Ages grew up with a parish church as their nucleus, Stepney
with St Dunstan's, Hackney (from about 1300) around St Augustine's,
and Whitechapel deriving its name from a small chapel of ease dedicated
to St Mary and achieving parochial status in the late thirteenth century.
Each community had small traders, operating free from the restrictive
practices imposed by guilds within the City itself. As soon as the Church
estates went up for sale in the mid-sixteenth century the eastern
approaches to London experienced the greatest land revolution they
had as yet known. Social climbers, from Court and City, scrambled for
advantage.

This new social order brought the fringe villages rapidly into London's
commercial life, not least because they still remained too far outside the
walls to fall within the monopolistic grasp of the livery companies or
other corporate authorities. Significantly the road from Essex across Bow
Bridge was paved at its western end through Whitechapel to Aldgate in
1542, just two years after the last abbey surrendered to the Crown.
Brewers, butchers, fruiterers, bakers and inn-keepers flourished; and so
did metalwork, the earliest of those 'nuisance trades' considered too
socially disruptive for crowded city streets. Already around Spitalfields
weavers were building up a textile industry; Protestant refugees, many
of them Dutch or Flemish, were introducing new skills. Not all good, true
English labourers welcomed their presence.

A clause in the Dissolution of the Lesser Religious Houses Act of 1536
stipulated that future owners or lessees should 'occupy yearly as much
of the same demesnes in ploughing and tillage of husbandry' as had the
monks or their farmers over the past two decades. So, to some extent
they did, at first. The great antiquarian John Stow, who lived near Aldgate
for over seventy years before he completed his *Survey of London* in 1598,
recounts what happened to the farmland now covered by Leman Street
and Prescott Street, off the Minories: he describes how land belonging to
the Poor Clares' nunnery – 'at the which farm I myself in my youth have
fetched many a halfpenny worth of milk … always hot from the kine' –
passed into the hands of Farmer Goodman, who kept thirty or forty cows
there, but whose son 'being heir to his father's purchase, let out the
ground for the grazing of horses, and then for garden-plots, and lived like
a gentleman thereby'. Stow's unfailing sense of right and wrong often

led him to denounce 'bad and greedy men of spoil': there were, for example, the brothers Owens who 'about the latter reign of Henry VIII' enclosed a field that had belonged to Holy Trinity Priory, Aldgate. There they built a gun-factory and attracted to the area 'divers others' who appear to have evicted 'poor bed-ridden people' from the 'homely cottages' where, before the dissolution, they had been comfortably maintained with 'charitable alms'. It is a familiar tale; the sad theme, varying in intensity, recurs many times during enterprising capitalism's onward march through the Tower Hamlets[1].

Poor Stow, out of humour with the 'scoffing, respectless and unthankful age' in which he wrote, anticipated gloomily the rapid spread of the 'continual building throughout' that he had seen in the past forty years; the lanes, stiles and hedgerows he knew would soon be gone, he feared. But Stow was unduly pessimistic. Not until the beginning of the following century did the houses go up where Goodman had kept his cows; the last acres of Goodman's Fields, long used as a place where woven cloth could be stretched to dry evenly, became building plots only when the first smuts of railway grime came to the district, with the opening of Fenchurch Street Station. Even in the 1660s, after the Civil War, Londoners had reason to be thankful that the property rights of the medieval Church had kept the countryside so near their walls.

For Samuel Pepys, who as Clerk of the King's Ships lived close to the Navy Office in the City, the fields and gardens beyond Bishopsgate and Aldgate held a promise of rural peace, little more than a mile from his home in Seething Lane. 'With my wife only to take the ayre, it being very warm and pleasant,' he wrote in his diary for 1664, on the second Saturday of June. 'To Bowe and Old Ford: and thence to Hackney. There light, and played at shuffle-board, eat cream and good cherries: and so with refreshment home.' This seven-mile excursion into the neighbouring countryside was popular with Londoners in Restoration England. John Stow would not have shared their delight; a century before there had been farms behind the white chapel of St Mary's, 'fair hedge rows of elm trees' where the market-stalls of Petticoat Lane now stand, and common land stretched northwards to the Bishop's hunting lodge at Bethnal Green. But tall elms still cast their islands of shadow over the quiet lanes off Mile End Common in Pepys's time and a windmill in Whitechapel would catch upriver gusts in its sails. There were, indeed, rubbish heaps on the road to Stepney and ribbon development had brought more cottages to the highway along which Will Kempe set out to dance his Morris to Norwich in the first February of the century; but there were good country smells as St Mary's, Bow, came in sight, for the village was dependent on unloading grain brought down the River Lea from Hertfordshire.

When Pepys reached the Lea he liked to turn northwards and seek the garden fragrance of Old Ford and Hackney, 'which I every day grow more and more in love with', as he wrote in midsummer in 1666. City worthies who did not wish to retire to the northern heights found the gentle slope up to Bethnal Green and Hackney acceptable and settled readily for an out-of-town country home within half an hour's ride of the Royal Exchange. Thus the hemp merchant, Sir William Rider, purchased Kirby Castle, an Elizabethan house facing westwards across Bethnal Green, within a month of Charles II's restoration to the throne and Pepys dined there in June 1663: 'A fine merry walk with the ladies alone after dinner in the garden; the greatest quantity of strawberrys I ever saw, and good,' he duly noted. Three years later, on the second night that the Great Fire raged through London, Pepys was back at Rider's mansion, hurrying there in his nightgown and trundling a borrowed cart filled with personal treasures, including the diary: he was not alone in making that journey eastwards from the City for everyone knew that, whatever way the flames might jump, the gentry's homes outside the walls lay safe in rural isolation. So quiet was Rider's garden that, on a June evening in 1667, the sound of distant gunfire could be heard at Bethnal Green and nowhere else in London; and it was from Sir William's servants that Pepys and the Navy Board, less than two miles away in Seething Lane, were alerted to the menace of a Dutch fleet in the Thames Estuary[2].

Yet, delightful though Pepys and his friends found the rural sur-roundings of Hackney and Old Ford, the eastern fringe of Middlesex as a whole was no arcadia in the later seventeenth century. There were workshops to service shipping along the reclaimed land beside the Thames and the outlying villages, overcrowded and lacking sanitation, were prone to epidemics. In 1603 the bubonic plague, which may have killed a fifth of the population of London, was said to have spread from Stepney, where 2228 deaths were reported, mostly among the families of seamen or those who serviced ships; and, although the different strain in the Great Plague of 1665 was first identified to the north-west of the City, it soon spread through Whitechapel and out to Bow and beyond. Even in plague years the good air of Hackney and Bethnal Green reputedly made them healthier places in which to live.

To Pepys the highway from Whitechapel across Mile End Common was a social demarcation line: cakes and ale and the delights of 'good refreshment' lay to the north, but to the south was all the bustle and industry of seamanship: houses of sea captains; homes of less dis-tinguished mariners; ropeyards and victualling stores to keep mer-chantmen and warships on the oceans for many months. In 1664, the year in which Pepys and his wife enjoyed the 'cream and good cherries' of Hackney, there were 14,185 households living in the Tower Hamlets: of these households 2482 lived in Whitechapel, 8292 in the riverside hamlets east of the Tower down to Blackwall and only 217 in Bethnal Green and 175 in Bow and Old Ford. The densest housing was in what Stow called 'the precinct of St Katharine', virtually in the shadow of the Tower, where there were forty households to an acre. By contrast there was an average of three acres to a household in Bethnal Green and five acres to one in Bow and Old Ford[3].

Later research pushes back in time this north-south social division across eastern Middlesex. Ships were built in Stepney parish in the fourteenth century, during the Hundred Years War, although not until the last decade of the following century, when Henry VII was encouraging overseas trade, did ship-repairing develop on a large scale. In Henry VIII's reign riverside hamlets expanded rapidly to meet the needs of seafarers. His ill-fated *Mary Rose* was fitted out at Blackwall, requiring the 'dykinge and castyne' of a special dock for shipwrights to work aboard her; and the *Henri Grace Dieu* was moored there, too, fifty-four mariners being boarded in Poplar to make sails for her[4]. When, late in Henry VIII's reign, the Dutch refugee Cornelius Vanderdelft completed draining Wapping marshes, a walled embankment was constructed along the waterside from Wapping itself through to Shadwell, where there were smithies and roperies. This 'Wapping Wall' was some 10 feet above the drained marshland and was kept in repair by those who lived in ramshackle wooden houses beside the river. A straighter highway, flanked in Stow's later years by rickety tenements certain of notoriety as soon as they went up, ran from St Katharine's to the south of St Dunstan's, Stepney, where a layer of reddish gravel beside a river landing-place had given the name Ratcliff (red cliff) to a thriving sea-trading community. The highway continued eastwards to Limehouse, the hamlet where lime burning served London's building trade since Edward III's reign, and on along a causeway, past the windswept empty fenland of the Isle of Dogs to the mouth of the Lea, at Blackwall, the most easterly riverside hamlet. All these villages, dependent on maritime initiative for their livelihood, were of constant concern to the Clerk of the King's Ships and there are many references to them in his diary.

'By coach to Captain Marshe's at Limehouse, to a home that hath been their ancestors for this 250 years, close by the limehouse which gives its name to the place', Pepys recorded on 19 October 1661; 'Here they have a design to get the King to hire a dock for the herring busses for herring fishing'. In December of the following year he was back at Limehouse to inspect the first two of these twin-masted broad-beamed smacks. For Pepys there was a succession of these professional visits to the riverside hamlets: to Whitehorse Lane, Stepney, and to Ratcliff for meetings of Trinity House, the guild of mariners of which Pepys was twice the Master; often to Ratcliff Cross Stairs to take a ferry across to Deptford, where King Charles's yacht was built, or to the royal dockyard at Woolwich, whose maladministration so perplexed him. On several occasions he went down to Blackwall where the East India Company had constructed the earliest of their fitting-out docks to shelter and prepare vessels for long voyages out to the Malay archipelago and the coast of Coromandel. Pepys was there in those mild January days of 1661 ('the rose bushes full of leaves') to admire the company's 'brave new merchantman' *Royal Oak*: she was, as he duly noted, wrecked four years later off the Scilly Isles, bound for Blackwall Reach from Bantam with a rich cargo from Java. In July 1664 he wrote warmly of the East India Company's fine storehouses and good dock, just as two months later he thought George Margett's ropeyard at Limehouse 'very fine'. He would travel down by coach or by water, sometimes coming by ferry from Greenwich to go on foot back along Wapping Wall and across Tower Hill into the City; we read of a hot Saturday in August 1663, spent 'in the King's service' at the dockyards south of the river when Pepys landed at Wapping and 'walked home, weary enough, walking over the stones'. Occasionally he gave detailed attention to technical skills: in February 1665, for example, he was at Limehouse to judge the effectiveness of the special stoves which, with their slow heat, made yarn waterproof; or he would visit Wapping to see draughtsmen at work on the plates from which the King's maps and charts were printed. He held the craftsmanship of the riverside hamlets in high esteem and, when he wanted a carved head shaped for his vial, it was to a marine carpenter in Wapping that he turned for service[5].

Already, however, there was a dark side to life along the north shore of Limehouse Reach and the Pool. The tenements in St Katharine's precinct and off the Highway teemed with vermin and smelt evilly. Sanitation – primitive enough in London as a whole – was virtually non-existent, for privileges said to date from the centuries of monastic rule allegedly exempted property owners from regulations which controlled buildings within the City. Almost inevitably, lodging houses for mariners seeking their next vessel or waiting for new sails and ropes became brothels; poor and irregular pay encouraged crime in a fast-growing community which multiplied four times over between the death of John Stow in 1605 and the death of Samuel Pepys in 1705. Locally brewed ale flowed readily to seamen and watermen in funds: a recent estimate suggests there were forty-four taverns for some 700 houses in mid-century Shadwell alone[6]. Moreover the craftsmen whom Pepys visited in Wapping were the gifted few among riverside labourers robustly defiant of authority. The sheriffs suspected that troublemakers found sanctuary amid the chandlers, bakers, shipwrights and seamen; and the Wapping mob was so easily swayed by the anti-papist demagoguery of the Duke of Monmouth's supporters that, in 1682, they figured prominently in the Earl of Shaftesbury's abortive plans for a Protestant coup. Seamen's wives from Wapping and Shadwell would shout abuse at Sir William Batten, the Surveyor of the Navy Board; and on at least one occasion the Captain-Commandant of His Majesty's Life Guards had to police Wapping with his troops to quell disturbances there – 'which', Pepys noted, 'is a thing of infinite disgrace to us'[7].

Perhaps Pepys – and the King's counsellors, for that matter – exaggerated the danger. Wapping was the home of London's ribald watermen, whose swift-moving wherries gave the Thames a taxi service. They were jealous of their rights, notoriously suspicious of any entrepreneur who might limit their trade by building a second bridge for London, and ready to demonstrate alongside seamen with a grievance. Written promises of payment rather than the chink of good money were enough to spark off mutinous protests. 'Upon Tower Hill saw about 300 or 400 seamen get together,' Pepys recorded six days before the first Christmas after the Great Fire 'and one standing upon a pile of bricks made his sign with his handkercher upon his stick, and called all the rest to him, and several shouts they gave. This made me afraid; so I got home as fast as I could.'

Over the following three centuries many others enjoying the cream and good cherries of comfortable living would catch a distant rumble of radical thunder from the East End streets and, like Mr Pepys, run for cover.

2

Suburbs – or Powder Kegs of Revolt?

B Y THE time of Pepys's death, in the second year of Queen Anne's reign, London had overtaken Paris as the most populous city in Europe. Some 600,000 people – one in ten of the population – lived in the capital and its outer fringe of villages, twenty times as many as in Bristol, the country's second largest town, and three times as many as a hundred years before. London, John Strype could write proudly in 1720, was 'the Metropolis and Glory of the Kingdom'; even those districts which the indefatigable antiquarian knew best, the hamlets east of the Tower, appeared to him to enjoy plenty, 'with wealth the crown of all'[1]. The early eighteenth century was an age of prosperous urban expansion and, with Chelsea and Marylebone creeping closer to the seat of sovereignty as satellites of Westminster, there was every reason to assume that the old manors of Hackney and Stepney, too, were becoming residential suburbs, serving the bankers and merchants of the City.

So at least it seemed to Strype who, for twenty-five years, would ride the three miles in from Leyton to preach regularly at Hackney parish church. And Daniel Defoe, in neighbouring Stoke Newington, was similarly impressed, even if concerned at the 'most straggling, confused manner' of London's growth. 'There is not anything more fine in their degree than most of the buildings this way,' Defoe commented in 1724; almost a hundred carriages 'are kept at this time' by prosperous merchants in Hackney and Clapton, he calculated. Within half a mile of Hackney church lived three recent Lord Mayors, two East India Company directors, several City liverymen and some rising lawyers. There, too, was the home of Richard Ryder, a linen-draper from Cheapside, whose law-student son Dudley noted down the high moments of Hackney life for 1715–16 in a diary which remained undeciphered until the eve of the Second World War. We read of gardens, bowling-greens, and coffee houses and of the daughters of gentlefolk in the finishing schools for which Hackney was famous from the reign of Charles II down to the Victorian reformers.

Dudley Ryder was to become Attorney-General and a Lord Chief Justice, but in 1715 he was only twenty-four, a social climber and an acutely self-conscious prig. His genteel Hackney had turned its back on the Thames and the Lea and looked towards Islington and the villages of London's northern heights. Only once in eighteen months did he take a trip on the Thames: he was rowed down to Greenwich from the Upper Pool by a waterman who surprised him by his Tory sentiments. There is none of the familiarity with the waterside that runs through Pepys, nor – more surprisingly – with the silk industry which was spreading along the roads Ryder followed back to his chambers in the Middle Temple. Except that from 1711 Hackney shared with Westminster and the City a regular threepenny postal service several times a day, Ryder could almost have been describing life in rural Surrey or Hertfordshire. Old Strype, whom Ryder heard preaching 'not politely, but tolerably good sense' from his Hackney pulpit, might list the village among his twenty-one Tower Hamlets, but those worthy citizens who kept their carriages off Mare Street and Dalston Lane knew better. Dudley Ryder chronicled the activities of a different community from the riverside folk of turbulent Wapping, the weavers packed into Spitalfields, or the newcomer labourers hoping for work in Ratcliff and Shadwell[2].

Over the eighteen months in which Ryder so meticulously entered up his diary, the master weavers of Spitalfields were still living comfortably in the wartime prosperity which flourished so long as government protection forbade imports from enemy France. The most successful of them were Huguenots who had escaped from religious persecution in France, some coming early in the seventeenth century but most after the revocation of the Edict of Nantes in 1685. The immigrants – many from Tours and Lyons – found a well-established silk weaving industry in London's East End, but they brought to it both an earnest, Calvinist sense of purpose and the perfection of new techniques: they showed how to give thin taffeta a glossy lustre and they supplied brocade encrusted with elegant floral patterns to delight a peacock society which preened itself in silks and satins. From Spitalfields, where there was already a thriving market for vegetables and poultry, the textile industry was reaching out northwards to Hoxton and Bethnal Green and eastwards through Whitechapel. Daniel Defoe remembered when Spitalfields Market was still 'a field of grass with cows feeding on it' but by 1724 he could only see 'numberless ranges of building' spread over an area almost as large as Hyde Park, 'all close built and well-inhabited'[3].

In Defoe's time Spitalfields and Whitechapel were therefore as compact a powder-keg of social unrest as Wapping. For while the more successful master weavers had sufficient capital to safeguard themselves against fluctuations of trade, there were too many journeymen apprentices earning such low wages that even a passing recession plunged them into poverty. With the ending of Marlborough's wars in 1713, cheap silk began to be smuggled in from France. More seriously, the industry was hit by a fashion for wearing printed calico which persisted through Queen Anne's reign despite ineffectual legislation, as early as 1700, to check importation of the cloth. Resentment at the way 'Ingy' (East India) nabobs flouted Parliament's protective measures came to a head in serious rioting during the hot summer days of June and July 1719 when a troop of Horse Guards was sent into Spitalfields, while reserves remained on the alert in the Tower. 'Shall Ingy calicos be worn while the poor weavers and their families perish?', ran a handbill distributed that summer; a woman wearing calico in the streets of London risked insult and even physical assault. The unrest died down with the coming of cooler weather, but when in the following spring East India Company interests delayed parliamentary attempts to strengthen the law on calicos, there was further trouble in the streets around Spitalfields. Only a new Calico Act in 1721 banning the importation and wearing of the cloth and the manufacture of home-printed cottons brought an uneasy calm back to Spitalfields. The troubles left a legacy of bitterness between master weavers and the poorer journeymen, who maintained that the masters' wives were filled with such boundless social ambition that, during the dogdays of summer, they had even worn printed calico themselves[4].

There was, too, another potential source of social discontent in the district in these opening years of George I's reign. The Calico Riots coincided with what was, in effect, a Government-sponsored building programme to benefit a particular section of the community. For in 1711 that rarity in eighteenth-century politics, a Tory Government, had passed the 'Fifty New Churches Act', a measure designed to combat religious nonconformity by imposing a tax on seaborne coal so as to provide funds for the building of fifty Anglican churches in London, Westminster or their suburbs. The Act stipulated that the churches should be built of stone and have towers or steeples. It did not specify where new parishes were to be formed, but priority was given to Stepney, Wapping, and Bethnal Green, an area densely populated, short of parish churches and sympathetic to Protestant dissent. Within three years, however, the Whigs were back in office: although the coal tax was retained, the church building programme was pursued with less vigour. Not fifty, but only ten entirely new churches went up in the following two decades, three of them dedicated to the patron saint of England and thus providing a felicitous way for the established Church to honour its Hanoverian King and Supreme Governor. The lack of enthusiasm for church-building was not entirely a consequence of the return of the Whigs, for the seacoal tax proved to have so low a yield that it needed to be bolstered by sup-plementary annual grants from Parliament. But there does seem to have been widespread apathy. When, on the last Sunday before Christmas in 1716, 'the walls of the old church' of St Leonard's, Shoreditch, 'were rent asunder with a fearful sound during Divine Service' and the con-gregation fled in panic, it was another twenty years before funds could be raised for work to begin on the church's reconstruction[5].

Something of lasting value to the East End did, however, emerge from the 1711 Act: the three magnificent churches of which Nicholas Hawksmoor was the architect – St Anne's, Limehouse; Christ Church, Spitalfields; St George's in the East, Wapping. Preliminary work had begun on St Anne's at Limehouse even while the Tories were still in office; by September 1714, when George I arrived from Hanover, the foundations had been dug for all three churches. Hawksmoor was an architect of independent mind, adept at imposing the fashionable stamp of baroque elegance on refined Gothic, and in designing the churches he enjoyed greater freedom than he did elsewhere in London, or indeed in Oxford: there was plenty of space, for he could build both St Anne's and St George's well away from the village houses and at Spitalfields he was fortunate in having an existing square to provide him with his setting. The three churches were characterised by idiosyncratic variations in their towers, which play tricks on a casual observer: the tapering 225-foot spire that catches the eye at Spitalfields is in reality not so high as the apparently squatter stump of St George's, less than a mile to the south. Another mile and a quarter down river the tower lantern of St Anne's owes something in design to the octagon of Ely Cathedral seen across the fens, but for mariners coming up Thames the church was well sited at the head of Limehouse Reach, for in composition its tiers suggest the topgallant, topmast and crow's nest of a square-rigged ship. Although critics complained that Hawksmoor's idea of steeple-building was to have 'a dull square rising out of another' there is no doubt that, whatever their inspiration, the towers of his three churches were by 1727 bringing a solid classical grandeur to London's eastern skyline[6].

They seem, indeed, to have stimulated an awareness of architectural good taste. It is still possible to trace in Newell Street and Narrow Street, Limehouse, the outline of Georgian terraces which date from the years immediately following St Anne's dedication. But more representative of their period are the houses in Spitalfields around Hawksmoor's rectory for Christ Church at what is now 2 Fournier Street (originally Church Street). Charles Wood and Simon Michell, two enterprising barristers, both of them from Somerset, leased some land in Spitalfields in 1708. Five years later, while the plans were being drawn up for Christ Church, they acquired more land, speedily and by dubious methods; this activity they continued for the following six years, until it was possible to call all the region to the east and south of the new church the Wood-Michell Estate. Other speculators might have rushed up buildings for cheap profit; but not Wood and Michell. The masons and carpenters of Fournier Street, and neighbouring Wilkes Street and Princelet Street, built houses worthy to stand beside Hawksmoor's rectory. Three outstanding houses on the southern side of Fournier Street (4, 12 and 14) survive as evidence of their good taste and of the wealth of the master weavers who, for the most part, lived here. Numbers 14 and 16 became both home and factory for the partnership of Sequeret & Bourdillion who had fourteen journeymen working on these premises twenty years later[7]. Except, perhaps, for a small community of Scandinavians, no other settlers in east London – from Ireland, Wales, the North and the West – fared so well as the Huguenot families of Spitalfields.

Yet the boom in fine house-building elsewhere in London during the first years of Hanoverian rule makes these developments in the eastern suburbs look puny by comparison. Orderly plans were creating a West End of squares and streets whose names affirmed loyalty to the new dynasty and whose houses, let by enterprising aristocrats on long lease with parliamentary backing, seemed a guarantee of social stability. Occasional attempts were made to follow West End practice in the East but, apart from the initiative of Wood and Michell in Spitalfields, without striking success. Their shrewd legal eyes had spotted ways of circumventing the restrictive manorial customs which hampered planned development over so much of the Tower Hamlets. Others were less astute: complex variations in the pattern of ownership of land and, in particular, the persistence of the ancient copyhold system of tenure ruled out rich rewards for speculative investment on a large scale. Semi-independent copyholders might lease their land for no longer than thirty-one years under penalty of forfeiture to the lord of the manor for any infringement of his rights[8]. So curious a restraint helped to make land cheaper, but it also favoured the spread of small houses, haphazardly packed into narrow streets.

There was, however, in the early eighteenth century one enclave in the Tower Hamlets where it seemed as if the pattern of development might run parallel to Holborn or Marylebone. Wellclose Square, elegantly centred on a Danish church and prospering from a timber trade boosted by the rebuilding of London after the Great Fire, actually antedated Mayfair planning. But Wellclose Square was less than half a mile from the walls of the Tower, and the combination of an enterprising foreign community and speculative builders was able to take advantage of a charter granted by James II in 1686 which extended the autonomous 'Liberties of the Tower' to the immediate vicinity of the fortress. Even Nicholas Barbon, the most roguish builder-financier of the age of Wren, had an interest in the leases of Wellclose Square, although it was for his ventures around Gray's Inn that this proto-tycoon son of Praisegod Barebone MP became notorious[9]. There was a parallel development a few hundred yards east of Wellclose Square, in what is now called Svedenborg Gardens. For in 1729, the Swedes followed the example of their fellow Scandinavians by building a church which they set in what was then a neat and demure square, named after the builder, John Prince. He, too, was an unpleasant speculator and left his mark on huge tracts of Marylebone, much as Barbon did in Holborn. But Barbon and Prince were ahead of their time. Not until the mid-nineteenth century did reforms in the law of copyhold encourage later developers, like Lord Tredegar, to build squares imitative of desirable residential districts elsewhere in the hopes of attracting prosperous middle-class families to Bow and Stepney. By then, however, it was too late to check the social differentiation which had created a fashionable West End and a mercantile and industrialised East.

Off Wellclose Square there was already, in Defoe's time, one of the foulest districts in London. A warren of alleys ran northwards from the Ratcliff Highway to Cable Street in which bawds offered insalubrious lodgings to seamen too drink-sodden to care where they fornicated. Throughout the eighteenth century the cheapest and most pox-ridden prostitutes in London plied their trade around Wapping and St Katharine's, a class of whore too low to satisfy the rakes who frequented Hogarth's 'houses of ill-fame' off the Covent Garden piazza. Yet there is no reason to suppose that a vicious lawlessness dominated the new riverside parishes; the most dangerous districts north of the river were around St Giles-in-the-Fields – where by 1735 one house in four was a cheap gin-shop – and 'Alsatia', the no-go area between Fleet Street and the Thames. Shadwell, only three-quarters of a mile further down river from the rough and tough warren around St Katharine's, had developed less haphazardly than its neighbours thanks largely to Sir Thomas Neale. This benevolent speculator of Charles II's reign virtually created the parish and, as early as 1669, ensured that the redbrick and wood-framed cottages which his builders put up were supplied with piped water pumped from the Thames by an engine worked, until 1750, by four horses. Shadwell and St George's in the East were not respectable suburbs, like Ryder's Hackney, but crime in these better-housed districts was spontaneous rather than organised, as in many of the alleys around St Katharine's; much of it was no more than petty pilfering by poor immigrants.

Popular prejudice blamed the Irish for every crime, major or minor. In their cottages along what became Cable Street they formed a compact community derisively nicknamed Knockvargis, after Carrickfergus, the linen port where William III landed before the battle of the Boyne. The Irish were assumed to be 'papists' and 'mumpers' (scroungers) who, it was said, would rather beg than work. That allegation, at least, was sharply refuted early in George II's reign, for Irish immigrants, flocking to London in great numbers, were so eager for work that they began to displace English labourers; and in the last week of July 1736 anti-Irish riots rocked east London.

Feelings were already running high that summer: Sir Robert Walpole, in his seventeenth year as Prime Minister, was known to favour measures to curb the cheap gin trade and was suspected of wishing to impose a bonded warehouse system on wines and tobacco; neither reform was welcome along a riverside where dram-shops were plentiful and smuggling profitable. But the immediate cause of the riots was a dispute in Shoreditch, where George Dance the Elder had at last begun to reconstruct St Leonard's Church; his builders, finding that the Irish would work for half the wages of the English, dismissed their labour force in favour of the immigrants. At the same time the master weavers of Spitalfields, greedy for quick profits, welcomed the coming of cheap Irish labour; rumour credited one master with taking on nearly 200 newcomers. On Tuesday, 27 July, after several evenings of shouting abuse, a mob of several thousand wrecked two Irish public houses and were dispersed only when panicking magistrates called out the militia, reinforced by fifty guardsmen from the Tower. On the Wednesday and Thursday evenings the mob was once more on the streets until assured by a local publican that the newcomers, both at St Leonard's and in Spitalfields, would be dismissed and English workers reinstated. The troubles, it seemed, were over. But the urge to teach 'papist bread-snatchers' a lesson persisted: on Friday night the rioters took the initiative, turned south from Spitalfields, pushed on through Whitechapel, and attacked every Irish ale-house or cottage dwelling they could find. 'On Saturday, 30, they rose in great numbers in the same parts to play the same game, but a detachment of our garrison marched out and surprised them,' noted the deputy Lieutenant of the Tower in his diary[10].

The Irish, denied opportunities in the building and textile industries, turned elsewhere for employment. Some 500 immigrants who had settled in Knockvargis and other parts of Shadwell found work as coal-heavers, for the capital's supply came entirely by sea from Northumberland and Durham and had to be unloaded from lighters. Pay, however, was so low that by the next generation the Irish were themselves in violent revolt against their conditions of employment. So serious were the disturbances in the spring of 1768 that five coal-heavers, put on trial at the Old Bailey for taking part in an armed affray, were hanged in Sun Tavern Fields, off the Ratcliff Highway. A crowd of 50,000 onlookers turned out for the occasion[11].

General narrative histories ignore the fate of these London Irish coal-heavers; and small wonder. For, in retrospect, the 1760s stand out as a decade full of incident: in that same spring, for example, King George's Governor in Massachusetts reported a restless air of defiance to taxation among his Bostonian subjects and, closer to hand, James Cook, the Yorkshire mariner who settled in Stepney, sailed from Blackwall Reach on a voyage in which he discovered Botany Bay. But in one famous long-running drama, enacted mainly in Westminster and the City, it was the petty craftsmen and labourers of east London who provided a vociferous chorus: 'Wilkes and Liberty' was as much a battle cry for the unenfranchised urban poor as for radical householders denied their democratic choice.

John Wilkes had tenuous links with London's eastern fringe: he was born in Clerkenwell, the son of a malt distiller who acquired an interest in land now covered by the railway lines at Bishopsgate; and a cousin, Nathaniel Wilkes, helped develop some of the area east of Spitalfields. 'Bawdy Jack' was first returned to the Commons, as MP for Aylesbury, in 1757 but it was another five years before he became notorious for the scorn with which his weekly journal, the *North Briton*, ridiculed Scotsmen in general and Lord Bute, George III's favourite Prime Minister, in particular. After being expelled from the House of Commons for sharply criticising the King's speech and also prosecuted for printing an 'obscene libel' Wilkes fled the country in December 1763 and was declared an outlaw. He returned for the general election of March 1768 and was elected MP for Middlesex, with overwhelming backing from all with a vote in the suburbs north of the river – the smaller gentry and merchants and any man in the outlying parishes possessing or occupying a freehold worth 40 shillings a year. Despite Wilkes's imprisonment and repeated expulsion from the House of Commons as 'incapable of being elected' the Middlesex voters remained loyal to their roguish demagogue: they supported him in three by-elections in 1769 (February, March and April), at the general election of 1774 – when he was at last allowed to take his seat – and in 1780 and 1784 as well[12].

Later generations respect Wilkes as the champion of a free press and the validity of democratic choice over a veto by the majority party in the Commons. But for the eighteenth century the Wilkes phenomenon in London's eastern suburbs had a wider significance; his cause became a catalyst of discontent. It was the Spitalfields weavers, in conflict with their masters against a cut in their wages, who swept down Piccadilly in March 1768 giving out cockades and broadsheets inscribed 'Wilkes and Liberty' and insisting that every householder should light up his windows in honour of their hero. A month later a different mob with a grievance demanded the illumination of poorer homes along the Ratcliff Highway: 'Wilkes and Liberty, and coal-heavers for ever!' was their cry. When on 27 April their popular idol, having been 'rescued' from the sheriff's officers on his way to prison, waved to his supporters from the upper window of the Three Tuns Tavern outside Christ Church, Spitalfields, it seemed as if mob rule would prevail throughout London. Wilkes, more sensible and far-sighted, than his would-be saviours, had to slip away from Spitalfields, in disguise and after dark, to surrender to his gaolers. Labourers in other skills also voiced their protest. Several hundred Thames watermen demonstrated outside the Mansion House on 9 May; and at least 5000 seamen from vessels in the Pool gathered angrily at Westminster next day: both groups had specific grievances over pay and conditions of work, but both, too, were taking advantage of new skills in mass agitation handed down by Wilkes and his friends to the mob[13].

Each of Wilkes's disputed elections coincided with industrial disturbances in the eastern suburbs. The most serious unrest came to the surface during the by-elections of 1769 and continued in Spitalfields and Whitechapel for the rest of the year, with violent protests of journeymen against master weavers who, for the past two years, had been importing engine looms from Holland. Louis Chauvet, a wealthy Huguenot living between Christ Church and Bishopsgate, had seventy-six looms smashed in a demonstration by some 1500 angry weavers. And, on 6 December, two prominent agitators – John Valline and John Doyle – were hanged at the southern end of Bethnal Green. 'There was an inconceivable number of people assembled and many bricks, tiles, stones etc. thrown while the gallows was fixing, and a great apprehension of a general tumult,' a reporter wrote on that same Wednesday. 'The unhappy sufferers were therefore obliged to be turned off before the usual time allowed on such occasions, which was about eleven o'clock, when after hanging about 50 minutes they were cut down and delivered to their friends'[14].

But, although a public execution was a grim warning to those who sought the destruction of new-fangled machinery, no amount of repression could bring peace to the silk industry. There were, fortunately, still some master weavers of sound common sense, and when food prices shot up in 1772, masters and journeymen made a joint approach to Parliament: passage of the Spitalfields Act of 1773 gave protection to the industry for another fifty years, not simply by strengthening the barriers against foreign competition, but by regulating the number of apprentices a journeyman might employ and settling rates of pay. After years of unrest it seemed as if the orderliness of good business was returning to the most industrialised of the eastern suburbs[15].

The calm was delusive; London's worst riots of the century were yet to come. Lord George Gordon, head of the Protestant Association, was a rabble-rouser but no organiser. In June 1780 he pandered to popular bigotry by exciting fears that anti-Catholic legislation would soon be repealed; and he was too foolish to anticipate the consequences of incitement. Defence of the Protestant Cause became an excuse for plunder and the settlement of personal scores against the Irish. 'I never till last night saw London and Southwark in flames,' wrote Horace Walpole in a letter of 8 June, contrasting the impact of the current riots with other troubles he had known in the capital over fifty years. The incidence of fire and looting in that terrible week fell more heavily south of the river and in the City and the north and west rather than on the East End; but there was, nevertheless, in Spitalfields, Whitechapel, and Wapping even greater violence than during the anti-Irish riots of 1736. The shops, taverns and private homes of those believed to be Roman Catholics were attacked, although in at least one case the victims would seem to have been Huguenots, gin-sodden arsonists having thrust flaming torches through their windows at the mere sight of a French name. A destructive hysteria emerged, as if from spontaneous combustion. In Whitechapel a crowd cheered on the circus strong man, Enoch Foster, who found he could rip up floorboards and hurl them through the window. Half a mile away Father Copps, priest to the Irish of Ratcliff, had to watch while his chapel ('Mass-house') in Virginia Street was destroyed and the homes of parishioners set ablaze. In London as a whole over 400 people were killed or seriously injured before the garrison of the Tower and the militia slowly restored order[16]. It is said that among the gangs who ran through the City streets and across the river freeing prisoners from five gaols were weavers from Spitalfields and mariners from Wapping. If so, they were adrift in a sea of communal hatred. During the demonstrations for Wilkes and Liberty there had, at least, been a hand on the rudder. But in June 1780, to the horror of the MP for Middlesex and his radical friends, no one kept control of the mob. To riot was an end in itself.

Among the propertied classes these years of upheaval left a lingering abhorrence of the 'Spitalfields mob' – although this generic term seems to have been applied by the socially secure to any marauding group of radical have-nots who made trouble on either side of the river. There is no doubt that, like the seamen of Wapping a century earlier, the Spital-fields silk-weavers and apprentices were highly mobile demonstrators, ready to protest in Westminster or Southwark as well as in the Tower Hamlets. Turbulent apprentices had been notorious trouble-makers since Tudor times, or even before. But the dissident silk-weavers were different. For the most part they were semi-skilled artisans, highly articulate and sharing a sense of communal unity – for how otherwise would masters and journeymen have come together in 1773 to secure the privileges of their trade by special act of parliament? The silk-weavers became London's proto-proletariat, the portent of a new threat to commercial society.

Yet, after 1773, statutory control of wages and protection against foreign competition made certain that, despite short-lived depressions, even the poorest weavers could stay off the lowest rungs of the social ladder. And Spitalfields was by no means London's blackest spot in the 1780s and early 1790s: there were sordid slums in Holborn; and Southwark had a worse tradition of violence. Yet since it is never the poorest of the poor who lead insurrections against the privileged classes, the improved living standards in Spitalfields for a generation after 1773 made the area a natural seedbed of revolution. But the seeds never broke surface. There was no major eruption of radical discontent in east London at the close of the century, despite the example set across the Channel in the faubourgs of Paris. Neither the weavers' mob nor foreign seamen ashore in Wapping were to blame for the fire which swept through riverside Ratcliff in 1794 although, as so often with such disasters, scaremongers encouraged tales of Frenchified incendiarists. Nevertheless, once Jacobinism triumphed in the French capital, those officials respon-sible for maintaining the king's peace, eyed the centre of London's silk industry with suspicion. And there, sure enough, Pitt's agents found a group of malefactors – the Spitalfields Mathematical Society. This emi-nently respectable body, a pioneer of adult education, was duly arraigned for committing a grave offence: it had dared to hold public lectures without a licence. Although, in October 1793, the earliest open-air demonstration of the radical London Corresponding Society took place in 'respectable' Hackney, it was thus over Spitalfields that an illiberal government continued to maintain eternal vigilance[17].

3

Life and Leisure

N O PEOPLES in eighteenth-century Europe rioted so readily as the
English and the Scots, whether in big cities, market towns or the
countryside. The continental empires might be shaken by major insurrections, but in Britain the grievances were localised; petty frustration
over conditions of work, a widespread suspicion of outsiders, and a
jealously possessive Protestantism prompted demonstrations which were
easily magnified into a lawless militancy, short-lived but highly destructive. With the country as a whole inclined naturally to violence, it is
hardly surprising if from time to time waves of passionate prejudice swept
angry crowds from the poorer districts into the streets of the capital to
burn and loot in support of a popular cause. Yet to see the East End as
ruled by mob fury for over seventy years is to mistake the occasional
sensation for the commonplace.

The everyday existence of most townsfolk remained drab and undra-
matic. Prosperous master-craftsmen, artisans, and casual labourers all
worked long hours, many of them from before six in the morning to after
six in the evening during the summer. In 1730 Lord Mayor Brocas

received a letter from a resident of Goodman's Fields which described,
with some satisfaction, the way of life of 'a careful honest man who is
industrious all day at his trade ... spends the evening in innocent mirth
with his family, or perhaps with his neighbours or brother tradesmen,
sometimes sitting an hour or two at an alehouse, and from there goes to
bed by ten and is at work by five or six'[1]. Habits, however, varied
from district to district. Semi-skilled 'mechanics' suffered considerably in
overcrowded Spitalfields; they were often confined to garret workshops;
but the worse treated and poorest paid were the women, particularly the
winders of silk and the young girls who would be put up for hire in
Spitalfields Market. From Wapping down to Blackwall hours and pay for
riverside workers fluctuated unpredictably, since their employment was
dependent, not merely on trade winds in the North Atlantic, but on calm
seas along the East Coast and up Channel too. For employers and artisans
alike the monotony was relieved by escape on Sundays and summer
evenings, sometimes to the gardens and surviving small fields in Hackney
and Stepney and frequently to the larger open spaces beside the lower
Lea. In 1795 the radical pamphleteer and poet John Thelwall – then
aged thirty-one – declared that he could remember the time when a
workman in Spitalfields 'had generally, beside the apartment in which
he carried on his vocation, a small summer house and a narrow slip of
a garden at the outskirts of the town' where he could spend his hours of
recreation, 'either in flying his pidgeons or raising his tulips[2]'.

Thelwall was, perhaps, writing in rosy reminiscence. John Rocque's
famous map of 1746 does, indeed, show gardens and fields and tree-lined
lanes coming to within a quarter of a mile of Christ Church, Spitalfields,
but there was also a common open sewer running from west to east
through what was known as Mile End New Town and the proximity of
lime-kilns, brickfields, piggeries, stagnant ponds and undrained marshes
must have diminished the arcadian charm of east Middlesex. Other
pursuits were certainly less idyllic than the cultivation of tulips. Thus
bull-baiting, which was in decline in Southwark and Marylebone long
before the coming of the Hanoverians, continued to command a following
beyond the City's eastern fringe; and bull-hanking, the pursuit of bullocks
through the streets on market days, remained a favourite sport at Bethnal
Green in Regency times. Some pastimes appealed to both West End and
East End. As late as the 1760s James Boswell commented on the extent
to which cock-fighting, in the old royal pit off Whitehall, was drawing
heavy wagers from young aristocratic bloods: the same sport was attracting far smaller bets from excited onlookers at cockpits in Clerkenwell,
Wapping and along the lower Lea. There – especially on Shrove Tuesday –
patrons were offered 'cock-throwing' as an alternative, the hitting with
a stick thrown from the length of a cricket pitch of a bird tethered to a

peg by a length of cord. In 1758 magistrates urged constables to check what they described as this 'barbarous' and 'shameful custom'[3].

'Anything that looks like fighting is delicious to an Englishman,' a French nobleman declared on a visit to London shortly before Paris erupted in revolution. Organised fisticuffs – the forerunner of boxing – had spread rapidly through England at the beginning of the eighteenth century. The earliest rules of prize-fighting were drawn up in 1743 by the Wapping waterman, Jack Broughton, who was to win such renown as a champion boxer that when he died, a wealthy octogenarian, he was buried in Westminster Abbey. But the origins of boxing lay south of the river, in the booths of Southwark Fair, and it was not until the last decades of the century that prize-fighting became especially associated with London's eastern suburbs. Less traditional bouts were popular at mid-century from Clerkenwell to Shadwell waterfront; at Stoke Newing-ton – to the north of eminently respectable Dalston Lane – an enterprising showman promoted a fight in 1759 between 'four natural bruisers', in which two women trounced two men; and, during the following decade, there were contests between 'battling women'. These fights remained uninhibited by Broughton's rules or, indeed, by any niceties of fair play whatsoever; and their promoters could count on good profitable returns from heavy betting. In 1768 – the year in which Joshua Reynolds became founder-president of the Royal Academy of Arts – a London newspaper was reporting, a few miles downriver, the triumphs of Bruising Peg, the most formidable of women pugilists[4].

Bruising Peg and her opponents first appeared in fair booths, as indeed had Jack Broughton. But until the early years of George III no fairs of particular note were held in what became the East End of London, although there are references to one at Stepney during the seventeenth century. Across the river there was Greenwich Fair every Easter and Whitsun and Charlton Horn Fair in mid-October, while the greatest of these gatherings in London itself was held for three days every August, beginning on St Bartholomew's Eve, at Smithfield, a mere half-hour's walk from Whitechapel. James II sanctioned another popular fair, to be held for the first fortnight of May in what is now Shepherd Market – an event which introduced the name Mayfair to London's topography. But in 1764 the Earl of Coventry, who had purchased 106 Piccadilly, secured the closure of the May Fair on the grounds that it constituted an annual disturbance at the rear of his property. As if anticipating more recent practices, the May Fair was thereupon moved out of London to the banks of the River Lea. Fairfield Road, running north from Bow Bridge to Old Ford, still recalls those two weeks each spring, when goods of every kind would be on sale while jugglers, fire-eaters, puppeteers, prize-fighters, freaks, acrobats and other booth entertainers brought a raffish vitality to the buying and selling of quack cures and tawdry finery. Bow Fair flourished for some seventy years. Then, late in the 1820s, neat terraced houses began to spread along the north side of Bow Road. Predictably, the newcomer residents, like Lord Coventry before them, complained how each spring the noise and bustle made their homes unbearable. And Bow lost its Fair[5].

In the middle decades of the eighteenth century the more comfortably prosperous families in Hackney or Bethnal Green or Whitechapel turned for their weekend amusements to the tea-gardens north of the City, especially at Bagnigge Wells (off what is now King's Cross Road) and White Conduit House, beside the fields of Islington, where cricket was played. Seamen and their womenfolk frequented alehouses around Stepney Fields and what remained of the common land in Mile End or crossed the Thames to Greenwich. In Wapping itself there were few open spaces, apart from the rope-walks and the confined area around Execution Dock, where until the 1780s pirates were still publicly hanged.

Long before then one group of riverside workers had begun to enjoy a summer Saturnalia of their own devising. Daniel Day, a block and pump maker from Wapping, had prospered so well from the business of London's river that he owned land some ten miles away in Essex, where the air was good and the countryside more genuinely verdant than in outer Stepney or Hackney. In the mid-1720s Day decided to combine the collection of rent from his tenants with a holiday outing for his employees and their friends. Thereafter, once every summer, all who made masts, blocks and pumps in Wapping accompanied Day to his fields at Fairlop, where a famous oak tree, 'overspreading an area of 300 ft in circumference', stood on the plain below Chigwell Row, about half a mile in from the western edge of Hainault Forest. Beneath this oak Day encouraged the establishment of a fair for the annual outing; and Fairlop Fair remained an East Ender's calendar date well into Queen Victoria's reign. On the first Friday each July the Wapping workers journeyed through Bow and Stratford and down the Romford Road to Ilford and up the lanes of Ley Street and Horns Road to Barkingside and the forest beyond; they rode, we are told, 'in two or three fully rigged model ships, mounted on carriage-frames, each drawn by 6 horses, with postilions and outriders, and attended by music'. Day died in 1767; the oak was damaged by fire in 1805 and blown down in the gales of February 1820; but it made little difference to the revelries. Fairlop Fair was still being held in its traditional clearing at the time of the Crimean War; and even when, soon afterwards, the site was enclosed, the annual carriage procession continued each July, with the neighbouring Maypole Inn at Barkingside as a destination. George Lansbury, the Labour Party leader in the early 1930s, could remember the fun of a Fairlop Fair procession

in his boyhood, sixty years before. Only with the decline of sailing craft
at Wapping and the coming of a railway to Fairlop in 1903 did the fair
die out[6].

Not all leisure pursuits were so roisterous. The Huguenot silk-weavers
brought a spirit of intellectual self-betterment to east London whether
they came directly from France or Holland or from the English West
Country, like the influential Tillard family of Totnes. The famous Spitalfields Mathematical Society was established in 1717 by a retired
mariner, John Middleton, who kept the Monmouth Head Tavern on land
now covered by Truman's Brick Lane brewery. It moved to Wheler Street,
Shoreditch, in 1725 but came back south to Woodseer Street ten years
later. John Dollond, a silk-weaver who invented an achromatic telescope
and founded a dynasty of opticians, was one of the many Huguenots
whose interest in the exact sciences was stimulated by the Society.
Thomas Simpson was a member when he wrote his treatises on fluxion
(1737) and the laws of chance (1740) and so, too, was his near-con-
temporary John Canton, who pioneered experiments in magnetism and
hydrostatics. Never again was the Society so distinguished. Its last home,
at 32 Crispin Street, was described in 1842 as 'lowly and inelegant';
three years later falling membership forced the survivors to hand over
their library to the Royal Astronomical Society[7].

There were at least five other cultural societies in Whitechapel and
Spitalfields in the mid-eighteenth century. They satisfied interests in
music, history, entomology, floriculture and the recitation of verse. The
Madrigal Society was formed in 1741 by John Immyns, an eccentric
lawyer; four years later it had fourteen members. They were 'mostly
mechanics, some weavers from Spitalfields, others of various trades and
occupations', wrote Sir John Hawkins, another lawyer member of the
Society. The 'mechanics' sang, he writes patronisingly, 'though not
elegantly, yet with a degree of correctness that did justice to their harmony'[8].

The Madrigal Society met above a tavern in the City, and their efforts
were supported by boy sopranos from St Paul's Cathedral, but there was
already a good musical tradition in the East End itself. Peter Prelleur,
organist of Christ Church, Spitalfields, from 1735 to 1755, was a distinguished composer and harpsichordist of Huguenot descent who had
anglicised his Christian name, Pierre. And John James, who became
organist of St George's in the East in 1738, composed voluntaries which,
as Hawkins remarked, were 'in the hands of every deputy organist of
London'; one of his surviving works was long ascribed to Handel.
Hawkins, a malevolent critic of others' foibles, blackened James's name,
perhaps jealous of his friendship with Handel: James allegedly enjoyed
watching bull-baiting and dogs being set to fight each other; and he

'indulged an inclination to spirituous liquors of the coarsest kind ... even while attending his duty at church'. But Hawkins concedes that he was a first-rate classical scholar and that, as an organist, 'James was distinguished by the singularity of his style, which was learned and sublime'.

Prelleur, too, could make music in the taverns, to the delight of an audience that was creating a folk-song tradition of its own. He lived in Rose Lane, a road long since swept away by the making of Commercial Street. A few hundred yards to the north was Christ Church, where he played the organ, and a few hundred yards to the south was the Angel & Crown, Whitechapel, with a tavern concert-room in which Prelleur was the star performer. An advertisement in the *London Daily Post* for 21 August 1739 shows the versatility of his musical taste; the public is invited to the 'Wells' in Wapping for:

> the usual diversions of rope-dancing, posture-masters, singing and dancing, serious and comic. The Whole to conclude with a New Entertainment called *Harlequin Hermit* or *The Arabian Courtezan* ... with a complete band of music, consisting of kettle-drums, trumpets, French horns, hautboys and violins. The Music by an Eminent Master. To begin at exactly five o'clock.

That 'Eminent Master' was Peter Prelleur; and *The Arabian Courtezan* is duly listed by modern reference works among his compositions, together with a *Harlequinade* completed two years later and a musical interlude, *Baucis and Philemon*[9].

At the 'Wells' in Wapping Prelleur was helping to preserve a theatrical association already well rooted in the eastern suburbs when the Puritan blight first fell on London, at the end of the sixteenth century. Twelve years before the coming of the Spanish Armada James Burbage, a leading actor with the Earl of Leicester's men, built London's earliest playhouse, called The Theatre, an enclosed wooden structure in Holywell Street, Shoreditch, a few hundred yards west of St Leonard's Church, where the Burbage family – and other actors, too – are buried. The Theatre was close enough to residential areas of London to attract patrons, but it had the advantage of being outside the jurisdiction of killjoy City aldermen. By 1595 Shakespeare was a member of the Lord Chamberlain's Company and therefore appeared at The Theatre and, almost certainly, in a second playhouse, The Curtain, built near to it. After James Burbage's death there was a protracted dispute between his eldest son, Cuthbert, and their landlord, Giles Allen, which induced the actors to pull The Theatre down three days after Christmas in 1598 and remove it upriver. There, on the South Bank, it became famous as The Globe. The theatrical connection with Shoreditch was, however, not broken, for The Curtain appears to have survived until 1642 when it was forced out of business by Parliament's general suppression of playhouses.

After the Restoration the people of the Tower Hamlets could see plays only at certain larger taverns or at fair booths. But in 1729 an enterprising minor playwright, Thomas Odell, converted a shop in Leman Street, Whitechapel, into a theatre which, in 1731, he left to the management of Henry Giffard, an Anglo-Irish actor, then in his mid-thirties. Giffard refused to regard Whitechapel as beyond the social pale. In that year John Rich, the theatrical manager who had made a fortune from staging *The Beggar's Opera* in Lincoln's Inn, was employing the fashionable architect Edward Shepherd to create a luxurious theatre for him at Covent Garden; and Giffard, in his turn, commissioned Shepherd to build what his friend Chetwood described as 'an entirely new, beautiful convenient theatre' in Alie Street, Goodman's Fields, where John Stow once fetched his 'halfpenny worth of milk, hot from the kine' – and where the Management Services Centre of the National Westminster Bank stands today.

On the first Thursday evening in December 1732 John Rich opened Shepherd's Theatre Royal at Bow Street, Covent Garden. Within a few months Shepherd completed the building of Giffard's Goodman's Fields Theatre, two and a half miles away, in the unfashionable east. Although small – less than half the size of what Hogarth dubbed 'Rich's Glory' – it must have been an attractive building, with an ornate painted ceiling above the auditorium, so that Apollo and the Muses could preside over the East End. Giffard engaged a good company which included Walker, who had created Captain Macheath in 1727, and Richard Yates, who was then a famous Harlequin but was later to become the first Sir Oliver Surface. 'Dramatic pieces were performed with the utmost elegance and propriety,' recorded William Chetwood in his biographical notes on the theatrical personalities of his day: the public paid two shillings for the pit and one shilling for the gallery; and for four years the theatre prospered. But Giffard was a cautious man, afraid of offending authority. When, in 1737, he received the manuscript of a satirical play, *The Golden Rump*, scurrilously attacking the Walpole administration, he at once dispatched it to Downing Street and received a gift of £1000 from a grateful Prime Minister. Soon afterwards, however, an Act of Parliament closed all unlicensed playhouses – with Giffard's Goodman's Fields Theatre among them. Only Covent Garden and Drury Lane were recognised by the Lord Chamberlain as patent theatres in the capital, although the King's Theatre in the Haymarket enjoyed special status, as the home of Italian opera[10].

Financially Giffard can never have enjoyed so rich a return on a play as when he squealed to Walpole about *The Golden Rump*. Professionally, however, his most successful year was still to come. For, like other theatre-managers, Giffard soon found ways of thwarting the Lord Chamberlain: his theatre re-opened as a concert-hall, the audience buying tickets for a musical performance which preceded and followed a, nominally free, play. It was in this way that, on 19 October 1741, Giffard presented *Richard III*, with a twenty-four-year-old unnamed actor in the lead. 'Last night I play'd Richard the Third to the Surprize of Every Body,' David Garrick wrote to his brother in Lichfield next day. Garrick had understudied Yates earlier in the year and widened his experience in a brief season, under Giffard's management at Ipswich; but, as the admiring Chetwood wrote eight years later, it was 'with the part of Richard the Third' that Garrick 'set out in full lustre at the Theatre in Goodman's Fields'. 'By the Force of Attraction', Chetwood added, he 'drew even the Court to the farthest suburbs of London'[11].

Throughout the season of 1741–2 Garrick provided a diversion between the musical entertainment at the Goodman's Fields Theatre. He acted in Restoration comedies as well as Shakespeare, with a curious triumph eight weeks after his debut when he played the ghost of Hamlet's father to Giffard's own Prince of Denmark. As early as 16 November Garrick let his brother know how Pitt was praising him as the greatest actor produced by the English stage and how the company was expecting a visit any night from the Prince of Wales; and in another letter, eight days later, Garrick was boasting that Goodman's Fields had more business than either Drury Lane or Covent Garden. To travel down to Alie Street was fashionable that winter; even Alexander Pope, by now a prematurely aged fifty-three, came out there on three evenings to see Garrick perform. 'The coaches of the nobility filled up the space from Temple-bar to Whitechapel,' Garrick's earliest biographer was to write a few months after his death. Garrick appeared more than 1720 times under Giffard's management, but he was too shrewd a businessman to remain in Goodman's Fields or risk becoming a casualty of a war of attrition with the patent theatre Establishment. By mid-April 1742 Garrick was assuring his brother he would appear at 'the other end' of London next season. As Chetwood recounts, with a discreet tact of omission, 'After making that remote part of the town as familiar to Courtiers of Quality as Wapping to Sailors he came with a blaze of light to Drury Lane'[12].

Garrick's departure marked the end of good theatre in the East End for at least half a century. The patentees at Drury Lane and Covent Garden were so powerful that they even secured the closure of the playhouse Shepherd had built for Giffard. Odell's converted shop in neighbouring Leman Street survived for another nine years as it provided what were, in effect, burlesque music-hall turns rather than plays. So, too, did Prelleur's haunt, the 'Wells' at Wapping, which promised free entertainment to patrons who bought a pint of wine, at two shillings a bottle. In December 1785, six years after Garrick's death, work began on a new playhouse, off Well Close Square, to be called the Royalty; it was under the management of John Palmer the Younger, a good Falstaff and Toby Belch at Drury Lane and an even better Joseph Surface. 'Plausibility Jack', as Sheridan dubbed Palmer, claimed that he was not bound by the Licensing Act of 1737 since the Royalty lay within the outer precincts of the Tower of London, from whose Governor he had obtained permission to build the theatre. On 20 June 1787 the Royalty Theatre opened, with performances of *As You Like It* and *Miss in her Teens*. But although Palmer was supported by a crowd of angry young apprentices, he was arrested and his playhouse restricted to the presentation of pantomine and bur- lesques. Palmer was soon released on bail, and he made a second attempt to present straight plays at the Royalty. Once again, however, he was threatened with imprisonment and gave up the fight. The Royalty passed into other hands and struggled on through the Napoleonic Wars, but later managers did not attempt to present 'legitimate' drama[13].

Chetwood maintained that his friend Giffard was 'obliged to quit' Goodman's Fields 'I may say, by Oppression'. So, too, was John Palmer, forty years later. Giffard and Palmer did not simply suffer from the possessive exclusiveness of Covent Garden and Drury Lane. Both man- agers had to contend with hostility closer at hand. For there remained in the inner eastern suburbs a residual local Puritanism which damned plays as a hindrance to the service of God, actors as corrupters of the young, and theatres as snares of vice, likely to spawn brothels around them. There was no strong tradition of specifically Anglican church- going in Stepney and Hackney, despite the creation of new parishes; indeed Hawksmoor's St Anne's, Limehouse, remained unconsecrated and unused for six years after it was built. But religious dissent had long been a powerful moral mentor in the Tower Hamlets, and by the middle of the eighteenth century there was an arc of nonconformist chapels and meeting-places from Hackney south to the riverside.

London's earliest dissenting academy was in Hoxton Square, on the borders of Hackney and Shoreditch, where many pastors received their theological training. The Quakers were established in Wapping and Ratcliff, the Baptists, Congregationalists and Unitarians in Spitalfields. As well as a famous Huguenot church in what is now Fournier Street, there was l'Église de l'Artillerie, tucked away in a poor alley south of Spitalfields market, where Jacob Bourdillon became minister on Christmas Day 1731 and indeed was still serving there during the Gordon Riots nearly half a century later. In Well Close Square was the home of the formidable Dr Mayo, an 'independent' pastor held in high esteem by Samuel Johnson, while in Stepney an organised pressure group of Protestant Dissenting

Deputies had links with the East India Company. There remained several freakish sects of 'ranters', the most active on the fringe of London being the Muggletonians, who reconciled a basic Unitarianism with a highly individualistic interpretation of the Book of Revelations. Strangest of all these groups in the 1780s were the Ancient Deists of Hoxton, earnest London craftsmen who dissented so far from the Dissenters that they convinced themselves they could maintain a transcendental hot-line with a galaxy of Messianic angels[14].

More lasting in its impact on the working population was the mission of Wesley. When in 1738 John Wesley accepted 'the world as his parish' and began his fifty years of evangelistic travels around the British Isles it was natural that he should seek to fire the Old Dissent of east London with a new zeal. His mother had been born in Spittal Yard and from 1740 until his death in 1791 Wesley made his headquarters barely half a mile west of the most densely packed alleys in the East End. Wesley's *Journals* show how often he preached in Tower Hamlets. Politically he was a High Tory and his sermons seem at first to have aroused strong hostility: in 1739 he 'was desired to preach ... morning and afternoon' but 'was not suffered to conclude my subject'; and in 1742 he was pelted with rotten eggs and missiles while preaching in the open air at Whitechapel; a stone struck him between the eyes on this occasion and a hostile mob 'tried to drive in a herd of cows' among those who were listening to his Gospel message – 'the brutes', Wesley notes in his diary, 'were wiser than their masters'.

Soon, however, John Wesley gained the magnetism which holds a crowd enthralled. Meeting-places were acquired where his followers might pursue the religious exercises he recommended, his 'Method' of worship. Wesleyan chapels were opened in Black Eagle Street, Spitalfields, before 1745 and in Wapping in the early 1760s. Eighteen hundred people heard John Wesley preach at Black Eagle Street in 1755 and he was there again in 1763, at a time when popular hysteria encouraged a belief the world was to end that very night. Wesley sought to show frightened East Enders 'the utter absurdity of the supposition'. But he chose as his text, 'Prepare to meet thy God', and it is possible that his theological distinctions were too subtle for the hundreds who hung anxiously upon his words. For, he admits in his diary, 'Notwithstanding all I could say, many were afraid to go to bed, and some wandered about in the fields being persuaded that, if the world did not end, London would at least be swallowed up by an earthquake'[15].

Sometimes Wesley's sermons confirmed popular prejudice. Thus, although his message fell short of a wild sectarian's inflammatory tirade, he left his listeners in no doubt that all 'papists' were wicked blasphemers. Yet in Wesley's East End it seems almost certain that Roman Catholic churchgoers outnumbered the active members of any other Christian denomination; by the end of the Napoleonic Wars priests reported that there were 14,000 Catholics in Shadwell alone. Most East End Roman Catholics were of Irish descent; many first arrived in London to travel out into rural Middlesex and Essex at harvest time and were then forced to seek employment as casual labourers along the riverside when winter came. They figure in the reports of eighteenth-century riots not only in the metropolis but as far out as the fields of Hendon and Edgware, where they were blamed for stealing jobs from good, Protestant English lads. Occasionally the Roman Catholics instigated the troubles. More often they were victims of the hatred, suspicion and resentment felt against any compact community of outsiders[16].

So, too, by the middle of the eighteenth century was London's rapidly expanding Jewish population. Wealthy Jewish immigrants from Spain and Portugal ('Sephardim') had settled in the City under the later Stuarts; at least ten families were prominent financiers in the City under George II. These Sephardic worshippers had been joined in the reigns of William III and Anne by the first 'Ashkenazim', followers of the northern ritual practised in Germany, Poland and the Netherlands. The concentration of Ashkenazim living on the eastern edge of the City was so dense that, before the death of Anne, they formed over a quarter of the population in the parish of St James's, Duke's Place. And there, close to Houndsditch and Aldgate, the Ashkenazim established in 1722 their first Great Synagogue, on a site in Duke's Place itself now covered by the Sir John Cass Foundation School. Despite civic disabilities, the Jews played a considerable role in local affairs, their mounting influence attracting more and more Ashkenazim to the area, especially after waves of persecution in Bavaria, in Bohemia and Moravia during 1744, and in partitioned Poland later that century. They found employment as jewellers, especially as diamond-cutters, they made pencils and they both made and sold watches and necklaces. Rich Jewish families gave such support to the Crown against the Jacobites in 1745 that the Duke of Newcastle introduced in 1753 a Jewish Naturalisation Act, to remove a few of the disabilities which marked out the Jews as aliens. But Newcastle's moderate measure aroused hostility and, with characteristic pusillanimity, the wretched Duke hurriedly repealed the Act in the same year that it went on the statute book[17]. The chief consequence of the act was a widespread suspicion, especially in the East End, that wealthy Jews would flourish as deceitful usurers and that frugal Jews – like those old familiar whipping-boys, the Irish 'papists' – would offer their services to unscrupulous employers as a means of undercutting English labourers.

Mob fury did not turn against London's Jews collectively, as it did against the Roman Catholics in the Gordon Riots. They were insulted in

the streets and occasionally attacked; and when any Jews were found
guilty of crime their racial ancestry and religious affiliation were
emphasised in newspapers and pamphlets. Young hooligans amused
themselves with Jew-baiting, a favourite pastime being the pulling of
beards. Quite apart from these insults, most Ashkenazim had a hard
struggle for existence: they were not confined within ghettoes, as in so
many cities on the continent, but they were still denied civic liberties and
they remained excluded from Christian education, from apprenticeship
to Christian master craftsmen, from succour in Christian almshouses,
and from treatment in Christian hospitals. The poor became a heavy
burden on the Elders of the Synagogue and, although generous gifts were
made by the wealthy Sephardim, the needs of the Ashkenazim aroused
a certain suspicion of these so-called 'German Jews' among their co-
religionists; the Elders of the Great Synagogue even supported attempts
to check immigration aboard the packet boats from Holland[18].

Butchers appear to have found particular satisfaction in heaping
insults on the Ashkenazim women of Whitechapel, no doubt from resentment at Jewish ordinances over the killing and preparation of meat. But
by 1778 this particular form of molestation was becoming a dangerous
pursuit. For one Jewish shopkeeper had a fourteen-year-old assistant who
was lithe, quick on his feet and prepared to hit anyone who insulted his
employer's Jewish wife very hard with his fists. 'In a short time', the boy
wrote many years later in his memoirs, 'I became the terror of these
gentry, and when they found that, young as I was, I was already to come
forward in her defence, they forbore to molest her'[19]. There were other
anti-social menaces, too, who felt the impact of those fists, the sailors
around the Stepney waterfront and St Katharine's among them. For
Daniel Mendoza, born in Aldgate in 1764, shrank from no challenge in
defending his co-religionists from insult and ill-usage. Once, so his
memoirs tell us, he was seized by a press-gang in Wapping and talked
himself off a ship's muster-roll within forty-eight hours.

'Mendoza the Jew', as he was billed professionally, emerged from a
series of prize-fights in Whitechapel, Stepney and Leytonstone to claim
the championship of England before his twenty-fifth birthday. He was
only 5 ft 7 in. tall and he would have been reckoned a middleweight a
century later, but in the 1780s and 1790s he was expected to take on
any comer of any weight. For success against taller and heavier men,
Mendoza relied on good footwork, and especially on neat sidesteps.

Unlike earlier prize-fighters, Mendoza sensed the value of publicity.
He was prepared to fight for a good purse in Edinburgh or in Yorkshire
as readily as in London. His first major championship bout, which he
lost to his former sponsor Richard Humphries, was staged at Odiham at
Hampshire in early January 1788. The return fight took place at Stilton

(near Peterborough) on 6 May 1789 and attracted 10,000 spectators. Mendoza's victory relegated to second place newspaper reports from Versailles of the opening session of the revolutionary States-General; and the third bout, at Michaelmas in 1790, was won by Mendoza in the full excitement of the Doncaster St Leger race-meeting. So great was the interest taken in this 'Light of Israel' that Mendoza was invited to Windsor, where it was arranged for him to meet King George III out walking in the Great Park.

Five years later Mendoza lost his title to John Jackson who was four inches taller than Mendoza, 40 lb heavier and prepared to hold Mendoza's black curly hair with one hand while punching him hard with the other. It was the end of Mendoza the champion, but not of Mendoza the prize-fighter. On the first day of spring in 1806, when he was in his forty-second year, Mendoza sparred for over 50 rounds in the open air at Greensted Green in Essex, a mere 20 miles from Mile End Road, where it had all begun[20].

After that gruelling 110 minutes of bare fisticuffs, Mendoza lived in retirement for another thirty years. Even in his lifetime it was recognised that he had lifted the self-respect of London's poorer Jews, showing them how to box scientifically so that quickness of thought might outwit brute force in any scrap. But, in the end, he must be remembered not simply as 'Mendoza the Jew'; he was the first lad from the densely crowded streets around Aldgate to exchange pleasantries with his sovereign at Windsor, and the first to become, for a few years, a national figure. It was a pointer to London's past and London's future that the earliest folk hero of the East End should be a Jewish fighter.

4

The Coming of the Docks & Railways

'**B**ELOW the three bridges, such a prodigious forest of masts, for miles together, that you would think all the ships of the universe were here assembled,' Lydia Melford wrote in her first letter back to Bath from London. The amazement which Smollett attributes to his heroine was a common reaction among visitors, whether from the provinces or abroad. No one looking at the Upper or Lower Pool could doubt London's claim to pre-eminence among the world's ports. By the end of the eighteenth century three times as much trade was being handled by the watermen of the East End as at its beginning. During 1791, the last year before Europe's commerce was disrupted by war, ships sailing up river from foreign ports would come in sight of St Anne's Church tower, Limehouse, at an average of one vessel for every hour and a quarter of daylight; and coasters bringing food or coal to the capital would, in theory, make their way through the wherries and cutters once in every 25 minutes between dawn and dusk[1].

There was no river in the world along which shipping moved with such neatly ordered regularity, and certainly not the long and sinuous

Thames. Passage upstream was dependent on the tide and on conditions out at sea, beyond the Nore: doldrum days, with winds in the wrong quarter, might be followed by the arrival in quick succession of a hundred or so vessels, bringing welcome employment to the riverside communities from Wapping down to Blackwall, but throwing London's port and its approaches into appalling chaos. For, by the autumn of 1790, the Upper Pool alone needed three times as many moorings as the City Corporation could provide. The 13,575 ships trading with London in 1791 were serviced by some 3500 lighters, hoys and barges; there were thus, in that one year, over 17,000 vessels plying on the waters of the Pool, a mere two and a half miles of river. An estimate made five years later suggested that, at any one time, there could be 'nearly 8000 Vessels and Boats of all kinds, occupying a space of four miles below, and two miles above London Bridge'[2]. It was not unknown for a ship to remain at anchor, within sight of Limehouse, for a week before finding a vacant mooring in the Pool. The congestion was especially bad between July and October, when westerly winds in the Atlantic would bring in a fleet of West Indiamen. Too often their cargoes of rum, coffee, ginger, cocoa and sugar were piled haphazardly in casks along the quay, waiting to be moved to warehouses before they were lost to rats, the variations in England's weather, or the organised depredation of pilferers.

Port administration remained a responsibility of the City Corporation, as it had been for almost seven centuries. Coasters, with flour, butter, cider, locally manufactured goods or fish, were allowed to come right into the city; some moored off London Bridge and discharged their cargoes into small boats; a few were able to go alongside the quay. Colliers made for Wapping and the services of the coalheavers, predominantly Irish. But any ships trading with a foreign or colonial port moored in midstream: the North Sea and Channel vessels off St Katharine's; the Baltic traders slightly further down river; and the West Indiamen in Limehouse Reach, off the desolate windswept pastures of the Isle of Dogs. The great East Indiamen, 'nearly equal in bulk to ships of the line in the Royal Navy', came no further up river than Blackwall Reach; and in the last years of the century they were lightened, and made safer, by unloading their gun-powder and any explosive cargo into hoys in Long Reach, a stretch of the Thames between Purfleet and Greenhithe, 19 miles from London Bridge. The Company's Blackwall moorings were close to the seventeenth-century fitting-out basin which, in 1789, was considerably enlarged by a private speculator who added to this 'Brunswick Dock' a Mast House 120 feet high. From Blackwall cargoes were taken, under armed escort, in a horse convoy to the East India Company's warehouse in the City, at Cutler Street. All other vessels, once they had found a mooring, were dependent on the lighters for transit of their cargoes. Most imports were carried up river to a licensed Customs quay. Until late in the eighteenth century the only landing points were those authorised by Parliament in 1558 and 1665, the twenty 'Legal Quays', spread along 500 yards of waterfront, around the Custom House, between London Bridge and the Tower. To ease the congestion twenty-one 'sufferance wharves', for goods bearing low duties, were established on the south bank of the river and for 250 yards east of the Tower; but not until 1789 was this concession regularised by law. Lighters were also used for loading exports, a slow process which left ships occupying moorings far too long[3].

The system was cumbersome, wasteful and monopolistic, bringing fat profits to those who owned the quays. Protests from merchants were received by the City Corporation as early as 1705 and in the 1760s there was another round of forceful complaints. But powerful associations ranged themselves against any change: watermen and porters; city companies with ancient rights; individual monopolists, like Lord Gwydyr, whose family claimed dues on every mooring chain used between London Bridge and Woolwich; and even two Oxford colleges, whose coffers benefited from wheeled vehicles passing across land they owned along the riverside. Yet there were also in the City two groups with a vested interest in creating, speedily and securely, a better port of London: the insurance companies; and the West India merchants. In 1793 William Vaughan, a forty-one-year-old director of the Royal Exchange Assurance Company, published *On Wet Docks, Quays and Warehouses for the Port of London*, a tract advocating the building of docks and protected warehouses at Rotherhithe, on the south bank of the Thames, and at three sites in the East End: around St Katharine's; at Wapping; and in the Isle of Dogs. Detailed proposals for docks were also put forward in 1794 by John Powsey, the district surveyor of Wapping and Limehouse, and by the Southwark-born architect and lighthouse-builder, Daniel Alexander. These arguments supplied the West India parliamentary lobby with ammunition for preparing a Dock Bill, presented to the Commons in January 1796. It was at once countered by petitions which emphasised that the West Indies trade represented little more than a seventh of the commerce of the port and complained that the proposed Bill threatened both the ancient rights of landowners and traditional occupations along the waterfront.

Had Britain been at peace in 1796, there is little doubt that the Dock Bill would soon have disappeared in the clash of rival interests within the Commons. But by January 1796 the nation was feeling the strain of almost three years of war against revolutionary France; hostile armies controlled not only the French Channel coast but the shores flanking Britain's northern trade-routes as well. In the previous winter – the most severe in living memory – a whole month passed in which only a single

Northumbrian coaster succeeded in evading French privateers in the North Sea so as to bring much-needed coal to snowbound Wapping; and at almost the same time a raid by Admiral Villaret Joyeuse's squadron in the Atlantic approaches lost Britain seventy merchant vessels. French frigates later in the year attacked a convoy from Jamaica and in the autumn of 1795 the Toulon squadron captured all thirty-one ships being (inadequately) escorted from the eastern Mediterranean into the Atlantic. At such a time of peril it was ridiculous for ships which had safely reached the Thames to risk losing their cargoes through the inefficiency of an antiquated system of mooring and unloading. William Pitt, the Prime Minister, appointed a Select Committee 'to Enquire into the Best Mode of Providing Sufficient Accommodation for the Increased Trade and Shipping of the Port of London'. Pitt was a member of the committee, but the chairman was the elderly and able President of the Board of Trade, Lord Hawkesbury (once Charles Jenkinson, and soon to be rewarded for his work on the Committee with the Earldom of Liverpool)[4].

Hawkesbury and his colleagues heard evidence about congestion, losses through theft, delays in unloading, fire risks, and the need for dredging a deeper channel in the Thames. They soon saw that docks were needed rather than any extension of wharves along the riverbank. Seven schemes for docks were laid before the committee: most of the proposals favoured docks in Wapping and Blackwall. It was commonly – and erroneously – believed that the only inhabitants of the Isle of Dogs were a cattle drover and a ferryman and strong arguments were put forward for turning the whole island into a series of docks; Samuel Wyatt suggested four basins between Blackwall and Limehouse accommodating 911 ships and 800 lighters, but drawings among his papers make the docks look as congested as the old Pool. The main report of the Hawkesbury Committee, published as early as May 1796, recognised that the port's resources were 'incompetent to the great purpose of its extended commerce' and urged the building of docks, but could not decide if they should constitute units administered by a single port authority, such as the City Corporation, or should serve only specialised interests, as the West Indian and East Indian pressure groups preferred. Three more years were wasted in discussion of dock plans, with each interest group marshalling its arguments and pouring scorn on its rivals[5].

The most forceful propagandist for walled and secure docks was Patrick Colquhoun, a former Lord Provost of Glasgow who became, in 1792, a London magistrate. Early in 1797 he published his *Treatise on the Police of the Metropolis*, a pioneer study which ran to seven editions in the following ten years. Colquhoun exposed the widespread 'criminal depredation' which afflicted the port of London and blamed the extensive

pilfering on the lumpers, those 'aquatic labourers' in the lighters responsible for 'discharging and delivering the cargoes of ships'. The West India
interest recognised in Colquhoun a valuable ally and he was encouraged
to supplement his original treatise by *The Commerce and Police of the River
Thames* (published in 1800). Colquhoun divided the marauders into
categories: 'river pirates', who attacked moored shipping in armed boats
at night; 'night plunderers', who raided the lighters; 'light horsemen',
who were corrupt ships' officers and revenue men and who ignored the
systematic robbery of a vessel by porters and watermen; 'heavy horsemen', who slipped stolen goods into their guernseys; and casual robberies
by groups of ratcatchers, mudlarks and warehousemen. He believed that
in 1797 – a time of threatened invasion, near national bankruptcy and
naval mutiny – the Thames plunderers stole £506,000 of goods from the
moorings and quays of London; this sum was nearly twice as high as the
amount spent by the Government that year in campaigns to secure more
sugar islands in the West Indies[6].

Pitt was, naturally enough, eager for some form of compromise over
the dock plans. At last, in the winter of 1798–9, the West India Company
abandoned its earlier preference for Wapping and settled for a site on the
Isle of Dogs, where the famous canal-builder William Jessop designed a
30-acre Import Dock and a 24-acre Export Dock. At the same time the
City Corporation accepted responsibility for a canal across the Isle of
Dogs, and the London Dock Company, representing City interests which
traded mainly with North America and Europe, received parliamentary
sanction in 1800 for a 20-acre dock at Wapping, planned by Daniel
Alexander and executed by John Rennie. Three years later an East India
Dock Act established a company which would develop the commercial
facilities of Blackwall.

The coming of docks to the Isle of Dogs was celebrated as an event of
national importance. When Lord Chancellor Loughborough laid the
foundation stone of the West India Dock on the second Saturday in July
1800 he was accompanied down Thames by the Prime Minister, William
Pitt, three other cabinet ministers and a 'numerous train' of City worthies,
making the unfamiliar journey to the Isle of Dogs in a procession of de-
corated barges. Twenty-five months later Pitt's successor, Henry Addington, was again at the Isle of Dogs to see a vessel bearing his name and
wearing the flags of all nations become the first ship to enter the dock.
On 4 August 1806 the East India Dock Company, too, staged a grand
opening spectacle for the benefit of 10,000 spectators. According to the
Gentleman's Magazine there were present on that Monday the Lord Mayor
and his attendant notables (barge-borne and uninvited), the Lords Commissioners of the Admiralty (barge-borne and late, having misjudged the
tide) and 'such an assemblage of British dames in all the pride of beauty,

grace, dignity and dress, as was scarcely ever collected together'. Three of the 'Honourable Company's Ships' entered the dock, to the salute of cannon and frequent salvoes of musketry. First in, reported the *Globe*, was HCS *Admiral Gardner*: 'As she passed in, she answered the salute of the Regimental Artillery, by firing her minute guns, while the company's band on her quarter-deck played "Rule Britannia" with full chorus from the ladies and gentlemen who crowded her decks.' The warmest cheers were reserved for the third arrival, HCS *Earl Camden*: she had fought off a running attack by the flagship of Napoleon's Indian Ocean squadron early in her homeward voyage; and nothing would induce her master to wait to be hauled into dock, like the earlier vessels. Proudly *Earl Camden* reached port 'under a press stay sail and part of her jib'. The whole ceremony, so the *Globe* assured its readers, was marked by 'the splendour and vivacity which distinguish every exhibition connected with the naval prosperity of this country'[7].

The City Canal, which cut two miles off the journey from Blackwall to the Pool, was also opened with some pomp; on 9 December 1805, a 500-ton West Indiaman was towed through by teams of horses yoked together on both banks. But Trafalgar Year had begun with a ceremony further up river when, on 30 January, the *London Packet*, a brig which had risked interception by French raiders off Ushant to bring wines of Oporto to England, became the first ship to enter the London Dock. On this occasion the *Gentleman's Magazine* was less enthusiastic: 'The Dock was nearly covered with a thin ice, the cold being intense, and a considerable fall of snow or sleet at the same time, together with the miserable dirty state of the banks of the Dock for want of pavement; all these circumstances contributed to lessen the effect and pleasure of this truly gratifying scene'[8].

This low-key coverage of what happened in Wapping echoed current prejudices. All had begun well enough; in June 1802 'genteel persons of both sexes' cheered the Prime Minister as he lay the foundation stone and threw down 'a purse of gold ... for the workmen'. But already the Company was unpopular; between 1800 and 1805 no less than 1300 houses were demolished to make way for the new dock and there were frequent complaints that the directors were offering miserly compensation. Nor was this the only charge against the 'Wapping gentlemen'. The chief engineer of the West India Dock alleged they had struck a bargain with the brickmakers, who would divert to the London Dock material required on the Isle of Dogs. The 'Wapping gentlemen' maintained that they had lost labourers to press gangs, so delaying completion of their work. There then followed an episcopal broadside accusing the Company of allowing work on Sundays; and there were dark hints that someone was encouraging the 'criminal classes' to turn their attention down river and threaten with plunder or arson the 'works at present in progress at the Isle of Dogs'. This was improbable, but rivalry between the dock companies remained intense, and from mid-May in 1802 a detachment of Guards was detailed to protect all building operations on the West India Dock and its licensed bonded warehouses. The first 200 dockers were armed and drilled as if they were an auxiliary regiment. The East India Company Volunteers could prevent trouble at Blackwall[9].

Financially the three docks on the north bank of the Thames were a success. For twenty-seven consecutive years the West India Dock Company paid its shareholders the maximum permitted dividend (10 per cent), and dock users found that cargoes were being handled expeditiously and at lower cost. As usual, the London Dock Company received a less favourable Press: dividends of no more than 3 – 4·5 per cent and occasional complaints of exorbitant charges for quay space and warehousing. But the improvement in trading conditions could be seen by anyone using the river. No longer did vessels have to lie off Limehouse or Blackwall clustered together, sometimes six abreast. Cargoes could be brought ashore within two days of reaching the Thames rather than three weeks or a month. And the massive walls – together with the paramilitary guards of the West India Docks and the East India Company and a Marine Police Force, established on Colquhoun's initiative at Wapping – effectively put an end to large-scale plundering. Other docks, smaller in size and run by several different companies, were constructed south of the river and specialised in the timber trade; and in 1812 the Regent's Canal Dock was opened between Shadwell and Limehouse for coastal vessels and barge traffic. Theoretically this small basin should have become England's chief canal port, linking the Thames to the Grand Union Canal at Paddington and so to the Midlands. But the Regent's Canal itself was not completed for another eight years, too late to catch the prosperity of the short-lived Canal Age. The 'Limehouse Basin', widened in 1819, succeeded Wapping's waterfront as the principal quay for coastal colliers.

There is no doubt that this comprehensive system of wet and walled docks became, for London, the most beneficial legacy of the long conflict with revolutionary France and Napoleon. The vast excavations – labourers digging with picks, spades and shovels and using horses and carts or barges to shift hundreds of thousands of tons of earth and alluvial clay and peat – were followed by the completion of some of the finest functional architecture in Europe, notably George Gilt's clinkered brick warehouses beside the West India Dock and the five stacks designed by Daniel Alexander for the London Docks, with their cast-iron columns and spacious vaulted cellars. These architectural and engineering achievements of Alexander, Gilt, John Rennie and Thomas Telford made

THE COMING OF THE DOCKS AND RAILWAYS

it possible for London to remain a great port throughout the following century and a half. Seventy years after the first ships berthed in the docks, one famous guide-book publisher could recommend to foreign tourists the 'interesting sight' of 'the Port, with its immense warehouses, the centre from which the commerce of England radiates all over the globe'; for 'nothing', Baedeker went on to explain, 'will convey to the stranger a better idea of the vast activity and stupendous wealth of London than a visit to these warehouses, filled to overflowing with interminable stores of every kind of foreign and colonial products'[10].

Yet the commercial prosperity brought to the City by these docks and warehouses was purchased at a cost impossible to calculate. The immediate human fatalities were few, although when a protective outer dam collapsed in July 1802 six labourers excavating the West India Dock were drowned as the river water burst down upon them. But the East End was changed out of all recognition. Homes were lost, not only in Wapping, but in Limehouse and Poplar. The East India and West India Dock Companies required a speedier and more direct route to the City than along the narrow Ratcliff Highway. They put money into the private company which, between 1804 and 1810, built the 'Grand Commercial Road', from Aldgate to Limehouse Church, where a West India Dock Road and an East India Dock Road led directly to the new quays. It was as broad and straight as one of Napoleon's *Routes Impériales*, sweeping its way through a corner of St Anne's churchyard as relentlessly as it cut across rope-walks or buildings which had sprung up since the consecration of the church. These new roads divided Limehouse into three parts, in each of which the communities developed characteristics of their own: Irish labourers in the north; 'Chinatown' in the centre; and, in the south, an industrial zone where, even before the opening of today's West Ferry Road in 1812, there was already established an iron works, an oil works and manufacturers of ropes, masts and tackle, and chain cables. Commercial Road itself remained a turnpike until the 1860s, with tolls charged on the vehicles using it, even the sixty covered wagons, each as elegant as a carriage, designed to bring tea chests from the East Indiamen to the Cutler Street warehouse. The West India Dock Company, too, had special means of transport. Passengers and light goods were conveyed to and from the City by short-distance stage-coaches in the 1820s and in 1830 a stone tramway of granite was laid at the side of Commercial Road; it helped horses to haul hogsheads of sugar to the so-called 'bakeries', the brick-built refineries five stories high grouped around Leman Street and Back Church Lane, where until 1870 Commercial Road ended. By 1825 the new thoroughfare was as busy as any along the approaches to London[11].

The West India, East India and London Docks all enjoyed monopolies during their first years of commercial enterprise. But other merchants were eager to profit from the coming of the docks and when, in 1813, Parliament declined to renew the East India Company's privileged trading rights it was a portent of what would follow the return of peace and a new scramble for fresh overseas markets. In 1823 a St Katharine's Dock Company was formed: it sought parliamentary approval to construct two basins, closer to the City than any existing docks. A rapid increase in shipping since the war was, the promoters claimed, causing new congestion and delays in the port; and they argued that all future docks 'should be established on the principle of free competition in trade, and without any exclusive privileges and immunities'[12].

The St Katharine's Dock Bill aroused more passion and protest than any previous building project laid before Parliament. Opponents maintained that the dock was not necessary: the new ships using the port were making short journeys around the coast or across to the near continent; such vessels needed wharves, they argued, not expensive docks. The great objection to the Bill came, however, not from the experts, but from a group of proto-conservationists. For there was no doubt that the scheme would involve great destruction of property: Georgian cottages, a brewery, and the medieval church of St Katharine-by-the-Tower, with its hospital and 13-acre precinct would all have to go.

For 700 years the Queens of England had extended their protection to the Liberty of St Katharine and its tenants – more than 2000 of them by the start of the nineteenth century. But in 1823–4 there was no Queen of England and the people of the precinct, like many in the City, had offended King George IV by their warm support for his estranged and uncrowned consort in the last stormy year of her life. They had, however, their champions: anonymous pamphleteers, radical booksellers and letter writers to *The Times* and to the *Gentleman's Magazine*, whose manager and editor from 1792 to 1826 was the idiosyncratic antiquarian, John Nicholas. Some correspondents – none of whom gave his name or precise address – insisted that it was time to clean up the neighbourhood: 'For many years a respectable female could not pass or repass certain parts of St Katharine's without being exposed to vulgar or indecent abuse,' one writer alleged. But there was in general a strong feeling against the Bill, a fear that part of London's heritage was up for sale to any speculative bidder: 'We might have some future Company petitioning Parliament to appropriate the "building called St Paul's Cathedral" for a pawnbroker's warehouse, or some other receptacle of lumber which they might require,' the *Gentleman's Magazine* declared[13].

Ultimately the campaign failed, although not until the original Bill had been withdrawn and amended. By the spring of 1826 St Katharine-by-the-Tower and the houses around it were rubble, although a new

collegiate church of St Katharine was established in Regent's Park and
the medieval fittings were saved. To make way for St Katharine's Dock
1250 houses and tenements were demolished and 11,300 people forced
to look elsewhere for a home – 'thus improving estates previously lying
waste in the eastern part of the Metropolis,' *The Times* assured its readers
with smug imprecision. Compensation was paid to freeholders and long
leaseholders, but not to the majority of displaced families, who were
simply thrown into the street. If labourers could find somewhere to live,
there was a good prospect of employment for them over the following
two years. Foreign visitors wrote with awed respect of 'the thousand men
and several hundred of horses' they could see excavating the land and
moving the earth to waiting barges. Exactly two years to the day after
the last service was held in the medieval church, a protective dam burst
late at night and the Thames flooded the workings to a depth of 30 feet.
No lives were lost; the workers even gained a few more months of
employment; but, as ever on such occasions, some saw in the accident
a sign of divine wrath. For, although the Dock Act of 1825 stipulated
that all coffins should be treated with decency and propriety, the developers had not spared the hallowed graveyard itself[14].

Yet apart from the church and its dependencies Thomas Telford and
Philip Hardwick had replaced what was, in effect, a Georgian slum with
a group of impressive and compact warehouses and quays; and even the
Gentleman's Magazine admired their work[15]. The brown brick walls were
offset by a Doric colonnade of cast-iron columns and the Doric theme
was retained in the elegant St Katharine Dock House, destroyed by bombs
in the Second World War. Along the quays, so the Company claimed,
there was room for 120 ships 'beside craft at one and the same time' and
the warehouses and vaults could give cover to 110,000 tons of goods.
The dock was opened on 25 October 1828, when the *Elizabeth* – an East
India 'free trader' as opposed to an EIC vessel – led a procession of ships,
dressed overall, through Telford's lock[16]. But among 2000 distinguished
guests there was not a single member of the Duke of Wellington's cabinet.
The building of docks, a national necessity in the days of Pitt and
Addington, had become by the end of George IV's reign merely one more
speculative gamble for the bankers and merchants of the City.

At St Katharine's it was a gamble that failed. In the first five weeks
after the Dock was opened eighty-one vessels unloaded their cargoes on
its quays[17]. But the dock was uneconomic. Costs were high, and the
entrance lock and basin were small. Investors received 3 per cent from
1829 to 1831 and then a mere 2·75 per cent. The dock's promoters had
assumed that large warehouses, holding goods landed close to the City
and its markets, would offset the disadvantages of limited quay space and
the consequent need for rapid loading and unloading. They failed to

anticipate the steam revolution in transport. Within a decade steam locomotives were making the conveyance of goods easier, cheaper and safer than ever before. Within a third of a century steamships, arriving regularly throughout the year, had cut out the need for stockpiling in warehouses. At the same time their greater tonnage meant that the steamships drew more depth of water than Rennie, Telford or any of the earlier engineers envisaged when they designed their lock gates.

It is curious that the St Katharine's Dock Company should have ignored the imminent transport revolution. For it was already in progress around them when they put their proposals to Parliament. The first steam vessel appeared on the Thames in the summer of Waterloo, and soon there were regular services, not only on the river, but around the coast to Ramsgate and, later, Harwich. As early as 1820 the iron steamship *Aaron Manby* was pioneering a passenger route from London down the Thames and up the Seine to Paris, chugging across the Channel at a steady 9 knots; and in the year excavations began on St Katharine's Dock steamships linked London and Portugal. Already, too, steam had outdated the City Canal; ships for the Pool preferred to rely on steamtugs rounding the Isle of Dogs rather than pay heavy transit dues to be slowly manhandled for 1400 yards by hauliers who sang doleful shanties as they pulled on their towing lines and warps. Only a few months after the opening of St Katharine's the City Canal was sold to the West India Dock Company for development as a timber basin[18]. Soon there were plans to give a cohesive unity to the port facilities in the Isle of Dogs, although it was not until 1838 that the East and West India Dock Companies were formally amalgamated.

By then merchants and bankers could judge for themselves the significance of the transport revolution in the capital. Most London labourers still walked everywhere, but by 1835 white collar workers were beginning to use the horse omnibuses which had recently come to the East End from the City and were plying regularly through Whitechapel, Poplar and Limehouse. The first steam trains in the London area ran from London Bridge to Deptford on 14 December 1836, six months before the accession of Queen Victoria. Soon fifty-six trains a day – one every quarter of an hour – were carrying passengers over the four miles of arched viaduct; more than 600,000 passengers used the line before it was extended to Greenwich fifteen months later. It was, however, essentially a middle-class suburban service benefiting, as *The Times* reported, those 'citizens of London whose villas adorned the picturesque scenes which abounded in the neighbourhood'[19].

Similarly, the earliest line in the East End was also intended for passengers rather than for commerce. Work began in March 1837 on the Eastern Counties Railway Company's route from Romford (and ultimately Norwich and Yarmouth) through Ilford and Stratford to a temporary station in Devonshire Street, between Bethnal Green and Mile End – still, in those years, on the edge of rural Middlesex. From Romford to Mile End the line opened at midsummer 1839 but plans to extend it to Shoreditch ran into difficulties, 'consequent upon passing through crowded building property, intersected with sewers, old ditches and numerous cesspools'. Although the Shoreditch extension was ready for service in November 1840, work continued on the terminus for another two years. In 1846 it was officially re-named Bishopsgate station and served travellers to Cambridge and East Anglia until 1874 when, after passengers had been 'frequently heard expressing their disgust' at the station's condition, the Great Eastern Railway provided them instead with the sepulchral amenities of Liverpool Street, a terminus less than a quarter of a mile from Spitalfields[20].

Proposals for a railway to run parallel to Great Commercial Road had aroused interest in the City and at Westminster even before the opening of the Deptford line in December 1836. Its promoters argued that such a line would attract passengers and make commercial transactions speedier and more efficient by bringing the City and the Docks into closer contact. The East and West India Companies backed the scheme; opposed to it was a powerful City lobby with interests in the London Dock, St Katharine's Dock, and the riverside wharves. Four years of prevarication delayed completion. Eventually, on 4 July 1840, the London & Blackwall Railway began services on a four-mile route from Brunswick Wharf through Poplar and Stepney to a terminus in the Minories. The new line was not, however, a steam railway. It used cable haulage and depended on more than 7 miles of hemp rope, operated by winding engines at each end. Trains did not stop at the intervening stations; they merely detached the rear carriage each time, picking it up again on the return journey. Because there was no steam to pollute the atmosphere, the City Corporation allowed the line to be extended 600 yards to the west in 1841, with a new terminus inside the City, at Fenchurch Street. Cables were used until February 1849 when the Blackwall line became a more conventionally operated steam railway. Three graceful 87-foot arches, built to carry the cable-hauled trains across the Regent's Canal at Limehouse, continue to serve the Docklands Light Railway a century and a half later[21].

The Blackwall line had interesting minor social consequences: it encouraged the popularity of steamer excursions down the Thames from Brunswick Wharf and, during the 1840s, made riverside taverns from Stepney to Blackwall fleetingly fashionable. Yet it seemed unlikely that this four-mile cable track would attain the economic importance envisaged by its promoters. Only if the London & Blackwall Railway were

linked to a major trunk route could it bring new trades and industry to
the districts it served. A spur built to Bow in the hopes of associating
the L&BR with the Eastern Counties Railway Company aroused little
response. But the directors of the London & North-Western Railway
Company were more far-sighted. To them it seemed that a new line
passing through the northern and eastern fringe of the capital and having
direct access to the docks would give London's commerce better links
with the Midlands than the slow-moving barge traffic of the Regent's
Canal and Grand Union Canal could ever provide. Accordingly in 1846
the LNWR and the L&BR established the East & West India Docks &
Birmingham Junction Railway – which in 1853 was re-named the North
London Railway – to build a line from the Birmingham to Euston trunk
route at Chalk Farm, through Hackney, Bow and Stepney to Millwall, at
the southern tip of the Isle of Dogs. From Bow passenger trains would
turn westwards into Fenchurch Street, where the platforms were within
half a mile of the heart of the City. By 1851 an average of 4800 people
a day were using the line, and goods trains were beginning to run along
the northern arc to the Birmingham Junction at Hampstead Road. When
the extension to Millwall was completed in 1852 the riverside industries
of the East End were drawn closer than ever before to the centres of iron
and coal production, while the factories of the Midlands were assured of
an outlet to the sea through the busiest port in the world[22].

The example of the LNWR was soon followed by other companies.
The Eastern Counties had second thoughts and in 1847 made its own
bid for dock traffic and freight from the riverside industries by a track along
the Essex bank of the River Lea from Stratford to North Woolwich. Short
branch lines, constructed solely for goods purposes, proliferated,
especially after the opening in 1855 of the Victoria Dock, which was
built by two of the great railway contractors, Sir Henry Peto and Sir
Thomas Brassey. The Midland and the Great Northern sought access to
the docks, not by cutting new lines through Hackney and Stepney, but
by negotiating running rights over existing tracks and constructing goods
depots and sidings of their own, notably in Whitechapel. But the chief
riverside passenger route north of the Thames – the London, Tilbury and
Southend line from Fenchurch Street to Shoeburyness, forty miles away
on the Estuary – belongs to a later period of railway enterprise.

Not only did docks and railways reshape the map of outer London;
their construction changed the whole character of social life and labour
in the East End. Skilled riverside crafts, furniture manufacture and traditional trades declined in competition with new industries: the cement
and chemical works; the making of soap, matches or confectionery; and,
above all, by work on the great slipways and stocks of the iron shipbuilding yards. Factories came to the open foreshore around the Isle of

Dogs and to what had been marshy pasture beside the lower Lea. William Cubitt – whose brother Thomas had developed Bloomsbury, Pimlico, Clapham and Camden Town – gave the family's name to wasteland on the south-eastern fringe of the Isle of Dogs which he purchased on long lease from the Countess of Glengall: Cubitt Town was laid out with timber wharves, brickfields, sawmills, a cement works, a parish church, and houses of two or three storeys in roads which followed the pattern of the old marsh drainage ditches. Elsewhere, however, homes were lost: the building of four miles of the Blackwall line in 1836 threatened 2850 dwellings; Farthing Street and Patience Street and Vine Street were lost beneath Shoreditch terminus in 1841; and 900 working-class tenements had to go, when the North London Railway cut two miles of new track[23]. Even more evicted families were left to fend for themselves in the 1860s and 1870s, during the second wave of railway expansion.

Railway trains, horse buses, river steamers and the Thames Tunnel – which, in 1843, at last gave pedestrians a link between Wapping and Rotherhithe – should have drawn the East End more closely into the life of London by making travel easier. Yet, paradoxically, these improvements in communications created more barriers than they swept away. The swing bridges at the entrance to the docks on the Isle of Dogs emphasised the self-contained sense of local identity which became a characteristic of the 'Islanders'. But from Hackney down to Stepney Green the coming of the age of steam led to a significant migration. Comfortably prosperous company clerks, minor civil servants and dockyard officials moved out of east London rather than see their houses covered with grime and soot; the railways allowed those who could afford to do so to travel to work from suburban stations along the Essex border, like Lea Bridge at Leyton (1840) or Forest Gate (1841). The withdrawal of these white-collar workers confirmed the character of the East End as a dormitory for the manual labouring class. At the same time the railways and steamers made it possible for more and more outsiders to come to London in search of a home, a refuge, and a place in the queues for casual labour.

It was natural that these newcomers, mainly Irish and Jewish but some Indians and Chinese, should keep together, preserving what was culturally familiar to them in a hard and precarious existence. But this tendency to remain isolated in particular quarters of the East End was intensified by the physical appearance of the town around them. Green fields still lay within easy walking distance of many close-built courts and alleys in Stepney, Whitechapel and Bethnal Green. After the First World War a former resident of Bromley-by-Bow could look back some 70 years and recall his childhood in Brunswick Road, 'Dear, charming beautiful Bromley ... with its trees, its blackbirds and thrushes, its fields, its lovely gardens with their beautiful scents, its strawberries which I used to gather and eat'[24]. Yet youngsters living half a mile nearer London were denied such idyllic delights. Occasionally, parts of historic parishes were separated by what a contemporary described as 'the deep gorge of a railway cutting'. But more often the impenetrable walls protecting dockyards and warehouses close to the river were matched inland by brick viaducts and embankments which supported the railways over a low-lying area. No openings or passages between tenements gave overcrowded families in Whitechapel or Bethnal Green that vista of a wider world that the 'Islanders' could still enjoy as they looked out across Greenwich Reach. The prevailing impression throughout the East End was claustrophobic: railways may have become the arteries along which flowed the life-blood of an industrialised nation; but where was the bloodstream to find its oxygen?

5

Crime and Cholera

'STRANGERS who act prudently will avoid the mixed company in a place like this, especially such as wish to escape the fangs of those called "kidnappers" or "East India crimps",' wrote the Welshman David Hughson in his *Walks through London*, an idiosyncratic guidebook published two years after the battle of Waterloo. The place to 'avoid' was the fittingly named Darkhouse Lane, which ran north-east from Billingsgate. It 'contained a number of public houses, used by watermen, fishermen, females and others' and was so 'confined' that 'candles are necessary all day'[1]. Hughson might well have advised his prudent readers to keep away from even more sinister alleys beyond Darkhouse Lane. But why look farther than Tower Hill? Visitors occasionally wandered up Rosemary Lane and through the old clothes market of Rag Fair ('their watches and valuables left at home'), but it was improbable that any would penetrate inner Spitalfields or risk robbery and assault along the Ratcliff Highway. Already it was rumoured that the inner eastern suburbs were safe havens for the lawless and the dissolute.

There is no doubt that London outside the city limits was inadequately policed at the end of the Napoleonic Wars. From 1793 there were paid magistrates, with six constables under their orders, at Shadwell and at Wapping but elsewhere policing remained a responsibility of parish vestries. Unpaid parish constables, paid beadles and, at night, hired watchmen were still expected to keep crime in check, despite the natural increase in population and labour migration. At Bow Street in the 1760s the Westminster stipendiary magistrate, Sir John Fielding, had augmented his brother Henry's 'thief-taker' runners by experimental patrols which were intended to safeguard travellers so long as they were within four miles of the City limits. This improvised system was still operating half a century later, although a posse of scarlet-waistcoated horsemen had begun to venture into Essex as far as Romford and Epping in the year of Trafalgar. Yet neither these 'Robin Redbreasts' nor the (much overrated) Bow Street Runners helped police the teeming back alleys in the East End. Apart from Great Commercial Road and the riverside waterfront – where, thanks to Patrick Colquhoun's initiative, a Thames Police Office and the dock companies' private constabularies safeguarded order and property – there were few districts in which law-abiding families could count on effective protection from the central government. Not until Michaelmas 1829 was the burden at last lifted from the parish vestries and the first Metropolitan Police constables appeared on the streets of inner east London[2].

Some crimes listed in contemporary reports were common to all the poorer and overcrowded quarters of London: garrotting, an assault akin to mugging, in which a thief's victim is rendered insensible by pressing on the throat with fingers or a stick, was as much a threat in Holborn, St Giles's and Southwark as in Spitalfields and Shadwell. And there were footpads between Kensington and Westminster as well as along Whitechapel Road. On the other hand, East End crime had its own peculiarities. Along the roads into town from Stratford and Old Ford unemployed casual labourers specialised in ambushing droves of cattle on their way to Smithfield Market. On Lady Day in 1818 a crowd of several hundred men seized a bullock and used it as a battering ram to attack a Spitalfields silk warehouse against whose owner they appear to have borne a grudge. The warehouse workers poured boiling water on their attackers and were defending themselves with shotguns when the frightened bullock ran mad and tossed and injured some of the crowd before falling dead. Four attackers, seized by a constable in the general confusion, appeared subsequently in court and received astonishingly mild sentences: one of six months, two of three months and one of only a month. More alarming to the community as a whole were a series of attacks eight years later in which gangs would drive terrified cattle into the narrow streets as night fell and use them to charge down anyone whom they met. Those who fell would be robbed as they lay on the ground. In a single fortnight more than fifty people were attacked in this way[3].

These curious affrays emphasised the lawlessness of inner Spitalfields. In themselves, however, they were not sufficiently serious to give the East End that flesh-creeping notoriety which it was never entirely able to shake off. That was the achievement of a motiveless killer who, in the miasmic murk of a dark December in 1811, claimed seven victims along the Ratcliff Highway. The animal bestiality of these murders shocked, not only the riverside community, but all who read their newspapers, whether in London or the provinces. More than forty years later Thomas de Quincey – living at Grasmere, nearly 300 miles away, at the time of the Ratcliff Highway murders – was still so fascinated by the killings that he wrote them up, at great length and with some imaginative licence, in his appendix to the essay on *'Murder considered as One of the Fine Arts'*[4].

Today these murders would rate SHOCK/HORROR/KILLING headlines in a tabloid daily and soon be forgotten as one of yesterday's sensations. But Regency London could count on a greater respect for human life among its hardened criminals. Moreover, despite the thievery of high-waymen and footpads, society was less accustomed to crimes of violence in the home or its immediate vicinity. For why, otherwise, would Thomas Marr, a draper living at 29 Ratcliff Highway, have risked sending his maid, Mary, out to purchase oysters when he was about to close his shop, shortly before midnight on Saturday, 7 December 1811? Not that anything happened to Mary: despite trudging around Shadwell and Wapping for some fifty minutes, she found no oyster stalls open and returned home unmolested. The shop was locked up and silent, but when she hammered on the door she thought she heard someone breathing heavily on the inside. Eventually neighbours and a watchman helped her to break in. They discovered Marr and his boy apprentice downstairs with their throats cut and his young wife and baby child dead upstairs. On the following Thursday week the murderer struck again, killing the publican of the neighbouring King's Arms tavern, his wife and their servant.

Public revulsion over these two incidents induced the government to take a rare interest in the affairs of Shadwell: the existing watchmen were dismissed, a new patrol was recruited and armed with pistols and cutlasses, and rewards were offered for 'the apprehension of the villain'. Local zeal led to forty arrests over Christmas and the New Year, but the magistrates released all except John Williams, a seaman lodging at the Pear Tree tavern. It was rumoured that Williams and Marr had once been shipmates on an East Indiaman; a bloodstained mallet, which Williams was said to have acquired from a Danish master-craftsman well known in the neighbourhood, was found at 29 Ratcliff Highway; and a seaman's knife, darkened by coagulated blood, was discovered among his clothing at the Pear Tree. Williams, fortunate to escape a lynching from the Shadwell crowd, was remanded in an isolated cell; and there, before he could be brought to trial, he hanged himself. The evidence against Williams was purely circumstantial, and for the King's Arms murders extremely thin; but it was assumed that suicide implied an admission of guilt. The corpse, with the mallet and the knife on show beside it, was loaded on to a cart and paraded through the main streets of Shadwell and Wapping. Ten thousand people are said to have watched the funeral procession of the Marr family; and at least that number execrated the body of their alleged killer. Eventually a stake was driven though the dead man's heart and the body was thrown into a hole dug at the corner of Cable Street and Cannon Street Road.

The murders, and the passionate feelings they aroused along the riverside hamlets, strengthened the uncomprehending suspicion with which government ministers in Westminster regarded this terra incognita to the east of Aldgate Pump. A minor incident during the last Christmas of the Napoleonic Wars well illustrates their fear of the unknown and the unfamiliar. On the afternoon of 27 December 1813 Lord Castlereagh set out from his home in St James's Square for Harwich. Never before had a Foreign Secretary left England for a series of summit conferences abroad. Ahead of him lay five months of trying negotiations on the continent and difficult journeys along two thousand miles of road ravaged by the final campaigns against Napoleon. Yet on that Monday evening it seemed momentarily as if the whole enterprise might founder within an hour of leaving Westminster; for as Castlereagh's four-carriage cavalcade reached Aldgate it was enveloped by an icy yellow fog which forced outriders to dismount and lead their horses cautiously down the Whitechapel Road by the light of flambeaux. Castlereagh was alarmed: what if footpads clambered aboard, cut the baggage loose, and robbed the envoys and their families of clothing, valuables and funds? Anxiously the Foreign Secretary ordered his servants to sit firmly on every trunk and box and be ready to repel boarders. They were not disturbed; the rivers Lea and Roding were crossed with relief and without ambush. All four carriages, and their contents, reached the safety of a Romford coaching inn before midnight and clattered into fogbound Harwich early the following afternoon[5].

Although Castlereagh's apprehension is understandable it was misplaced. Petty crime flourished in the cramped courts and alleys off Whitechapel Road, but the people were too destitute for organised brigandage, or indeed for the radical insurrection which the government feared in the aftermath of the wars. During January 1812 – the month in which

Shadwell and Wapping execrated Williams's corpse – in Brick Lane, less than a mile to the north of Ratcliff, 6000 people a day were dependent for sustenance on the ladling spoons of a soup kitchen, maintained by a predominantly Quaker charity; and in the year of Waterloo an official survey on 'mendicity in the metropolis' reported that there were 828 Irish beggars in Whitechapel alone[6].

In the immediate post-war years, there was relative prosperity for the hand-loom weavers of the silk industry, but the boom failed to raise living standards in Spitalfields itself. The more fortunate weavers took the opportunity to migrate to the southern edge of Bethnal Green, where new, two-storey, terraced houses were quickly built for them in Cheshire Street and the adjoining roads. But it proved to be a bubble prosperity: complaints of unfair competition led William Huskisson, as Chancellor of the Exchequer, to introduce fiscal reforms in 1824 which destroyed the protection offered to weavers by the Spitalfields Act of 1773 and removed the prohibition on foreign finished silks. Although the imports were subject to a tariff of 30 per cent, an influx of overseas goods led to a sharp decline in handloom weaving. By 1830 the 'extreme distress', which was recognised as 'peculiar to the poor of Spitalfields' as early as the winter of 1806–7, had spread the length of Brick Lane to envelop much of Bethnal Green, especially along Hackney Road. It was in this decaying part of a sprawling parish that in 1831 Bishop and Williams, the Burke and Hare of east London, pursued their trade. A fourteen-year-old Italian, and probably two other youngsters, were drugged and drowned in a well behind a house in Nova Scotia Gardens. Their bodies were then hawked around the anatomists of London's hospitals[7].

In the 1820s and 1830s, however, Bethnal Green was notorious not so much for murder as for corruption. Until the Metropolis Management Act of 1855 there was no all-embracing local authority for London. Administration was left to the officials elected at the vestry meetings of ecclesiastical parishes; these gatherings might be attended by all rate-payers or by a select few. This cumbersome and archaic arrangement was easy to abuse; and for a third of a century it was systematically manipulated in Bethnal Green to benefit Joseph Merceron and his family. Originally Merceron was a clerk in a lottery office. During the harshest years of the Revolutionary Wars he emerged as a charitable champion of Bethnal Green's poor and by the winter of 1796–7 was chairman of the Watch Trust, responsible for law and order in the local community. The bounds of his personal empire spread rapidly: control of the paving trust, commissioner of sewers, treasurer of the Poor Rate funds, and magistrate. He also owned eleven public houses and received rent – or possibly protection money – from eleven other beer shops. When the vestry met in St Matthew's Church, Merceron would pack the assembly with several hundred artisans and, a contemporary reported, 'instigate his creatures to riot and clamour' so that 'the will and opinion of the major part of the parish were subservient to Mr Merceron's views and interests for a long course of years'. In 1813 he was accused of illegalities in raising and administering the poor rate, but the charge was dropped. However five years later – in the third week of May 1818 – Merceron went on trial for 'corrupt conduct as a magistrate in re-licensing disorderly public houses, his property' and for having defrauded the 'poor rate funds of St Matthew, Bethnal Green ... of £925 1s 3d'; and he was gaoled for eighteen months. By the following summer, a shorthand account of his trial could 'be had of all booksellers', the reader also being able to follow the proceedings against the former rector and others, who were found not guilty of conspiring with the disgraced Treasurer of the Poor Rate Funds. Boss Merceron, it seemed, had fallen[8].

But not, however, the pillars of his empire. By 1822 Merceron's son-in-law was vestry clerk and was re-elected as head of one of the commissions. Within a year he was sharing control of the vestry with his son and son-in-law. Soon the family was again in charge of the Watch Board and the paving trusts, self-perpetuating guardians of a parish which had already risen from 22,310 inhabitants at the start of the century to over 50,000 twenty years later. There were complaints of atrocious conditions for boys in Bethnal Green workhouse and allegations of neglect in maintaining fences, banks and ditches around the Green itself. Fourteen years after Merceron's conviction, the commissioners investigating the working of the Poor Law noted that the parishioners of Bethnal Green 'have seen a person's condition greatly improved after having served the office of overseer', there being 'no ostensible reason' for this new prosperity 'except that he has been in office'. Only at his death, in the year of Victoria's accession, did Merceron relax his grip on the affairs of Bethnal Green. By then alarm over the health hazards of what were beginning to be called 'slums' was inaugurating a new era in local administration[9].

In the second week of February 1832, while Westminster was rapt in battle over parliamentary reform, cholera came to London for the first time. From Rotherhithe it crept along the south bank of the Thames to Southwark and Lambeth and soon leapt the river to Ratcliff, Limehouse, Whitechapel and Hoxton. No one was surprised at its coming, for it had ravaged huge tracts of the continent, spreading westwards from Moscow in 1830 to cover much of eastern and central Europe within fifteen months. Doctors were, however, puzzled at the way in which the disease seemed to jump from district to district, for it was not realised that the bacillus could thrive for a fortnight in the capital's rudimentary water system. Emergency Boards of Health were established, with authority from the Privy Council to close cesspools and order the scouring of sewers and the cleansing of slaughterhouses. For a few weeks medical reports from London's eastern suburbs went directly to the centre of government, revealing the appalling standards maintained by Merceron and his fellow 'Commissioners of Sewers'. By the autumn of 1832, however, the threat of cholera had receded and the Boards were disbanded. Only a few reformers who believed in the need for scientific government intervention to cure social ills heeded the lessons of the epidemic. Among them was Edwin Chadwick, the Secretary of the new Poor Law Commissioners.

Chadwick, aged thirty-two at the time of the first cholera epidemic, became the greatest pioneer of sanitation and public health in England, receiving a belated knighthood in his ninetieth year. Few contemporaries liked him, for he was ill-tempered, impatient and mistrustful; not until sixty years after his death did he begin to get a good press from historians, and there are still some who regard his methods as disastrous[10]. But it is clear he possessed the keen eye of a good reporter and the analytical mind of a ruthlessly efficient bureaucrat. When typhus swept through London in 1837 he was disturbed by the burden thrown on the poor rates, arguing that it would cost less to improve living conditions than to provide passing relief for the sick, the widows and the orphans each time pestilence struck the great cities. Characteristically he called for detailed reports from the districts where there were the heaviest claims for relief: Dr Neil Arnott and Dr James Kay would examine health hazards in Ratcliff, Stepney and Wapping; Dr Thomas Southwood Smith would study conditions in Bethnal Green and Whitechapel.

The Poor Law Commissioners published the doctors' reports in May 1838, Southwood Smith subsequently completing an additional street-by-street survey of the filthiest districts, 'where the very worst forms of fever always abound'. Yet, as he wrote, 'Even in Church Street, Bethnal Green, the main thoroughfare, there is no drain, the water runs off as it can, and now and then the parish authorities send round a mudcart to gather up what becomes so thick as to block the way'. And the report concluded, 'It is not possible for any language to convey an adequate conception of the poisonous condition in which large portions of both these districts always remain, winter and summer, in dry and rainy seasons, from the masses of putrefying matter which are allowed to accumulate'[11].

Much of the material in these reports Chadwick had expected: the ill-ventilation of back-to-back cottages; the absence of sloping sewers; the appallingly cramped conditions in lodging-houses for seamen and migrant labourers. Perhaps, too, at Westminster some peers and MPs anticipated grim reading of the Commissioners' bluebook, for by now there were many members of the propertied classes to whom east London

was familiar as a fictional concept, thanks to the early writings of Dickens:
more than a year before, *Sketches by Boz* had described the Ratcliff
Highway, 'that reservoir of dirt, drunkenness and drabs; thieves, oysters,
baked potatoes and pickled salmon'; and in the same weeks that the
doctors were compiling their reports successive instalments of *Oliver Twist*
portrayed low life in seediest Whitechapel. But to turn from Dickens to
the realities of the bluebook was to make his account of Nancy's murder
read like fantasy melodrama. What shocked those who lived comfortably
distant from the East End was the doctors' painfully comprehensive
catalogue of putrefaction: the unemptied cesspools and privies; open
sewers; stinking slaughterhouses; and the physically nauseating burial-
grounds, where decomposing bodies were inadequately interred. Even in
death an East Ender could be certain of overcrowding.

The coldly unemotive propaganda of Chadwick and his doctors stirred
a slothful Parliament into a semblance of action. A Commons select
committee was established in order to report on the health of towns. The
House of Lords accepted a proposal by the Bishop of London that Chadwick himself should report on the 'sanitary condition of the labouring
population'. Southwood Smith urged the Commons select committee
to establish a Board of Health to take over tasks too great for local
commissioners: 'These poor people are victims that are sacrificed,' he told
the committee, as he recalled his experiences in the East End. 'The effect
is the same as if twenty or thirty thousand of them were annually taken
out of their homes and put to death; the only difference being that they
are left in them to die.' Chadwick, too, concentrated on the East End,
although he was so obsessed with the need for outdoor drains and sewers
that he missed the significance of too many people in too few rooms.
There are only two maps in his report: one illustrated sanitary-conscious
Leeds; the other was a mortality map of Bethnal Green parish to show
how poor sanitation allowed disease to flourish in particular streets[12].

The hungry forties were a time of hardship for the labouring classes
throughout the nation, not simply in the East End, and governments,
Whig or Tory, had to remember the mines and mills in the North and
Midlands as well as London's open sewers and cesspools. So impressed
was Lord Melbourne's Whig government with Dr Southwood Smith's
studies that he was asked to help draw up a report on child labour in the
coal mines. He was, however, on hand when, in 1840, the Marquis of
Normanby, Melbourne's Home Secretary since the previous summer,
became the first cabinet minister to set out on a fact-finding tour of the
slums of Bethnal Green and Whitechapel. And Southwood Smith was
again an escort when, in September 1841, the dedicated humanitarian
Lord Ashley (from 1851 onwards, the seventh Earl of Shaftesbury) made
a similar journey. 'What a perambulation have I taken today in company

with Dr Southwood Smith!' Ashley wrote in his diary. 'What scenes of
filth, discomfort and disease! ... One whiff of Cow Yard, Blue Anchor or
Bakers Court outweighs ten pages of letterpress'[13].

Something was already being done to bring order into one aspect of
local government. The Poor Law Amendment Act of 1834 established
Boards of Guardians, elected by ratepayers, to take over from parish
vestries all responsibility for workhouses and pauper relief. The Guardians
were expected to treat able-bodied vagrants as the parasites of a thrifty
society; workhouses became, in Chadwick's notorious phrase, 'uninviting
places of wholesome restraint'. The system of elected Poor Law Guardians – which, with structural modifications, survived in metropolitan
London until 1929 – started badly in the East End: because of the
relatively small number of property owners, the Guardians had to levy a
high poor rate which they sought to keep under control by the most
grudging economies. To discourage able-bodied 'scroungers' by making
them undertake heavy and monotonous work was in keeping with the
general philosophy of Chadwick and his Poor Law Commissioners; but
to refuse money for preventive sanitation was not. The Guardians were
also hampered by further social upheaval in their 'sickly, pauperized and
vicious ... area'[14]: the coming of the railway to Shoreditch in 1840 and
the cutting of Commercial Street northwards from Whitechapel through
Spitalfields over the following five years made many evicted families
destitute; and a new influx of poor Irish, made desperate by the potato
blight of 1845–6, increased the number of able-bodied unemployed
seeking outdoor relief. By 1847 – when the Poor Law Commissioners
were replaced by a Poor Law Board of five privy councillors – it was
becoming clear that the constant stream of jobless wanderers, abandoned
children, widows, sick and aged were becoming too great a burden for
the elected Guardians and their limited resources.

In that year Dr Hector Gavin, lecturer in forensic medicine at Charing
Cross Hospital, visited many of the streets which had been surveyed
in 1838 by Southwood Smith. Gavin, a meticulous and indefatigable
observer, developed these field studies into a book which, while noting
recent changes, was intended primarily to support the agitation for
sanitary reform. When, early in 1848, his *Sanitary Ramblings: Being
Sketches and Illustrations of Bethnal Green* was published, much of its detail
made familiar reading. Yet there had been two major improvements
since 1838: private companies had provided new cemeteries at Bow in
September 1841 and four years later, on a smaller scale, in what is now
Meath Gardens, on the borders of Bethnal Green and Mile End; and the
East Enders had acquired their first state-sponsored recreational 'lungs'
with the opening in 1845 of James Pennethorne's Victoria Park on
Bonner's Fields, the site of the old episcopal deer park on the southern

edge of Hackney. Three new and wide converging streets, also planned
by Pennethorne, made the Park accessible to space-starved Londoners.
But if there was by now an almost suburban salubrity on the eastern
fringe of Gavin's Bethnal Green, elsewhere the picture remained starkly
depressing. Streets were cleaned only once a quarter and 94 per cent of
them were still without underground sewers. Dr Gavin found that in the
southern and western parts of the parish there was such overcrowding
that people were often packed fourteen to a room. He estimated that life
expectancy among the labouring class was sixteen, with 22 per cent of
the children born in 1847 dying within that same year. Sometimes
privies were shared by forty or fifty people; thirty houses could depend
on a single standpipe with an intermittent supply of water. Gavin pointed
out that there were 'highly coloured deposits' present in the water. This
was an ominous comment; for, as Gavin well knew, all the signs from
the provinces and the continent suggested that another wave of cholera
was about to attack London[15].

It was through no fault of Lord Normanby that so little had changed.
His escorted tour of the East End in 1840 made so deep an impression
on him that he secured the rapid passage through the House of Lords of
a Borough Improvements Bill and a Drainage of Buildings Bill. These
measures would have bolstered local authorities in their struggle for
better housing and sanitation. But the Bills never became law. For in
May 1841 Melbourne's Whig government fell, Normanby went out of
office, and Peel's Tories had no inclination to take up their predecessors'
programme. Ashley likened Sir Robert Peel to 'an iceberg with a slight
thaw on the surface'. He accepted the need for reforms 'to promote the
health and comfort of the poorer classes', but the improvised expedients
favoured by Normanby and his Whig friends did not attract him. Ideally
Peel believed in carefully planned policies, based on the wise precepts of
a Royal Commission. But time was against him. In July 1846 Peel, too,
fell from office and it was left to Lord John Russell in August 1848 to
hurry through a reform which satisfied nobody, by creating a General
Board of Health, of which both Ashley and Chadwick were members. The
Board, however, had no direct authority in London: it might recommend
action; it could never compel it.

Had Parliament not been preoccupied with the Irish famine and
confused over repeal of the Corn Laws, an effective public health act
could have ended the sanitary anarchy before midsummer in 1849,
when the second cholera epidemic reached the East End. The imminence
of disaster did indeed win for the General Board of Health a right to
direct local authorities anywhere in the country to clean up particularly
noisome districts, but this grudging concession was no more than a
temporary measure. Moreover the Board still could not compel the Poor

Law Guardians to obey its instructions. At the start of the epidemic the Guardians in both Whitechapel and Bethnal Green scornfully flouted the Board's recommendations to cleanse infected houses and open emergency dispensaries. Local worthies sometimes feared centralisation more intensely than the killer disease[16].

This second epidemic lasted in London for only four months, but it was worse than its predecessor. Doctor Gavin, whom the General Board appointed Medical Inspector of Bethnal Green, Hackney and Shoreditch, found that the high-intensity areas depicted on Chadwick's map for 1838 were, once again, the most grievously hit; there were deaths in almost every house in the Nichol Street area, between Shoreditch and the northern end of Brick Lane. Gavin's familiarity with the district enabled him to visit homes likely to become infested and treat cholera in its earliest stages. He calculated that out of 85,000 people in Bethnal Green, 10,000 received free medical treatment for cholera and less than one in ten of them died from the disease. To have contained the cholera in this way, despite the slow pace of reform and the hostility of the Poor Law Guardians, was a notable achievement; it emphasised the value of detailed knowledge of a particular area, street by street. South of the river Rotherhithe and Southwark had a higher mortality rate than anywhere on the north shore. In London as a whole there were some 30,000 cases of cholera, with 14,000 of them proving fatal[17].

Once again, as in 1832, the government and general public became complacently indifferent to health problems as soon as the cholera threat receded. Even the closure of ancient burial grounds and the provision of large cemeteries across the Essex boundary provoked bitter controversies which rumbled on for seven years. Disputes over the need for a main drainage system filled many columns of The Times between 1848 and 1850; they discredited Chadwick, who had made the disastrous mistake of ordering existing sewers to be systematically flushed, thus causing infected excrement to be emptied into the Thames and its tributaries. Legislation which required water companies to filter any supplies drawn from the rivers entered the statute book in 1852, but little was done to enforce the new regulations. A year later a Smoke Nuisance (Metropolis) Act gave hopes of thinning the grimy wreath from factory chimneys which, on so many days, would hang cheerlessly over Hackney and the Tower Hamlets.

It was not until 1855, when the Metropolitan Board of Works brought London's local authorities together in suspicious and uneasy collaboration, that serious attention was given to a comprehensive drainage system. Even then little progress was made before the coming of the 'Great Stink' in the hot summer of 1858 when, as The Times recorded, the 'pestilential odour' of effluence in the Thames drove both Disraeli and Gladstone from a Commons committee, with handkerchiefs to their nostrils[18]. At last, in 1865, the Prince of Wales opened the first section of Joseph Bazalgette's engineering triumph, a main drainage system for the whole of London. The piped sewerage of the riverside was carried to lower Stratford, where a pumping station, heavily disguised as a Byzantine basilica, was sited on the former mead land of the Cistercian abbey. It then ran parallel to Bazalgette's northern outfall sewer, both drains finally reaching his filter beds at Barking Creek. Surely there was no longer any need for what Disraeli called 'a pervading apprehension of pestilence' in London's eastern approaches?

Cholera, however, devastated the expeditionary force sent to fight Russia in 1854–5, and several specialists who had combated cholera in the East End travelled out to the Crimea. Among them was Dr Gavin, who died at Balaclava from a shooting accident when unbuckling his uniform. In London another cholera epidemic, which coincided with the start of the Crimean War, claimed more than 10,000 victims; the heaviest mortality rate fell in Soho, Vauxhall and Southwark rather than in Bethnal Green, Whitechapel or along the north shore riverside. But at least this third visitation enabled the physicians to identify the means of propagation of cholera; the observations of Dr John Snow, the Queen's obstetrician, showed convincingly that cholera was water-borne rather than inhaled as a poison produced by putrefaction, the assumption of many earlier medical theorists.

Clean, filtered water would, it was clear, prevent the spread of another epidemic. But with an estimated one in five of MPs holding shares in water companies it was difficult, as Chadwick complained, to have health matters discussed impartially in the Commons. Moreover, in the poorer districts the supply system remained primitive. There were still public wells in some parts of the East End and considerable areas solely dependent on standpipes for their water supply; many families having to let the water stand in pails, buckets or jugs for most of the day. In 1862 a health inspection of 133 overcrowded courts in the Whitechapel slums revealed that in forty-eight of them the families had to scramble to draw their water from stand taps which were turned on for periods varying from fifteen to thirty minutes a day, and never on Sundays. On an average each of these stand taps served sixty-seven people[19].

Despite improved understanding in the medical profession and apparent progress in public health legislation, for the East End the worst cholera epidemic was still to come. Unexpectedly on 18 July 1866 a cholera death was reported in Poplar. Within three days it was clear that the disease was spreading rapidly, especially along the length of Whitechapel Road and Mile End Road. During the following week, on average, eleven people died from cholera every two hours in the Tower Hamlets. By 28

July it was realised that the line of mortality coincided closely with the area to which the East London Water Company supplied water from the River Lea, 'not a drop ... unfiltered' so their chief engineer asserted. But in one house, in which two children died, their father found a putrid eel fourteen inches long blocking his pipes; and there was at least one similar incident elsewhere in the East End. By the end of the first week in August few people doubted that the Company had, indeed, supplied unfiltered water to their consumers[20].

'If the cholera comes, Lord help us' had been an inner prayer of working-class Londoners for more than a third of a century. After 1866 that supplication could disappear from the private litanies; despite a sudden scare twenty years later, the scourge was gone for all time. But no fewer than 4276 people died from the disease that summer between the City boundaries and West Ham, eastwards across the Lea. A private government inquiry confirmed that the East London Water Company had committed a breach of the 1852 Metropolitan Water Act[21]. No prosecution was ever made over a crime which, for its magnitude, makes the killings in the Ratcliff Highway and the bestiality of the Bethnal Green body-snatchers seem like everyday aberrations.

6

The Problems of
Freer Trade

FROM early May to mid-October in 1851 the 'Great Exhibition of the
Works of Industry of all Nations' in Hyde Park proudly affirmed
Britain's primacy as a manufacturing country. More than six million
people wandered through Paxton's 'Crystal Palace' over those twenty-
four weeks, almost 42,000 admissions for every day that it was open.
Some visitors made the journey from the eastern fringe of suburban
Middlesex; and John Knight, whose Wapping soapworks had flourished
for fifteen years, was awarded a medal for the excellence of his products.
But the Great Exhibition was essentially a City and West End affair; it
was no festival for dockers or labourers from Bethnal Green, Whitechapel
or the riverside hamlets. Although honour was officially accorded to 'the
working bees of the world's hive', the Exhibition celebrated the middle-
class virtues of sobriety, self-dependence and happy family life. Above all
it was a triumphant advertisement for the Free Trade theories which, so
Richard Cobden prophesied, would enable town and country to flourish
side by side for the rest of the century.

   Free Trade, however, brought little benefit to east London. If Huskisson's tariff reforms in the 1820s had sent the silk industry into sharp decline, the Cobden-Chevalier commercial treaty with France of January 1860 virtually killed it, leaving only a few high-quality weavers in Spitalfields, their work too good to suffer from the competition of Paris and Lyons[1]. Sugar refining, sack-making, and the monopolies of the old privileged merchant companies in tea and coffee were early casualties. Other traditional industries followed them unexpectedly in the third quarter of the century, causing hardship from Wapping eastwards to Limehouse and Blackwall.

At first it was hoped London would prosper as a port from the increased trade likely to follow the abandonment of Protection. Some City investors also believed that the riverside wharves must benefit from the Customs Consolidation Act of 1853, which simplified the levying of duties in the Pool as a whole; and, indeed, over the following twelve years as many as fifty new wharves were constructed, most of them on the south bank of the Thames. Many built jetties out into the river so that moderate-sized steamers could berth alongside them: all, whether on the north or south bank, challenged the continued viability of the dock companies.

But this threat was slow to emerge. Not only the moneyed men of the City were optimistic at mid-century. An assumption that there would continue to be a huge demand for casual labour along the riverside attracted jobless 'men of every calling' to seek employment there, especially after 1855 when the railway-linked Victoria Dock was opened, the largest in the country. As well as the thousands of immigrants who had crossed from Ireland, there were unwanted farm labourers, failed misfits from the City, released convicts, and, after the collapse of the revolutions of 1848, refugees from central Europe as well. Whatever might be happening in the Pool itself in the late 1850s, the trading figures of the Victoria Dock looked good. Plans were drawn up for further expansion down river, although it was not until June 1880 that the Duke of Connaught opened the extension and the Queen gave permission for the 'finest docks in the world' to be known as the Royal Victoria and the Royal Albert. So modern were the 'Royals' that their quays remained illuminated all night by electricity[2].

There was, however, no 'modernisation' of riverside labour. Free-trade policies removed the duties on over a thousand imported goods between 1842 and 1860, thereby making the bonded warehouses largely superfluous and reducing the need for so much porterage. Increased wharfing facilities and the spread of the port across the Lea into West Ham also emphasised the need for change, especially the greater security and discipline afforded by a permanent staff of labourers. But the old reliance on casual labour, criticised by outside observers in the 1840s, remained basic to the systematic working of the port throughout the

1850s and 1860s – and, indeed, a hundred years later.

The atheist Friedrich Engels – not yet Marx's partner – shared with the evangelical churchman William Champneys a deep disgust at the demoralising absurdities of the casual labour system. 'Hundreds of the poor appear every morning in winter before daybreak, in the hope of getting a day's work,' Engels quoted Champneys as saying. 'They await the opening of the gates; and, when the youngest and strongest and best known have been engaged, hundreds, cast down by disappointed hope, go back to their wretched homes[3].' 'Call-on' normally came twice a day, soon after half-past seven in the morning and again five hours later, if work was still available. Casual labourers, whether dockers or stevedores, would rush forwards through the dock gates to stand waiting behind a chain at particular spots on the 'stones', desperately seeking to catch the eye of a foreman or an overseer in order to find work.

Even after the coming of steam, the prospects of earning a basic living wage still depended considerably on the weather. Ice on the river in the notoriously bitter early months of 1855 meant no work on offer at call-on for week after week. 'The distress amongst the labouring class caused by the suspension of labour is appalling and there are not fewer than 50,000 men out of employ, who have been for several days past subsisting on the scanty relief doled out by the parishes and the unions,' a radical newspaper declared on the last Sunday in February. Bread riots followed in Whitechapel within the week[4]. Six years later another newspaper reported how, on the evening of 16 January 1861, conditions had become so desperate after a full month of heavy frost, that 'thousands' of dock labourers 'congregated in the principal streets' of Whitechapel and Mile End. They then attacked bakers' 'shops and eating houses, and every morsel of food was carried away'; the mounted police found that 'it was impossible for them to act against so large a number of people'[5].

Changes were at last made, cautiously and inadequately, at the top of the industry: in 1864 the London, St Katharine's and Victoria Dock Companies amalgamated. But this act of managerial common sense could bring little benefit to the dock labourers so long as the call-ons were dispersed over a huge area. And although the merger may momentarily have relaxed the cut-throat rivalry between the dock companies, it did not end it. The conversion of the old City Canal into the South-West India Dock in 1866 and the opening two years later on the Isle of Dogs of the Millwall Dock – railway linked, but only a third as big as the Victoria – increased the competition. Although Britain's exports multiplied rapidly in volume between 1850 and 1880, the docks and wharves of London remained inefficient, hampered by internal rivalries, rashly over-capitalised and with a labour force which was starkly underemployed[6].

One traditional riverside industry flourished throughout the 1850s and into the 1860s. The shipbuilders of Limehouse, Millwall and Black-wall seemed at first to have adjusted well to the demand for big, iron vessels. The largest merchant ship in the world, the *Himalaya*, was launched at Blackwall in 1853, became a troopship in the Crimean War, and was still in Admiralty service off Portland when sunk by German bombing in the Second World War; and HMS *Warrior*, the first ironclad battleship in the Royal Navy, came from the Blackwall yards seven years later. It is sometimes said that in November 1857 the bungled launching of the *Great Eastern* – more than an eighth of a mile long and with three times the displacement of other large vessels – discredited Thames shipbuilding, giving an advantage to the Clyde and the Tyne. But in 1864 thirteen vessels were under construction in the yard which had built the *Great Eastern*, among them the armour-plated warship *North-umberland*, and a new yard, Dudgeons of Cubitt Town, had profited from orders for blockade-runners from the Confederate South. That scrupulous observer, Thomas Wright, commented in a book published in 1867 on the notable way in which the Isle of Dogs had so recently become a centre of iron shipbuilding and marine engineering, providing work for some 15,000 men and boys: 'There are more than a dozen ship and marine engineering establishments, among them being the gigantic one in which the operations of the Millwall Iron Works are carried on,' he reported[7]. But Wright's comments were out of date even before his book went on sale. For in the closing weeks of 1866 the Thames shipbuilding industry collapsed like a ziggurat of playing cards. With the coming of the New Year in 1867 *The Times* had to report that 30,000 unemployed were seeking relief in Poplar alone. The weather was again particularly cold that month and soon afterwards, for the third time in twelve years, there were bread riots in the most hard hit districts. Significantly, there was trouble in various streets hitherto considered lower middle class in character[8].

Historians of the nineteenth century customarily emphasise the political and military events of 1866, when Bismarck's Prussia became the master Power within Germany. But, nearly a century and a quarter later, it is possible to argue that the most significant day of that year was not 3 July, when Prussia defeated Austria at Königgrätz-Sadowa, but 11 May, the first of those 'Black Fridays' on which commercial panic swept through the greatest of the world's money markets. For in Lombard Street on the previous afternoon insolvency had forced the doors to close on Overend, Gurney & Company, for almost forty years principal supplier of short-term capital in the City. As London had three times as many bank deposits as New York and ten times as many as Paris, the collapse of such a respected institution threatened widespread distress and caused Friday's panic among creditors and investors. Even though the great merchant banking dynasties of Rothschild and Baring were buttresses against total disaster, dozens of smaller financial concerns were in danger; and within six months the consequences of Black Friday had hit the working population of east London[9].

Samuel Gurney, senior partner in Overend, Gurney & Company from 1827 until his death in 1856, had known the East End well. Like his sister, Mrs Elizabeth Fry, he was a Quaker reformer and philanthropist; on every working day his carriage would bring him to Lombard Street through Bow, Stepney and Whitechapel from Ham House, his home on the borders of Plaistow and Upton Park; and, with other members of his family, he would attend the Friends' Meeting House in Plaistow, barely five miles east of Aldgate Pump. Gurney, although sympathetic to any entrepreneur who could offer a prospect of employment and sober living to the poor around him, was too shrewd a businessman to advance money to highly speculative ventures. After his death, however, his company rashly provided backing for railway speculators, a fleet of steamships, and the new shipyards and iron works along the Thames. *The Times* of 28 November 1866 reported that nearly half a million pounds had been advanced to C. J. Mare of the Millwall Iron Works; James Ash, a former naval architect who, as late as 1863, opened a new yard in Cubitt Town, was another heavy borrower. Both companies went bankrupt[10].

Their failure was not entirely a consequence of over-investment and rash speculation: coal, iron and labour were cheaper and ready to hand in northern England and on the Clyde. The Thames shipbuilders were too ambitious: yards specialising in repairs and the construction of small vessels weathered the economic storm; thus, Yarrows – who came to Cubitt Town only a few months before Black Friday – were still building torpedo boats there at the turn of the century. But whatever the cause of the collapse of 1866–7, it was a blow from which the industry in Poplar and Millwall never recovered. Within little more than a year the big shipyards were deserted, 'the birthplace of the *Great Eastern*' was 'a grass-grown waste', and the shadow of pauperism hung heavily over streets which had so recently enjoyed a comfortable prosperity. 'There was more poverty and misery and suffering in the East End of London in that winter (1868–9) than I have ever seen since', the writer F. W. Galton recalled a quarter of a century later[11].

It was unusual in southern England to find an industry so closely localised as iron shipbuilding on the Thames; when it collapsed, there were few alternative jobs for the semi-skilled. Boiler-makers and expert metal-workers might still find work in the Isle of Dogs or, over the following decade, in the new factories across the River Lea, in Stratford and West Ham. The destitution did not drag on for so many years as in the later depressed areas of the 1930s and 1980s. But it lasted long enough to change the face of the East End for all time. During the early years of Victoria's reign speculative builders in Bow and Stepney had sought to attract white-collar workers, and even some flourishing merchants, by following the fashion of other parts of London and building small houses in imposing terraces set at right angles to a main road. Thus in Ratcliff, between Commercial Road and Cable Street, there was an Albert Square, downgraded to Albert Gardens long before television soap-opera revived the name for a fictional Canning Town; and, to the north of Bow Road, Tredegar Square has still not entirely lost a stuccoed façade of Corinthian-column security. But the scourge of cholera in 1866 and the collapse so soon afterwards of a major local industry ruled out all possibility of creating a genteel Canonbury or Pimlico between the Great Eastern Railway and the docks. The lower middle-class quill-pushers began to move to the Essex suburbs, following a pattern of migration which was to continue for over a hundred years. Some became rack-renting landlords of their old homes, subdividing them so as to accommodate the poor who were turned out of the City or Holborn by the building of offices and the cutting of new roads. A drab uniformity seemed, by Victorian social standards, to bind together the people of Bethnal Green, Mile End, Stepney and Poplar in demoralised pauperism[12].

At the same time east London was trespassing out of Middlesex, across the River Lea, and into Essex. Although breweries, distilleries and some small manufacturing firms had long functioned close to the City's eastern limits, there had never been large industrial areas of sprawling factories within metropolitan London, as in the Midland cities and the North[13]. But by the late 1860s a belt of 'nuisance industries' stretched southwards from the paintworks and dyers of Hackney Wick through Stratford to Silvertown, a township east of Bow Creek, built around the rubber and telegraph works of S. W. Silver & Co., and perpetuating their name. These new enterprises were not subject to the provisions of the Smoke Nuisance Act of 1853, which had sought clearer air within the metropolis itself. Barely a quarter of a mile beyond Bow Bridge the five high stacks of the Imperial Works were, as early as 1860, belching out smoke over the former mill meads of Stratford. The Gas Light & Coke Company – granted a royal charter as early as 1812 – failed to secure the site it wished in Hackney marshes, but in 1868 its enterprising director, Samuel Beck, acquired 150 acres of lowlying land south of East Ham, beside Barking Creek and Gallions Reach. There within a few years the Company established the largest coal gas works in the world. The works closed in 1976; Beckton, like Silvertown, survives as a placename[14].

'Many branches of the Lea are pleasing to none of the senses' commented James Thorne in 1876. 'Chemical works, varnish manufactories, match mills, candle factories, manure works, cocoa-nut fibre and leather-cloth factories, and distilleries, are on a large scale[15].' Prevailing westerlies carried the stink of these factories down river, but if the wind was in the east the smoke settled on Bow and grimed the bay-windowed respect-ability of upper Clapton and old Hackney. Already a sooty fallout was attacking the stonework of the two most attractive buildings in Mile End Road: the Trinity Almshouses of 1695 for 'decayed Masters and commanders of ships' and the Georgian Drapers' Company almshouses and school known as Bancroft's Hospital. The pollution rapidly became worse. For seventeen weeks between November 1879 and March 1880 a grey, yellow fog lay drooped over east London; and in 1881 yet another choking Christmas gave way to a wheezy New Year.

Despite the absence of large industrial areas within the East End itself, there were plenty of smaller factories. Proximity to the docks and inland waterways gave relatively easy access to raw materials, and there was always a superfluity of cheap labour. Some companies – like Allen & Hanbury, the famous pharmaceutists of Bethnal Green – expanded gradually from eighteenth-century beginnings. Several soap manu-facturers followed the example of John Knight and set up business in Wapping or east of the Minories, but most soon preferred the more spacious wastelands of the lower Lea; Knight's themselves eventually moved to Silvertown in the early 1880s.

The largest East End factory in those years was Bryant & May's. Their match works had been built in 1861, in what was then still a verdant part of Bow. They relied on timber brought in barges along the Lea Navigation Canal and on unskilled labour; and this was mostly supplied by the unmarried daughters of casual workers who were themselves so poorly and irregularly paid that the family needed supplementary earn-ings in order to subsist. A similar labour force was employed at the many confectionery works in east London, where jam and marmalade were produced as well as sweets and candied fruits. At the start of the economic Depression in the mid-1870s Batgers of Ratcliff were employing 450 regular workers and taking on 100 casuals for the Christmas rush and 250 casuals in May, June and July for the English fruit season. Sometimes the jam factories would need women workers for only a day or even a few hours, and there was as much rough-and-tumble hustle at the gates as at a dockers' call-on[16]. Since fewer matchboxes were required in summer than winter, some women found work both at Bryant & May's and in a jam factory. And if they were able-bodied, they might also count on 'hopping' for two weeks' pay. By the final quarter of the century an expanding railway network was enabling thousands of families to leave London at the end of August for a fortnight of hop-picking in Kent or east Sussex. In 1877 there was an exodus of 35,000 men, women and children from both sides of the river, according to the *Pall Mall Gazette*[17]. Some hoppers walked to their destinations, for the railway companies were notoriously slow to accept the need for cheap train fares.

If life was hard for the casual labourer in the docks and factories, it was even worse for those dependent on the so-called 'sweated trades' for their livelihood. Since the days of the Regency, many clothing firms in the City and West End had been accustomed to give out work for women to complete in their homes in the poorer districts of east and south London. By the middle of the century competition from the factories of Lancashire and Yorkshire – and, with freer trade, from across the Channel, too – was leading to an expansion of this form of home industry, designed to provide ready-made clothing for the general market. The invention of the sewing machine and of the toothed steel belt known as the band-saw encouraged a trend towards mass production, without the heavy overheads associated with the factory system. A middleman (a 'sweater') would arrange for women, and often for men and children as well, to work on clothing under his supervision, generally in a room or basement at his own home. As places of work these 'sweat shops' were deplorable: starvation wages, long hours – over ninety a week for some workers in the late 1860s – and unhygienic conditions. Most sweat shops were hidden away in garrets or cellars, so that factory inspectors never discovered them. Successive waves of poor immigrants, accustomed to a low standard of living in the lands they had left, accepted the system because poorly paid work in a sweat shop was better than no work at all. The sweaters showed ingenuity in exploiting weaknesses in the factory legislation so as to prevent inspection and condemnation. Sweated clothing dens proliferated in the side streets of Whitechapel and Shadwell. Not until 1901 did the Factory & Workshop Consolidation Act afford workers in the sweat shops some protection. By then a method of production, devised in the first instance for the clothing trade, had long since spread to the making of footwear – and, to a lesser extent, of cheap furniture – in parts of Bethnal Green, Hoxton, Shoreditch and Stepney[18].

No attempt was made by workers in the sweated trades to organise a serious protest against their exploitation until the late 1880s. But throughout the period 1850–75 – allegedly years of Cobdenite prosperity – trade unionism was growing rapidly in the whole of Britain and particularly in London. One East Ender by adoption, William Newton, played a distinguished rôle in building up trade unionism. Newton, who was born in Cheshire, was working as a foreman engineer when he was sacked in 1848 for his disruptive radical agitation[19]. He then became a publican in Ratcliff, and in January 1851 was co-founder, with the Scotsman William Allan, of the 11,000-strong Amalgamated Society of Engineers. In 1852, at the age of thirty, Newton stood unsuccessfully for the Tower Hamlets as an independent radical, the first working-class labour candidate for Parliament. He stood again in 1868 and 1875, but for most of his active political life he interested himself in the affairs of Stepney, as a long-serving member of the Metropolitan Board of Works. He helped build up the ASE, trebling membership in sixteen years and making it a model union, which others were to copy. The ASE was so well organised that it was able to give considerable financial support to London's builders when they went on strike in 1858. It was natural that Newton, with his Ratcliff waterside connections, should seek to encourage trade unionism among the dockers. Significantly John Burns and Tom Mann, two of the three outstanding dockers' leaders at the end of the century, were both originally engineers.

Yet Newton achieved only limited success among the dockers. The fault was not of his making: the casual and unskilled character of so much labour along the wharves and quays made it extremely difficult to organise. Eventually, in December 1871, it was an unemployed Irish tailor, Patrick Hennesey, who brought together the prototype union of London's dockers, the Labour Protection League. A fortnight after the foundation of the LPL its Secretary, a compatriot of Hennesey, disappeared with its funds. By the following midsummer the morale of the LPL had improved and its members were able to bring all the docks in the East End to a standstill. This first large-scale dock labourers' strike of 1872 raised the hourly wage by 25 per cent so that the more fortunate members of his League – those who found work every day – could bring home £1 for a forty-eight hour week in summer and 17s 6d for a forty-two hour week in winter. But the employers made this concession only after imposing new conditions for increasing the amount of work expected each hour. When four years later the dockers who handled grain at Millwall struck for better conditions, management brought in 'fine, powerful' blacklegs from the fields of Dorset, Wiltshire, Hampshire and Gloucestershire, and were thus able to replace the strikers with non-union labour from the countryside[20]. The dockers – consistently the poorest paid heavy labourers in the metropolis – deserved inspired leadership, capable of winning support throughout the East End and beyond. For this they had to wait another dozen years.

The era of Cobdenite prosperity saw trade unionism achieve legal respectability. In 1871 Gladstone's first Liberal ministry granted any Trade Union whose rules did not advocate a criminal act the status and protection of a 'Friendly Society'. Attempts to enforce observance of a strike remained forbidden until 1875, when Disraeli's Conservative Government showed Tory confidence in the stability of the unions by amending the criminal law, so as to permit 'peaceful picketing'. Yet there remained deep misgivings over the growth of unionism among some company directors and managers. This hostility was particularly strong in two industries long established in the East End – gas supply and brewing. Both Beck (of the Gas Light & Coke Company) and the London brewing dynasties sought to safeguard their employees from the beguiling dangers of an industrial age by a paternalistic protection of their interests. Had the general prosperity continued, it is probable that the paternalism would have become so embracing as to separate a respectable working class, comfortably housed and adequately insured, from the great mass of east London's casual workers. But the pressure of foreign competition burst the bubble of Free Trade prosperity in the mid-1870s: export values declined; jobs were lost; the returns on investment fell; and the City adjusted itself as a world money market from pre-eminence to mere eminence. By the early 1880s uncertainty and fear linked the casual labourer, the unionised worker and the independent artisan in a common mistrust of capitalist society. And, amid the propertied classes, fear and uncertainty conjured up the forgotten spectre of social revolution.

7

Church and Charity

THROUGHOUT the first half of the nineteenth century all British governments were haunted, in varying degree, by the bogey of French Jacobinism. The risk of revolution was less real than in Metternich's Austria or Tsarist Russia, and refugees from the Continent could find sanctuary in London without searching scrutiny of their radical past; but the nightmare of an angry mob sweeping into the capital from its poorest quarters continued to disturb the comfortable assurance of Victorian minds. When arms were found in January 1840 at the Trades Hall in Bethnal Green the police were put on the alert for fear of a Chartist insurrection, and in June 1848 the announcement of a coming demonstration at Bonners Fields brought the Life Guards to Shoreditch Goods Station and the Royal Horse Guards to Victoria Park, while 400 specially mobilised army pensioners were quartered in the Bethnal Green workhouse[1]. An uprising in the London of steam power and the penny post was unlikely to follow a Parisian pattern fifty years out of date, but a spate of memoirs and reminiscence ensured that the great Revolution remained an apocalyptic vision for the reading public long after it receded

into history. The future Cardinal Newman would avert his eyes from
tricolour flags, as if the precision of their stripes mocked the severed heads
of the faithful; and as late as 1850 the thought of 'the red fool fury of
the Seine' in flood ruffled the measured stanzas of Tennyson's *In Memoriam* with a frisson of apprehension.

Ways to contain and repel the Jacobin assault on English minds had
been proposed before Newman and Tennyson were born. Repressive
legislation delayed the emergence of trade unions and working-men's
associations. More positively, it was proposed to set aside money for the
establishment of churches in the poorest and most troubled districts of
English towns in the belief that 'The true Christian will ... never listen to
French politics or French philosophy[2]. In 1818 and 1824 Lord Liverpool's
government granted one and a half million pounds towards the building
of 'new churches in populous places'. But after the 1832 Reform Act,
Parliament became less well disposed towards the Established Church
and Charles Blomfield, Bishop of London from 1828 to 1856, set up two
diocesan funds of his own to provide places of worship for 'the most
ignorant and neglected of the population' within the metropolis. The
second of these funds was specifically intended to build ten churches in
Bethnal Green, where only St Matthew's, completed in 1746, and St
John's – dedicated by Blomfield in October 1828 – served 70,000 people.

Although the Bishop was far from popular with any class in the
community, he gave generously himself, and the City and rich patrons
individually answered his call. An anonymous wealthy clergyman contributed £6000. There remained, however, among urban workers and
their families a deep suspicion of organised religion as a repressive instrument of the ruling class. A local church-goer, seeking sixpences for the
fund from the more fortunately housed parishioners of Bethnal Green,
was told that while they would give a shilling to hang the Bishop, there
would be no sixpences to build a church. This hostility came to the
surface in August 1840 when the Lord Mayor laid the foundation stone
of St Peter's, Hackney Road, the first of the ten churches. The protest
took a locally familiar form; an infuriated cow bore down on a line of
children gathered to sing a hymn, and the ceremony was disrupted.
Fortunately the children were not hurt, and neither Blomfield nor his
fund's benefactors were deterred by the incident[3].

By training Blomfield was an Oxford Classicist, who had edited Aeschylus; in character he seemed an ecclesiastical Edwin Chadwick. He was
an austere diocesan who, if he deigned to smile, made certain that he
was smiling episcopally. It was difficult for him to find clergy to serve his
new parishes. Even married men with an earnest vocation were reluctant
to bring families to such a filthy, disease-ridden part of London, while
celibates were subjected to attacks and insults in the streets. Yet some

notably enterprising young men felt called to Bethnal Green. Among them was the Reverend James Trevitt of St Philip's, in the notorious border streets linking Bethnal Green, Spitalfields and Shoreditch. In 1860 – shortly after Blomfield's death – Trevitt won the approval of the journalist, John Hollingshead, for helping hard-pressed weavers financially and running two church schools, an infants' school, two 'ragged schools' for the destitute, and a Sunday school attended by 800 children who were at work on weekdays[4].

Blomfield may well have allowed his zeal for bricks and mortar to outweigh his common sense. More than half the free pews in the new churches remained empty, and too much of their fabric became a financial liability, even before the end of the century. Whether the building programme in any way checked the dissemination of radical doctrines is highly questionable. More sympathy was shown for Chartism in Bethnal Green than elsewhere in the East End. But during Chartism's most active phase – from September 1847 to June 1848 – the movement seems to have been dominated locally by Roman Catholics from the militant Irish Democratic Confederation of London[5].

The Bishop's energy certainly brought some material good to Bethnal Green. By mid-century ten new spires relieved the drab skyline of the district, and schools sponsored by the 'National Society for Promoting the Education of the Poor in the Principles of the Established Church' gave the youngest boys and girls the rudiments of primary education. Evidence presented to a Select Committee of the House of Lords in 1857–8 suggests that, by then, the people had come to recognise how Blomfield's building programme was making their lives safer and more 'civilised' than a quarter of a century before. Shortly afterwards Thomas Okey, a lad born in Spitalfields, entered St James the Less National School, Sewardstone Road, one of Blomfield's foundations to the west of Victoria Park. Some fifty-five years later Okey became the first Professor of Italian Studies at Cambridge[6].

In 1845 Friedrich Engels declared confidently that 'All the writers of the bourgeoisie are unanimous on this point, that the workers are not religious, and do not attend church'. That was not the experience of William Champneys, the Evangelical clergyman whose condemnation of the casual labour system at the dock gates Engels quoted with sympathetic approval[7]. Champneys, the earliest of the great slum pastors, became vicar of Whitechapel in the year of Victoria's accession and remained in east London until 1868, when he was appointed Dean of Lichfield. There were, in 1837, 33,000 people living in his parish, many of whom were Irish and some Jewish. On an average only 1 in 66 of his parishioners would attend the main Sunday morning services, but by the time of the Crimean War he was drawing an evening congregation of

1500 men and women to old St Mary's, Whitechapel. He cut the incidence of juvenile crime by setting up the earliest of London's ragged schools and by organising a bootblacks brigade. Moreover he could claim to have checked drunkenness and street brawling in what Hollingshead described as 'the closely packed nests' around the church, 'full of overflowing with dirt, and misery, and rags'[8].

Some 1500 yards from St Mary's, Whitechapel, was Hawksmoor's St George's in the East, where Bryan King became vicar five years after Champneys. The church stands in a rectangle formed by Cannon Street Road, Ratcliff Highway, Dellow Street and Cable Street. At the start of King's incumbency there were within that block 733 houses, of which 154 were brothels. King himself belonged to that group of churchmen who, even before he came to east London, had already been dubbed 'Puseyites', 'ritualists', 'Tractarians', 'Anglo-Catholics' – and much else besides. After fourteen uneasy years at St George's he was joined in August 1856 by a vigorous curate, Charles Lowder, and soon afterwards by yet another churchman of courage and principle, Alexander Mackonochie. When churchwardens who were hostile to King and his curates secured the appointment of an Evangelical lecturer at St George's, the troubles of the parish received widespread publicity, and from June 1859 to May 1860 'anti-papist' protesters disrupted the services. Not for the last time, a compact site in the East End, easy to reach from other parts of London, became an arena of battle, in which a passionate rabble upheld the traditional customs of England with an Englishman's customarily traditional violence.

Even the calm prose of the parliamentary report into these disturbances makes sensational reading: hounds let loose in the aisles; hassocks thrown at the altar; clergy kicked and tripped; boys supplied with fireworks and pea-shooters; a pew used as a privy; and a Protestant League who would meet locally on Tuesday evenings to plan next Sunday's assault. For seven weeks in the autumn the church was closed, reopening when King gave an undertaking not to wear vestments. Fifty uniformed police were on duty at Sunday services for the next six weeks. The clergy thereafter relied on a personal bodyguard from outside the parish, among whom was the author of *Tom Brown's School Days*, a good boxer. But the Sunday afternoon Flashmans proved incorrigibly unrepentant and, after twelve months of troubles, the police presence had increased to seventy-three[9]. At that point Bryan King's health gave way and he left St George's in the East, eventually accepting a country living in Wiltshire. But Father Lowder and Father Mackonochie stayed on in London; they were the first of the many Anglican priests in the East End accorded such titles of canonical respect by their congregations. Nearly thirty years later a correspondent in the *Church Times* recalled[10]:

one Sunday afternoon, passing with Father Mackonochie and one or
two others along Ratcliffe Highway, and being assailed with abuse by
a handful of roughs who were drinking in company with a couple of
women dressed in the costume which at that time still prevailed there
among those of their avocation ... The two women went for the men
like a couple of tigresses; swearing, in language by no means quotable
in your columns that, if one of them laid a finger on Father Mackonochie, they would 'have their blood'.

Alexander Mackonochie soon moved to the slums of Holborn; he died
in a blizzard at Glencoe more than a quarter of a century later. Charles
Lowder remained in dockland, converting a tin mission chapel into St
Peter's, Wapping Lane, where he served for more than twenty years.
From 1857 onwards he was assisted by a courageous Anglican sisterhood, headed by Elizabeth Neale. Lowder's 'papist practices' were still
denounced from time to time in the local press, as were the colourful
innovations of other Anglo-Catholic priests in the East End, notably in
Shoreditch at Haggerston and Hoxton; but Father Lowder won widespread respect for the care and compassion which he showed in 1866
during the last major cholera epidemic. So indeed did Blomfield's successor as Bishop of London, Archibald Tait, after whom a road was named
in one of the worst afflicted districts of dockland.

Other denominations suffered from what a Methodist newspaper was
to call 'the general migration of the prosperous'[11]. In Spitalfields the
Wesleyans had purchased, in 1809, the former Huguenot chapel at the
corner of Fournier Street and Brick Lane, but its congregation 'dwindled
away to nothing'; it was sold to a Jewish immigrant society and became
a synagogue in 1897 (and, more recently, a mosque). Attendance fell
away, too, at Wesleyan chapels in Limehouse, Poplar and eventually
Bow, which in the 1870s was still rated 'the most flourishing Methodist
church in East London'.

The Roman Catholics had lost one church when the London Docks
were built and they had to wait until 1850 for the consecration of St
Mary and St Michael's in the Commercial Road. St Anne's, Underwood
Road, followed five years later, but it was 1880 before St Patrick-in-the-
East came to Wapping. The Irish, used to going to Mass regularly, were
glad to hear a comfortingly familiar Latin in a city which treated them
with hostility and suspicion. At mid-century Henry Mayhew jotted down
the complaints of an Irish woman who told him, 'Oi have little harrut to
go into the public houses to sill oranges, for they begins floying out about
the Pope and Cardinal Wiseman, as if Oi had anythink to do with it'[12].
From 1865 the communal loyalty of the immigrants was strengthened
by the leadership of Wiseman's successor as Archbishop of Westminster,

Henry Manning, who gave much time to the problems of what he called 'the Irish occupation of England'. One group, in particular, held his attention: those dependent for their living on the docks, the wharves and the maritime industries. Engels the Atheist, Champneys the Evangelical, Lowder the Ritualist, and Manning the future Cardinal were at one in deploring the human degradation caused by the vagaries of labour along the riverside throughout the middle decades of the century.

These years saw, however, some improvement in living standards, especially within the inner East End. Much of the initiative was taken by private benefactors, frequently backed by a reforming churchman. The Metropolitan Association for Improving the Dwellings of the Industrious Classes was founded as early as 1841 and, within ten years, it had built two tenements in the Albert Street area of Spitalfields, one for single men and the other for sixty families; many other semi-philanthropic housing trusts were established in the second half of the century. By the 1880s at least a dozen of these trusts were seeking to ease the housing problem in east London[13]. Baroness Angela Burdett-Coutts, the daughter of a radical MP and granddaughter of the founder of Coutts' Bank, was encouraged by Charles Dickens to have the slums east of Shoreditch Church cleared for the construction of Columbia Square Buildings. These four mock-Gothic blocks, completed in 1862, housed 183 families at very low rents. Seven years later the Baroness added Columbia Market to her original project. It was a huge building intended to attract costermongers and stallholders out of the streets and into regulated market buildings, but within five years the Baroness acknowledged that this venture was a failure; the small traders preferred all the rough, tumble and chance of the streets[14].

Her munificence was matched by the generosity of the Massachusetts-born philanthropist George Peabody who, in the year that the first families moved into Columbia Square, established a fund to house the poor of the metropolis and improve their material comforts. The earliest of the 'Peabody Buildings' was opened in Commercial Street, Spitalfields, in 1864; four more Peabody blocks were completed in Shadwell by 1867; and, in London as a whole, over the following thirty years, the Peabody Trust provided homes for some 20,000 people. Critics complained that the rules for Peabody tenants were strict and that the barrack-like blocks resembled reformatories, but so, too, did the blocks erected by other housing trusts. Aesthetically there was nothing to choose between Peabody buildings and the apartments put up for Sydney Waterlow's Improved Industrial Dwellings Company in riverside Wapping. The fault did not lie in the failure of Peabody, Waterlow or their architects to understand the needs of the working class. London's first purpose-built block of flats, the fourteen-storey Queen Anne's Mansions, was not completed until 1889, and for more than eighty years could be reckoned the ugliest building in Westminster. If architects were as yet unaccustomed to designing apartment blocks for the wealthy, there was little hope they would find creative vision in any strictly economical commissions for the industrious poor.

The most respected of philanthropic housing reformers was Octavia Hill, a granddaughter of Dr Southwood Smith. For her, every block dwelling – whether administered by the Peabody Trust or one of the other societies – was, by its nature, 'the negation of a home'[15]. Living standards could best be raised, she argued, by purchasing and repairing old houses and reforming the habits of those who lived in them; tenants needed to find in their landlord an example of sober and enlightened management. Through her Charity Organisation Society Octavia Hill sought to domesticate the labouring classes; her volunteer middle and upper class managers were both rent collectors and pioneer social workers – although the virtuous condescension with which they chose to help the 'deserving' rather than the 'undeserving' poor would not, as yet, win widespread acceptance today. Several homes in the East End followed Octavia Hill's rule of life even if they were not themselves owned by the COS; notable among them were Katharine's Buildings, near St Katharine's Dock. Her arguments were to make a considerable impression on Richard Cross, the Lancastrian-born reformer appointed Home Secretary in 1874, when the Conservatives returned to power with their first clear majority for a third of a century.

By then there was also an influential group of missionising philanthropists at work in Tower Hamlets. The most famous among them was William Booth, the salvationist who promised 'Heaven in east London for everyone'. In thirteen years the mission he had launched at Whitechapel in 1865 grew into a Salvation Army of which he became 'General'. The first 'Sally Army' hostel, a converted warehouse by the West India Docks, was not opened until February 1888, but long before then the hungry poor of Whitechapel and Mile End had come to depend on Booth's soup kitchens for sustenance. At the same time Dr Thomas Barnardo, who had received his medical training at the London Hospital during the last cholera epidemic, was beginning his work to relieve the plight of homeless children whom he found in the streets of Stepney, Poplar and Whitechapel. In 1870, with the backing of Lord Shaftesbury, Dr Barnardo was able to open his first Home for Destitute Boys at 18 Stepney Causeway. A third benefactor, Frederick Charrington, great-great-grandson of the founder of the brewing dynasty, was working in the family's Anchor Brewery in Mile End Road when he, like Barnardo, was appalled by the vice around him. He found lodgings at Stepney Green, began addressing temperance meetings in 1873, and set up a shelter for women in distress.

Charrington money – much of it from London's pubs – was used to lead a crusade against prostitution and to build the Mile End Assembly Hall, where no drinks headier than coffee and cocoa were served[16].

William Booth, Dr Barnardo and Frederick Charrington were all impelled to fight poverty and vice as crusaders of social action. So too, less dramatically, were Samuel and Henrietta Barnett, the husband and wife partnership who over the last quarter of the century blazed a trail for settlers in London's Wild East. 'The worst parish in my diocese, inhabited by a mainly criminal population,' the Bishop of London warned the future Canon Barnett in 1872, on offering him the living of St Jude's, Whitechapel. When, early next year, the newly married vicar arrived in Commercial Street he was at once mugged by a parishioner and robbed of his watch. Such incidents were commonplace in so lawless a district; two incumbents of neighbouring Christ Church suffered breakdowns in health, worn down by the violence around them. But the redoubtable Barnetts accepted the challenge. 'We came to Whitechapel attracted by its poverty and ambitious to fight it in its strongest fortress,' the Canon's widow recalled forty years later[17].

Toynbee Hall, the Whitechapel Art Gallery, and the Passmore Edwards Library next door to it survive today as memorials to their initiative. But these were the achievements of later years. Samuel Barnett was only twenty-eight when he came to St Jude's from the fashionable parish of St Mary's, Bryanston Square, and his principal concern at that time was with housing. At Bryanston Square he had come to know not only his future wife but also her close friend, Octavia Hill, and the Barnetts played a prominent role in the early activities of the Charity Organisation Society. In 1874, five years after the COS was established, Barnett was among the members of its Council who presented a detailed memorandum to Richard Cross, the Home Secretary, on 'the Improvement of the Dwellings of the Poor'. And when Cross made a private tour of inspection of the East End he had Samuel Barnett as his guide. In February 1875 the Home Secretary responded positively to the COS council's report and presented an Artisans' Dwellings Bill to Parliament. Within five months the Bill was on the statute book. Momentarily it looked as if a firm initiative from central government would achieve more than a charitable organisation could hope and sweep away the slums[18].

There had been earlier attempts in Parliament to end the crisis of overcrowding in the great cities, notably the so-called 'Torrens Act' of 1868, named after the independent Radical who was its sponsor. The Cross Act, however, possessed the teeth which had been drawn from Torrens's original bill when it was amended by the House of Lords. In London, outside the City, the Metropolitan Board of Works was for the first time empowered to carry through a vast scheme of slum clearance.

Housing declared insanitary by the local medical officer of health would be taken over by the Board. They would then compensate the owners, demolish the slums and sell the land to the Peabody Trust or one of several companies which promoted 'model industrial dwellings'. A supplementary act, by which Cross clarified the responsibilities of the Board and the rights of landlords for compensation, became law in 1879, a few months before, in the spring of 1880, Gladstone and the Liberals returned to office[19].

Within ten years, however, the Cross Act was recognised as a bungled disaster, at least for east London. Samuel Barnett himself was complaining that in St Jude's parish 'the houses of several thousands of the poor have been destroyed without any reconstruction'. There had been clumsy mismanagement and thoughtless planning. Slum clearance in the East End was promised for parts of Shadwell, Whitechapel, Limehouse, and Poplar. But most of the homes condemned as uninhabitable had housed casual labourers, costermongers, waterside workers and lightermen – a difficult community to shelter. Moreover, there was a long gap between condemnation and demolition, during which landlords would spend nothing on upkeep or repairs and this delay was followed by an even longer interval between demolition of the slums and completion of the working-class homes to replace them. By then it was often found that many evicted tenants could not manage to pay the revised rents. In Limehouse, by the time that the new Peabody Buildings were ready for occupation, no more than a dozen dehoused families could afford to live in them[20].

Despite his strictures, Barnett himself was among the over-zealous muddle-heads. As one of Whitechapel's Board of Guardians, he had taken the lead in urging slum clearance as early as February 1876, convincing his sixteen colleagues that every court and alley between Fashion Street and Whitechapel High Street should be condemned. So vast a scheme would have displaced 4354 people, and it was gradually modified until, in May 1877, the Home Secretary personally approved proposals to demolish about a third of the area, much of it afflicted by a typhus epidemic in the preceding winter. But the Metropolitan Board of Works then discovered that if action were taken on all the schemes for east London pending in that summer, another 13,000 homeless would be needing shelter by Christmas; and nothing was done.

Nor indeed was any progress made along this borderland of White-chapel and Spitalfields over the following six years, partly because of the contraction of business enterprise following the long price-fall of the late 1870s. At last, in the autumn of 1883 – a year of false hopes of economic recovery – clearance work began in Flower and Dean Street, described in that summer as 'the foulest and most dangerous street in the whole metropolis'. Even so, only a quarter of this notorious rookery came down. It was not until 1887 that the East End Dwellings Company, formed on Samuel Barnett's initiative in 1884, and the Four Per Cent Industrial Dwellings Company, set up by Baron Rothschild to house Jewish labouring families a year later, began to provide, however imperfectly, homes for the dispossessed[21].

By then the social problems of the inner East End were a familiar talking point at Westminster and in the older universities. Queen Victoria let Gladstone know of the distress she had felt on reading about 'the deplorable condition of the houses of the poor'[22]; and when the liberal radical cabinet minister, Sir Charles Dilke, established his Royal Commission on the Housing of the Working Classes in 1884 the Queen welcomed the presence on it of the Prince of Wales; he even found time – some fifty-seven hours of it – to attend more than a third of the commission's meetings. The inclusion of Cardinal Manning, Lord Salisbury, Lord Shaftesbury, Sir Richard Cross and William McCullagh Torrens among the Prince's colleagues made this Commission the most prestigious inquiry ever instituted into the housing of the poor. To emphasise the importance of the East End, the Royal Commissioners also included the Rt Revd Walsham How, who, as Bishop of Bedford, was from 1879 to 1888 the first area bishop with responsibility for east London (later suffragans receiving the title Bishop of Stepney). The Commission was as concerned with tenements in Liverpool, Bristol and Newcastle as in London and as much with the slums of Holborn, St Pancras, Southwark and Bermondsey as with the Tower Hamlets, but it gave particular attention to overcrowding in Whitechapel. Significantly, it looked, too, at a new problem: the changes taking place in Hackney, where a village which horse buses and the North London Railway had converted into a dormitory suburb was rapidly being encroached upon by speculators building shoddy homes for the factory workers of the lower Lea valley. The chief discovery of the Commissioners was the superficial inadequacy of earlier social legislation; 'the existing laws' on housing and public health 'were not put into force, some having' always 'remained a dead letter'. Too much, it seemed, was left to charity: too little imposed by firm paternalistic central government[23].

The Commission met twice a week for some ten months in 1884, with a long break for the summer season. Its report was published in May 1885, condemned by some critics as 'state socialism', hailed by the *Pall Mall Gazette* as 'epoch making' – and very soon forgotten[24]. The mouse brought forth in labour by this particular mountain was the Housing of the Working Classes Act (1885), an unmemorable statute which merely re-defined terms used in earlier legislation and, in London, strengthened the powers of the Metropolitan Board of Works.

Nevertheless the Housing Commission Report, much of the press comment, and the 1885 Act itself all implied tacit recognition of an important new principle: that a central municipal authority should be responsible, not merely for slum clearance, but for creating housing schemes and erecting working-class dwellings under its own management. It was significant for the metropolis, and especially for the fragmented communities in the East End, that within three years of the Report Lord Salisbury's Conservative Government should have brought into being a unitary County of London, with a council elected directly by the ratepayers. Eleven years later the same prime minister created the Metropolitan Borough Councils, among them Bethnal Green, Hackney, Poplar, Shoreditch and Stepney. Comprehensive municipal housing enterprises, capable of accommodating far more families than could the Peabody Trust, the COS and the other semi-philanthropic societies, were attainable only through the leadership of a strong and democratic local government. Whether the Conservative municipal reformers of 1888 and 1899 perceived this, remains open to question.

8

Years of Sensation

THE East End, as a collective concept meriting the use of initial capital letters, was an invention of the early 1880s. It was created by the London Press at a time of falling sales and thwarted political endeavour. Reporters of the previous generation – Dickens, Mayhew and Hollingshead among them – vividly described particular areas on both sides of the Thames, but recognised differences between Whitechapel, Bethnal Green, Wapping and Limehouse as well as between the Tower Hamlets and Bermondsey or Deptford across the river. Their successors, turning aside from news stories from a troubled Ireland and a militantly Islamic Khartoum, felt a call to amplify the cries of the poor within walking distance of Fleet Street itself. Yet in concentrating on this inner ring of poverty in outer London these writers of the 1880s distorted past and present, giving an artificial unity to old parishes, traditionally distinct from each other. Frequently they exaggerated the squalid wretchedness of outcast London[1]. It was not until the end of the decade, when Charles Booth began to analyse systematically the social condition of the people, that 'the peculiar flavour' of each district was again recognised. By then the dark and narrow alleys of Whitechapel had yielded a new sensationalism for the penny Press to exploit.

This trend towards a generalised picture of the East End was set in December 1882 by a socially instructive novel, rather than by any newspaper or periodical: Walter Besant's *All Sorts and Conditions of Men* was a three-volume fantasy which soon became a best-seller. It was followed in June 1883 by a series of articles in the *Pictorial World* on 'How the Poor Live', written by George Sims, author of that tear-stained ballad, 'In the Workhouse, Christmas Day'. Sims's articles – like Besant's novel – were illustrated by Frederick Barnard, whose artistry had already made a striking impression on the public in the later works of Dickens. Not surprisingly, the combination of Sims's compassionate investigative reporting and Barnard's gift for graphic simplicity attracted widespread attention, and Sims was soon commissioned by the *Daily News* to write another series, exposing conditions in 'Horrible London'. Meanwhile 'How the Poor Live' was reprinted as a shilling pamphlet. In this form it was used extensively by the Congregationalist minster, Andrew Mearns, in his famous and anonymous twenty-page penny tract, *The Bitter Cry of Outcast London*, which went on sale in the third week of October 1883. So great was the impact of *The Bitter Cry* that on the last Sunday of the month the Headmaster of Harrow, the Revd Montagu Butler, could brandish a copy of the tract from the pulpit of the University Church at Oxford: 'God grant', he declared, 'that it may not startle only, but that it may be read and pondered by thoughtful brains, as well as by feeling hearts'[2].

The Bitter Cry was taken up and exploited by W. T. Stead, the new editor of the *Pall Mall Gazette*, within a few days of publication, thereby attracting nationwide attention and giving Stead his first journalistic scoop. Less than a month later even Lord Salisbury, the joint-leader of the Conservative Party, unexpectedly contributed an article on the housing of the poor, published in a new periodical, the *National Review*. By the end of November 1883 the *Daily Telegraph* had its own bitter-cry column ('Why Should London Wait?'); and a tetchy second leader in *The Times* complained of 'highly wrought accounts' and condemned the haste with which 'everyone who can write or speak a few consecutive sentences' was exposing the slum housing, 'with more or less fervency of rhetoric'. 'Nothing is ever done in this country without a good deal of blowing off of waste steam,' *The Times* leader added[3].

There was a considerable difference in the content and form of all this prolific writing. Walter Besant's novel, for example, was strong on the rhetoric and discreetly reticent on the horrors. Angela Messenger, the heroine of his lack-lustre fairy tale, was a brewing millionairess from Newnham, Cambridge, with a belief in the beneficent virtues of dressmaking and a premature fixation on lawn tennis. Her fortune she used to sweep away 'a whole four-square block of small houses' before anyone could so much as murmur 'George Peabody', conjuring up in their place a 'Palace of Delight', covering more than seven acres beside Mile End Road. Here Miss A. Messenger had the 'very beautiful dream' of uplifting with the joy of self-fulfilment the day-to-day existence of 'two million' East Enders. Hitherto they had been content, poor blighted souls, 'never to know what pleasant strolling and resting-places, what delightful interests, what varied occupation, what sweet diversions there are in life'. Now 'Angela resolved ... to awaken in dull and lethargic brains ... a craving for things of which as yet they knew nothing'[4].

Angela's creator was persuaded by his friends to give *All Sorts and Conditions of Men* the sub-title, 'An Impossible Story', a reasonable suggestion. Yet Walter Besant was so gifted a propagandist that his fantasy palace soon became a reality. For within five years of the novel's publication the Queen's Hall of the People's Palace was opened by the sovereign herself; east Londoners possessed, for the first time, their own centre of 'intellectual and material advancement, recreation and amusement'. The Queen's Hall grew into a 'palace' which was still offering cultural enrichment during the Second World War, although the original building had been destroyed by fire a few years earlier. Not all the credit for this transformation scene rests with Besant, even if his readers did subscribe many thousands of pounds towards the project: the land was provided by the Drapers' Company on a site left vacant in 1886 when Bancroft's School – which the Company had maintained in Mile End since 1738 – moved out to Woodford Green; and further grants from the Drapers' Company were matched by endowments from the trustees of J. E. Barber Beaumont (died 1841), whose bequests had founded a Philosophic Institute near Stepney Green forty years before. But, even allowing for the generosity of the Drapers' Company and the Beaumont Trustees, the initiative in setting up a People's Palace in Mile End Road rests with Walter Besant and the pasteboard characters with whom he peopled Mrs Burmalack's boarding-house on Stepney Green. Few novels as bad as *All Sorts and Conditions of Men* can ever have had such beneficial consequences[5].

Besant had no wish to sully his pages by hinting that within an idealised East End there might lurk dens of vice. But Sims and the Congregationalist minister Andrew Mearns were realists. 'Were I to go into the details of ordinary life in a London slum, the story would be one which no journal enjoying a general circulation could possibly print,' Sims declared. Mearns was even more explicit. He warned his readers that 'seething in the very centre of our great cities, concealed by the thinnest crust of civilization and decency, is a vast mass of moral corruption'; in these overcrowded slums, Mearns explained, 'incest is common, and no form of vice or sexuality causes surprise or attracts attention'[6]. Stead's use of imaginative typography in the *Pall Mall Gazette* drew attention to these 'unspeakable horrors and abominations', for prurience always pushes up sales. But the crusade of Sims, Mearns and Stead had a double consequence: it encouraged Parliament to look seriously into the housing conditions of the poor; and it gave added impetus to the movement in the older universities for the settlement in Whitechapel and Stepney of a benevolent 'gentry', who by finding homes for themselves in the East End would raise the level of life around them.

To later generations this attitude seemed both priggish and patronising. But already many deeply sincere graduates from mid-Victorian Oxford had felt a vocation to serve, in varying forms, the dispossessed of east London. The young Christian Socialist, John Richard Green, held a tough curacy in Stepney from 1860 to 1869 before becoming Librarian at Lambeth Palace and completing his famous *Short History of the English People* – in itself a historian's protest against the drab poverty around him. And the publication in 1873 of posthumous letters written by the young and tubercular layman, Edward Denison, from lodgings he had deliberately taken in Philpot Street, Whitechapel, aroused a sense of social concern among his Oxford friends. Samuel Barnett, at St Jude's, had been welcoming undergraduate helpers inspired by the example of Denison and others for several years before Mearns's *The Bitter Cry* rang out across the land, and he was to deplore the sensationalism with which the newspapers covered 'much talked-of East London'[7]; but when Barnett spoke at St John's College and at the Oxford Union Society in Michaelmas Term 1883 he used the press revelations to encourage the formation of a permanent Universities Settlement in the East End. In June 1884 it was established in a disused boys' school close to St Jude's, taking its name from Arnold Toynbee, the young economic historian who had died in March of the previous year. Dissentients in both of the older universities favoured more specifically religious missionary settlements: Oxford House, with a predominantly Tractarian tradition, opened in Bethnal Green some three months after Toynbee Hall; and in 1890 Oxford's Congregationalists founded Mansfield House in Canning Town, rightly recognising that the social problems of the East End had by now bridged the Lea[8].

The early residents of Toynbee Hall accepted civic responsibilities as Poor Law guardians, and on school boards and the committees of philanthropic societies while also running classes for vocational training and cultural enlightenment. Although Samuel Barnett was both Warden and Vicar of St Jude's, Whitechapel, until 1906 he continued to emphasise that Toynbee Hall was a civilising rather than a christianising mission.

In later years the settlement influenced a far wider area than the East End: it is fitting that both the Workers' Educational Association and the Youth Hostels Association should have been launched there, in 1903–5 and 1929 respectively[9].

Other settlements, too, became social service nurseries, but with more specific, limited objectives. Arthur Winnington-Ingram, principal of Oxford House from 1889 to 1898, was consecrated Bishop of London within three years of leaving Bethnal Green, and by the coming of the Great Slump in the 1930s every leading Anglican churchmen had gained their first experience of a depressed area while in residence there. Both Mansfield House and Oxford House encouraged a multiplicity of clubs, distinguished from older social gatherings in east London by their total ban on beer and betting. There was, however, a certain rivalry between these cultural mission stations and some duplication of effort, especially with the growth of musical activities at the People's Palace in the early 1890s. Occasionally the teaching in the settlements had strange consequences: in 1886–7 Ben Tillett, then a tea warehouseman lodging with his wife's family in Bethnal Green, was attracted to some lectures at Oxford House on the strategy and tactics of Napoleon's wars. By the summer of 1889 Tillett was applying what he had learnt of 'routes for marches, lines of communication ... and methods of attack' in managing London's first major Dock Strike. The lectures were given by a Mr C. G. Lang, then reading for the bar, but destined to become Bishop of Stepney within fifteen years. Within fifty, as Archbishop, he would bury one sovereign, hasten the abdication of another, and crown a third.

Yet, helpful though Tillett found this pre-archiepiscopal grounding in military history, he was highly critical of 'slumming' as a way of dissolving class barriers and promoting harmony and brotherhood: 'The middle classes, some with sincere motives, others with a cynical interest in what promised a new sensation, went down to the East End and learned something, if not much, of the wretchedness and destitution that existed,' he recalled in his memoirs[10]. There was, too, some resentment at the attempt to impose middle-class attitudes on working-class habits, to stamp out an indigenous cockney culture because so much of it had flourished, vocally and often crudely, in saloon bars and taverns. A liking for theatre persisted, particularly in Shoreditch and around Goodman's Fields, where the memory of Garrick was preserved by a playhouse named in his honour, although rarely presenting the works with which he was associated. From the early years of Victoria's reign the most popular form of dramatic entertainment had been the so-called 'penny gaffs': a small stage would be put up in an empty shop, warehouse or stables along Mile End Road, Ratcliff Highway or Commercial Road; melodramas were mounted for an audience of about two hundred, who would pay a penny each for an hour's entertainment. And, by the time Walter Besant was campaigning for his Palace of Delight, music-halls had spread from Lambeth, by way of Drury Lane and Camden Town, to Wilton's (off Wellclose Square) and the 'Brit' in Hoxton High Street, round to The Queen's in Poplar and across to 'Relf's', Canning Town (the Royal Albert Music Hall, known as the 'Imp' from 1909 to 1931). The halcyon days of fringe-London music-hall coincided with the turn of the century, but by the late 1880s it was already accepted as the chief Saturday night diversion for a working man and his family, with sixpence or a shilling to spare at the end of the week. Music-hall depended on audience participation, sometimes critical, frequently vulgar and always robust. It accustomed East Enders to more vigorous ways of self-expression than were offered by lectures on Morality and Metaphysics, or by the considered reflections of Cosmo Gordon Lang on Napoleon's massing of his Guards on the plateau before Austerlitz.

There was indeed a world of difference between the well-intentioned endeavours of the Barnetts and Besant and the cycle of passing elation and despair experienced by so many families in east London during these years. Some turned to a different type of middle-class onslaught on their way of life and welcomed the top-hatted Marxism spread among them by H. M. Hyndman and H. H. Champion of the Social Democratic Federation. Both men might be reckoned as born-again Socialists, their ready acceptance of capitalism shaken by a misreading of Marx and Engels in French translation: Champion was a retired army officer who owned a printing press; and Hyndman was a company director, a Cambridge graduate and amateur cricketer, who played thirteen first-class innings for Sussex in the two summers that Marx was struggling to finish *Das Kapital*, volume I. They were good propagandists; and, although Hyndman was perversely critical of trade unionism, they soon won to the SDF cause the gifted open-air platform speaker, John Burns, of the Amalgamated Society of Engineers. The SDF leadership made a formidable trio in 1885–6 when East End unemployment reached a new peak. The press may have exaggerated the power of socialist oratory, but there is no doubt that it remained a beguiling instrument in this harshest winter of the trade recession.

Newspaper reports still conjure up a genuine fear in the West End of the bogies in the east. On the second Monday in February 1886 – the coldest February for thirty years – SDF speakers encouraged unemployed dockers and builders to break away from a protest meeting in Trafalgar Square and march to Hyde Park, but as the demonstrators were moving down Pall Mall the SDF leaders lost control; windows were broken and there was looting in Piccadilly. Disturbances continued over the following two days, with the capital blanketed in dense fog. Alarming rumours maintained that a mob was advancing westwards through Whitechapel from Commercial Road and that another march of the 'roughest elements' was heading for the City from Bethnal Green Road. On Wednesday *The Times* reported that 'some 100s of the dock labourers proposed to join others from the East End in further attacks upon the property in the West'. It announced that troops were standing by, and warned its readers that 'such a state of excitement and alarm has rarely been experienced in the Metropolis'. An indignant Queen complained to her Prime Minister of 'the monstrous riot ... which risked people's lives and was a momentary triumph of socialism and disgrace to the capital'[11]. Yet all this fearful froth and fury was undeserved: the only serious trouble lay south of the river, in Deptford and New Cross; the police kept order without calling out the army. Hyndman, Champion and Burns were among several speakers prosecuted for inciting riots in the West End, but in April all were acquitted by an Old Bailey jury.

There was widespread sympathy for the distress in east and south London and a ready response to an appeal for charitable relief sponsored by the Lord Mayor. But for most reformers another round of philanthropic palliatives seemed inadequate; the SDF was not the only socialist group in the East End to call for fundamental changes in the social order. The poet and artistic craftsman William Morris – who, mistrusting Hyndman's leadership, formed the Socialist League in 1884 – enjoyed a considerable following in Tower Hamlets, addressing Sunday morning meetings outside the Salmon and Ball at Bethnal Green and large gatherings at Poplar, Victoria Park and Mile End. Vigorous support to the reformers was also given by the Guild of St Matthew, a moderate Christian socialist Anglo-Catholic movement founded by the Revd Stewart Headlam, curate of St Matthew's, Bethnal Green[12]. Headlam, a pioneer churchman in breaking puritanical taboos on music-hall and ballet, spent forty years of his life improving primary education in Hackney, Bethnal Green and Whitechapel; but in 1886–7 it was as an ally of the secularist radicals that he first attracted public attention.

Sensational rumours of imminent revolution continued to disturb West End property owners throughout 1886 and into the Queen's Golden Jubilee Year. Tennyson's wearily unconvincing celebration of

> Fifty years of ever-broadening Commerce,
> Fifty years of ever-brightening Science

held no promise of ever-burgeoning exports, and the recession was still biting hard. A fine and warm summer attracted sleepers-out to the parks and Trafalgar Square – unemployed dockers, builders and farm labourers driven to seek unskilled work in London by the agricultural depression. In October, however, the nights turned frosty and tempers became frayed;

the police sought to clear 'vagrants' out of the West End; there were jobless marches on Westminster and a succession of SDF meetings in Trafalgar Square. When the Metropolitan Radical Association, supported by the SDF and the Socialist League, called on 'the democracy of London' to show 'help for our brethren in Ireland' by gathering in Trafalgar Square on Sunday afternoon, 13 November, to protest at the imprisonment of an Irish radical MP, the police at once prohibited the meeting; the Chief Commissioner feared that it would draw out the East End Irish as well as committed socialists. But the MRA and SDF went ahead with the protest, despite the ban. The police tried to prevent columns from entering Trafalgar Square; there were scuffles in the approaches to the Square; Foot Guards and Life Guards were called out of barracks; and some policemen and many demonstrators were seriously injured.

Resentment at the repression on this first 'Bloody Sunday' in 1887 lingered long in working-class London. Folk myth transformed a protest over an Irish MP's imprisonment into a peaceful meeting of the unemployed; and within three years Wiliam Morris, who was there, could declare 'There was no fighting, merely unarmed and peaceable people attacked by ruffians armed with bludgeons'[13]. Legend has, however, run together several demonstrations, in particular confusing the rioting in Trafalgar Square with what happened on the following Sunday. For on 20 November another open-air meeting, again primarily concerned with Ireland, was called in Hyde Park. Processions converged on Speakers' Corner from Hammersmith, south London and the East End, a drum and fife band marching from Poplar through the City and clashing with the police in High Holborn. More serious was a clash in Northumberland Avenue, when mounted policemen prevented a column entering Trafalgar Square; Alfred Linnell, a 'law writer' from Cursitor Street, Chancery Lane, was so badly injured that he died twelve days later. His funeral, on Sunday 18 December, became in itself a solemn assertion of the deprived East Enders' claims for social justice, with Stewart Headlam leading a procession which included many secularists and pantheists from Soho through Leicester Square, Long Acre, Fleet Street and Cheapside to interment in the Tower Hamlets Cemetery at Southern Grove, Bow. An unusually hostile account of the funeral in *The Times*, commenting on the presence along the route of 'the roughest elements in London', acknowledged that at Whitechapel, 'The densely populated districts here had turned out their people to see the march'. The procession took one hour to pass down Aldgate High Street[14].

The immediate effect of Bloody Sunday, and the weekend demonstrations which followed it, was to intensify political awareness among the casual poor of east London. Nevertheless within the SDF feeling hardened against Hyndman's inflexible leadership. The social tension in those closing months of 1887 strengthened the influence of the moderate Fabian Society (founded almost four years before) and encouraged social-ists to seek a radical exposure of iniquitous working conditions rather than provoke the earliest skirmishes of a red revolution. It was Hyndman's right-hand man, H. H. Champion, speaking to Fabians seven months after Bloody Sunday, who drew attention to the appalling working con-ditions of the match girls at Bryant & May's factory in Bow. By 5 July 1888 the girls were on strike. For the first time in British industrial history unorganised female labour, at the lowest level of employment, was defying the management. Once again the 'densely populated' East End made the headlines in national dailies.

It was Annie Besant – Walter Besant's free-thinking sister-in-law – who first exposed this 'white slavery' at Bryant & May's, writing in her weekly, *The Link*, on 23 June; and without her organisational skill and the assistance of her companion, Herbert Burrows, there would have been no strike at Bow. Adult match girls were receiving eight or nine shillings a week, youngsters half as much. Some 1400 of these underpaid workers came out, and they found East End labour solidly behind them. So, too, were some influential figures elsewhere in political life: Annie Besant recalled, a few years later, the help they had received from Sidney Webb, Frederick Charrington, Bernard Shaw, Stewart Headlam 'and many others'[15]. Nursery memories of Hans Andersen may, perhaps, have inclined some members of the middle class to look more sentimentally on little match girls than on other female workers. But there was little doubt that the strikers had a just cause. After a fortnight the company gave in: outside arbitrators secured higher wages for the girls and the abolition of a system by which fines could be deducted from their earnings. Above all, a Matchmakers' Union was established, the earliest organ-isation set up to protect the interests of unskilled women workers.

Within three weeks of the match girls' return to work, an early morning market porter found a woman's corpse in an alley off Commercial Street, close to the Barnetts' vicarage and Toynbee Hall. The body of Martha Turner, a thirty-five-year-old prostitute, was perforated with twenty-nine frenzied knife wounds. On the last day of August, half a mile away, the mutilated body of another prostitute, Polly Nichols, was discovered in Bucks Row, now Durward Street, north of Whitechapel station. Eight days later a third prostitute, Annie Chapman, was knifed behind 29 Hanbury Street, Spitalfields. At one o'clock in the morning of 30 Sep-tember the body of Elizabeth Stride was found in Berner Street and half an hour later yet another prostitute, Catherine Eddowes, died in Mitre Square, off Houndsditch. The dismembered body of a seventh victim, Marie Kelly, was found at a house in Dorset Street, Spitalfields, on 9

November. All these crimes were attributed to the killer whom the sensationalist press first described as 'The Monster of the East End', settling later for 'Jack the Ripper'. It is generally assumed that Marie Kelly was his last victim. But the death in July 1889 of Alice McKenzie suggests the Ripper may have struck once more before passing, unidentified, into macabre legend. For Alice McKenzie, too, had sought customers in the Dorset Street area, and her knifed torso was spread-eagled across an alley off Whitechapel High Street, close to the scene of the first murder. If she was killed by the Ripper, he cannot have been the mentally disturbed Wykehamist barrister, Montague Druitt, with whom some investigators identify him; for Druitt's body was dragged from the Thames in the previous December[16].

Too much has been written about the Whitechapel murders, more than on any other unsolved crime in British history. Public houses traditionally honour popular heroes, living or dead, but the strange appeal of this sinister whodunit encouraged Truman's brewery to change the name of the pub where one victim was last seen alive: in 1974 the Ten Bells, at the corner of Fournier Street, became Jack the Ripper. While the brewers' gesture gratified some tourist agencies, it aroused the indignation of many campaigners against violent crime. But the protracted horror story still exercises a morbid fascination: it has come to the screen in a dozen films; and, through the medium of a German dramatist, it brought East End crime to the theatre, to opera and to ballet. Speculation over the Ripper's identity continues: among candidates put forward by the fanciful have been Queen Victoria's least attractive grandson, the Duke of Clarence (second in line of succession to the throne), and – even more improbably – Dr Barnardo[17].

Yet if all the murders were committed by one man, he must almost certainly have been an outsider with a knowledge of surgery or dissection, not a native East Ender. Perhaps he had come as an immigrant, only to find his social code affronted by what he found in darkest Whitechapel. More likely he was a fanatical slummer whose wrath burst through the seals of reason when he perceived around him the moral corruption of which Sims and Mearns had written. It is significant that the murders took place in the furthest west, and already most publicised, black spot of the East End. Fortunately the crime cycle had beneficial consequences: gaslighting was extended into the alleyways of Spitalfields and Whitechapel; the re-housing programme, which the Board of Guardians had been pressing for so long, received a belated fillip; and, in an interesting concession to humane sensitivity, new regulations restrained bestiality in the slaughter-houses, to which – as Henrietta Barnett had noted with dismay – 'scores of frightened cattle' were still led through the densely packed streets.

The newsboys shouting 'Murder, murder, 'nother 'orrible killing in Whitechapel' did not deter the women who felt called to serve in the East End, whether their humanistic vocation was religious or secular in inspiration. The 'Salvation Lassies' continued to picket bars along Mile End Road as they had been doing for the past ten years, with copies of *War Cry* ready for distribution. Henrietta Barnett organised a women's petition to the Queen, seeking royal support for ridding Whitechapel of its dens of vice; and she received a private message of sympathetic encouragement from the Palace. That formidably middle-class intellectual Beatrice Potter, not yet married to Sidney Webb, disguised herself and sewed by the hour in sweaters' dens, enabling her to infuse a struggling vitality into the dry-as-dust statistics of her pioneer social surveys[18].

Also working in Whitechapel at this time was Eleanor Marx, whose father had died in north London five years before. In March 1889 she began to help Will Thorne create a union among the unskilled gas workers of Beckton. By midsummer the London Gasworkers' Union had 20,000 members and was so well organised that the mere threat of a strike forced the gas companies to concede a reduction in the basic working day from twelve hours to eight and a corresponding rise in the hourly rate of pay. Eleanor Marx – 'slovenly picturesque ... curly black hair flying about in all directions ... fine eyes, full of life and sympathy'[19] – was a distinctive figure. She spoke at open-air meetings in Victoria Park and along Barking Road; she accepted the burden of clerical work in building up the Union; and yet she found time to give Will Thorne that basic education which an inadequate schooling had denied him. In personal terms she achieved in those four months a greater success than had her father in his forty years of public polemic. Eleanor Marx also possessed the gift of inducing the workers of her small world to unite. For, although there was no general wave of sympathy for the Beckton workers as there had been for the 'white slavery' victims at Bryant & May's, Thorne was able to count on support and advice from two experienced SDF speakers, John Burns and Tom Mann, both members of the Amalgamated Society of Engineers. To some distant observers, particularly at Westminster and in the City, Thorne's reasoned presentation of his gasworkers' case made the new trade unionism seem yet another manifestation of self-help, an acceptable discipline which might reconcile deserving East Enders to the more virtuous Victorian standards of life. This attitude of mind was to prove important a few months later when, for the last time in the 1880s, the affairs of east London became a passing sensation in the daily press.

The success of match girls and gasworkers encouraged the growth of a new unionism among the largest, basically unskilled labour force in the metropolis, the dockers. Many casuals among them found employment during the winter months at Beckton or Bromley-by-Bow and saw for themselves the success of Eleanor Marx and Will Thorne. In the 1870s Hennesey's Labour Protection League had achieved only partial success in uniting stevedores, dockers, porters and watermen; it proved easy for shipowners to bring in blacklegs and exploit old rivalries between the various grades of dock labourers. Low pay and long hours for 'permanent' workers and the humiliating uncertainty of 'hanging about the docks and starving' for the casuals continued to burden dockers' lives. Ben Tillett, who had already been a seaman and quayside casual, was working in the tea warehouses in Cutler Street when, in 1887, he organised a union of Tea Operatives which, within two years, was attracting membership from dockers at Tilbury as well as in the Pool. The summer of 1889 was a good moment of joint industrial action: a long spell of hot and fine weather and improved trade prospects promised fuller employment than for many years. It would be harder than in 1872 for the dock company directors to find blackleg labour.

On Monday 12 August 1889 dockers unloading the sailing ship *Lady Armstrong* in the South-West India Docks walked off the ship, demanding 6d rather than 5d an hour and an end to the system by which 10 per cent of the piece rate earnings of speedier workers was pocketed by 'sweater' agents responsible for finding them employment. Within two days Tillett made the strike official, soon winning the support of Tom McCarthy, the stevedores' leader; by Friday Tillett knew he could count on the backing of Tom Mann, John Burns and the Engineering Union; and by the following week the port of London was strikebound.

There followed perhaps the strangest four weeks in the history of English trade unionism; the shipowners and directors of dock companies soon found that they were among the most unpopular men in the country. For a month a procession would form up each working-day outside strike headquarters at the Wades Arms public house in Poplar. Behind a brass band and waving flags and banners lent by trade societies, several thousand strikers would then march to the City, in a column never more than five deep and dutifully keeping to the left-hand side of the road. The broad straight route built by the East and West India Dock Companies to speed the transit of goods made a natural processional route. The marchers tramped resolutely along West India Dock Road and Commercial Road to Aldgate, on to Leadenhall Street and down to Tower Hill for what *The Times* described as 'lay sermons' from Burns, Tillett or one of their other leaders. There, as an eyewitness wrote a few weeks later, 'the docker heard the plain unvarnished truth about himself, that this strike was being fought that he might have some chance of becoming less of a brute and more of a man than heretofore, that his wife and children and home might have more care'. The discipline and orderliness of the demonstration made a great impression: 'The strikers had marched through the City without a pocket being picked or a window being broken', recalled H. H. Champion, who was, in effect, Tillett's public relations man[20].

Small wonder if the 'pavements became black with every description of city man from the magnate to the office boy'. East Enders had long since taken naturally to street theatre and, about these dockers' processions, there was a strong element of summer carnival. Again eyewitnesses noted the peepshow as it passed the end of city streets;

> burly stevedores ... permanent men got up respectably, preferables cleaned up to look like permanents, and unmistakable casuals, with vari-coloured patches on their faded greenish garments ... a stalwart battalion of watermen marching proudly in long scarlet coats, pink stockings and velvet caps, with huge pewter badges on their breasts, like decorated amphibious huntsmen ... coalies in wagons fishing aggressively for coppers with bags tied to the end of poles ... skiffs mounted on wheels manned by stolid watermen ... Father Neptune on his car in tinsel crown and flowing locks[21].

Poor Linnell's mourners, trailing eastwards from Long Acre under a darkening December sky, had booed and hissed the police in Bow Street. Now, less than two years later, the strikers' band played 'Auld Lang Syne' as the Metropolitan force handed over escort duties to the City police at Aldgate. 'The strike procession', it was recalled, 'had its moods – was merry on some days, taciturn on others, laughed at the Dock House sometimes, howled at it at others, but it never lost command over itself or caused serious anxiety to its leaders or to the citizens of London'[22]. Reporters representing foreign newspapers, as well as the British press, would ask for statements from the strike headquarters. 'Our cry for help had run like a prairie fire through England, the Continent, America to Australasia,' wrote Tillett some years later[23]. Money came in from many European cities, including Berlin and Paris. At times the strikers' band is said to have played *La Marseillaise* – for it was, after all, the centenary of the most dramatic summer in France's history. The *Star*, a sound radical newspaper, started a fund for the strikers which quickly mounted to £6000. But the largest contribution to the strike fund, £30,000, came from the wharfies of Australia.

With such support, it was almost impossible for the strike to fail. Tillett established what he claimed was a virtually 'Napoleonic' system of picketing; there was even enough money to buy off some would-be blacklegs. But the principal spokesman for the management, C. M. Norwood, was a tougher opponent than the gas company directors who had accepted Thorne's demands earlier in the year: 'A man of Herculean proportions', said Tillett, who was as diminutive as his hero, the great Emperor of the French. 'The very embodiment of the insolence of capitalism ... stout, well-fed and arrogant,' the *Star* declared, less generously[24]. But the City and the Churches were prepared to seek a reconciliation between the formidable Norwood and that increasingly resolute trio of Tillett, Burns and Mann. When the strike entered its fourth week the Lord Mayor established a Mansion House Committee, under his own chairmanship and including both the Bishop of London (Frederick Temple) and the Cardinal-Archbishop of Westminster (Henry Manning), for a high proportion of the marchers were Irish Catholics. Even so, it still took a week for this powerful committee to persuade Norwood to make concessions and there was then a final visit by the Cardinal to the strike committee in a Poplar schoolroom before a compromise was worked out. John Burns had demanded 'The full round orb of the dockers' tanner'; and, in return for a pledge of no victimisation against blacklegs, this was conceded – sixpence an hour, eightpence for overtime, and no more subcontracting to 'sweaters'. On Sunday, 15 September, one final procession marched the length of the Commercial Road and through the City to a triumphant rally in Hyde Park.

'The London dockers were marching to that brilliant victory over their employers which changed the whole face of the trade union world,' Sidney and Beatrice Webb declared four years later. The judgement was, perhaps, premature. Tillett's creation, the cumbersomely named Dock, Wharf, Riverside & General Labourers Union represented the interest of his workers in the East End and Tilbury until after the First World War, but there remained an independent Labour Protection League for the docks south of the river. Tillett, unlike Will Thorne or Ernest Bevin in later years, never became a national leader; and his critics maintained that he had achieved little for the casual poor, since from 1890 onwards the dock companies refused work to applicants who failed a medical examination[25]. Moreover, the port employers, shipowners and (later) the railway companies supported the establishment in 1893 of a National Free Labour Association to supply blackleg labour; three vessels were even fitted out as a strike breaking fleet, to sail non-union workers to any port closed by a dispute. Yet, if a long war of attrition lay ahead, Tillett, Burns and Mann had at least won the opening battle, 'the fight for the dockers' tanner'.

There was, too, something of general significance for the people of Plaistow and the Isle of Dogs, Poplar and Limehouse, Stepney and Wapping to celebrate on that third Sunday in September 1889. Never before in London's history had the East End successfully imposed its will upon the metropolis. That it did so now, with the active sympathy of moderates among the propertied classes, gave a final twist of irony to a decade in which journalistic extravagance of phrase had been regularly matched by the shocks and surprises of everyday events.

9

Strange Exotics

IN FEBRUARY 1886 the *Pall Mall Gazette* encouraged the spread of yet
another sensationalist scare. It warned the public that a racial conflict,
provoked by 'fifteen or twenty thousand refugees of the lowest type' was
about to break out in east London. 'Foreign Jews of no nationality
whatever are becoming a pest and a menace to the poor native born East
Ender', ran a reader's letter cited by the newspaper. Here was a new and
ominous note for any London journal to strike. And within little more
than a year it was echoed in the Commons[1].

Although individual Jews were verbally – and even physically –
attacked from time to time, there were no sustained outbursts of anti-
semitism in the capital during the first half of Victoria's reign. In the East
End itself the Jews' fiercest critics were the Irish Catholics, their reaction
prompted by a fear of being upstaged as street-traders rather than by
racial or religious prejudice. When the great prize-fighter Daniel Mendoza
died in Petticoat Lane in 1836 there were about 17,000 Jews living in
London. Some were so wealthy that they had homes in Piccadilly or Park
Lane; one, David Salomons, was in that year Sheriff of London and

Middlesex; but almost every eminent member of the community, irres-
pective of where his principal residence might be, still possessed property
in the district in which Mendoza had spent his last days. For two centuries,
from the late 1740s onwards, a compact zone on either side of Aldgate
and Whitechapel Road remained the nucleus of Anglo-Jewry, almost as
if preserved as a symbolic ghetto after the removal of the last civic
disabilities on Jewish believers.

By mid-century the Jewish population of London had increased to
about 20,000 and over the following thirty years the numbers more
than doubled. Immigrants arrived as refugees from central Europe, as
enterprising job-seekers from the Netherlands, and in the late 1860s and
the 1870s as fugitives from Poland. Many reluctantly accepted poor
earnings in the garment sweat shops, but changes were already taking
place in the structure of Jewish trade. Large ready-made clothing establishments came into being: as early as 1848 the Aldgate firm of E. Moses
& Son was so well known that when the deposed King of the French
allegedly went to Aldgate High Street to replenish his wardrobe, Thack-
eray sent *Punch* some satirical verses for the occasion: 'The cloth was
first-rate, and the fit such a one as only is furnished by Moses & Son'. By
1860 Jews from Whitechapel were also working for Moses Moses, king
of the second-hand clothes trade and father of the 'Moss Bros', who were
to open a famous shop in King Street, Covent Garden. Probably the
biggest single employer of east London Jewish labour in these years was
the manufacturing clothier, L. Hyam, of Gracechurch Street in the City.

Tailoring, however, was only one of many trades followed by the
immigrant Jews at mid-century: the Dutch newcomers became London's
principal cigar makers, while others built up specialist crafts, making
meerschaum pipes, umbrellas, or coconut matting, for example. One in
five working-class Jews was engaged in street-trading, from stalls,
barrows or small shops; one in ten made boots or shoes; and less than
one in ten was employed by furriers or jewellers or in the furniture
trade. Few East End Jews seem as yet to have acquired professional
qualifications, but many were general traders, especially at the fruit and
vegetable markets[2].

It was during the early 1880s that the composition of London's Jewish
community changed dramatically, largely as a result of events in Russia.
Twenty years earlier, when Tsar Alexander II's reign still held promise
of enlightened reform, old restrictions on the work and movement of his
Jewish subjects were considerably relaxed. But Russian resentment at
the Jews' social advancement, together with a suspicion that Jewish
intellectuals were dangerous revolutionaries, soon revived latent anti-
semitism, encouraging a steady flow of emigrants to seek sanctuary in
the West. Tension mounted in southern Russia after 1871, when the

Jews of Odessa had their property destroyed and their shops looted in an
outburst of unrestrained 'Jew-baiting', the earliest 'pogrom'. Ten years
later, in the spring of 1881, rumour held Jewish terrorists responsible for
the Tsar's assassination. Within seven weeks of Alexander II's death, the
first of a series of pogroms took place at Elisavetgrad (now Kirovograd),
an important trading centre in the Kherson province, where a third of
the inhabitants were Jewish. The pogroms spread rapidly through the
Ukraine, with tacit support from the government, until in May 1882 the
'Temporary Orders concerning the Jews' were issued in St Petersburg.
These 'May Laws', so far from affording protection against the assaults
of fanatics, imposed savage restrictions on all Jews, hampering their
ownership of land, their opportunities for education and their participation in business dealings. The persecution fell particularly heavily
on the Jewish population of Russian Poland and encouraged a mass
exodus. Some journeyed no further than Germany, but most hoped to
reach America, a haven for many Jewish refugees already during the
previous decade.

Anglo-Jewish charities assumed that many refugees would merely
pass through Britain. They were prepared to give them aid, but there
was a powerful lobby among influential Jewish leaders which firmly
opposed any new large-scale settlement in England, particularly in
London[3]. In July and August 1882, however, such a tide of immigrants
swept into the country that the existing Jewish institutions for handling
newcomers were overwhelmed. Some refugees were fleeced and exploited
as soon as they stepped ashore at Hull or Harwich and many more were
determined not to travel further across the seas. In 1885 Rothschild
money enabled a Poor Jews' Temporary Shelter to be set up in Whitechapel so as to prevent the immigrants being defrauded and cheated on
arriving in England. Representatives of the Shelter met ships from
Germany and Holland as they docked in London and GER trains from
Harwich arriving at Liverpool Street Station.

By February 1886, when the *Pall Mall Gazette* sounded its tocsin
warning, the Poor Jews' Temporary Shelter was well established. Later
that year Bismarck sought to force Polish Jews in Prussia back to their
villages, many preferring to make their way to the coast and take passage
in crowded steamers bound for England. By 1890 each week there would
arrive in London alone four regular ships from Hamburg, three from
Bremen and from Rotterdam, and a Danish steamer direct from Libau
(Liepaja) in Russian Latvia. Over the following twenty years, from its
headquarters' hostel at 84 Leman Street, the Poor Jews' Temporary
Shelter sought to meet a succession of emergencies. For what had begun
in the Ukraine in 1881 spread to Romania and parts of Austria-Hungary
by the end of the century; and the decision taken by the Tsarist authorities

in the spring of 1891 to eject Jews from Moscow, Kiev and other Russian cities led to yet another wave of emigration, with thousands of families uprooted. In all, between 1870 and 1914, 120,000 Jews sought refuge in England[4].

Almost all the immigrants settled in recognised Jewish districts within the principal English cities and particularly in London. As Whitechapel and Mile End were so close to their point of disembarkation, many were content to go no further. Rapidly the Jewish quarter expanded eastwards into old Stepney and northwards into Spitalfields. As early as 1889 Charles Booth could comment on the way in which 'the Jews have flowed across the line' separating 'the Jewish haunts of Petticoat Lane and Goulston Street' from the 'rougher English quarter'. 'Hanbury Street, Fashion Street, Pelham Street, Booth Street, Old Montague Street, and many streets and alleys have fallen before them ... they live and crowd together and work and meet their fate independent of the great stream of London life surging around them'[5].

Families from the same town or village in Eastern Europe tended to herd together, perpetuating old habits of thought, speech and worship in an alien environment. They also frequently prompted the older Jewish families to move out northwards to Finsbury Park or along the suburban railway route to Walthamstow, Tottenham and Enfield. This internal migration intensified the distinctive character of the newcomers: Yiddish newspapers and Yiddish drama flourished; and ultra-Orthodox religious societies and a separatist union of small synagogues clashed with the less ritualistic traditions of the Chief Rabbinate. The younger generation of immigrants assimilated English habits while proudly declining to abandon their sectarian heritage and be anglicised. There were plenty of Jewish clubs which they could join, learning not only the language but football, cricket, swimming and other sports as well. A Jewish Girls' Club was set up as early as 1886, and in 1895 a Jewish Lads' Brigade was established 'for developing the physique, for inculcating habits of obedience and self-restraint and for fostering a spirit of true patriotism'[6]. At weekends Jewish youngsters sought to escape to dance halls or the theatre. There was for them a good choice of melodrama, burlesque and pantomine both at the Standard Theatre in Shoreditch and at the Pavilion, Whitechapel Road. In later years the Pavilion became an exclusively Yiddish playhouse but, from the mid-1870s to 1904, the theatre was owned by Morris Abrahams and flourished under the enterprising management of Isaac Cohen[7].

Israel Zangwill, born in the East End of parents who had come to London from Russian Poland in an earlier exodus, successfully depicted the different strata of these Jewish newcomer 'greeners' in his three-volume novel, *Children of the Ghetto*, which was published in September

1892. It was set in and around the 'dull, squalid, narrow thoroughfare' which 'a dead and gone wag called ... "Fashion Street", and most of the people who live in it do not even see the joke'. Zangwill portrayed, with wry affection, the strictly orthodox Sons of the Covenant:

> Strange exotics in a land of prose, carrying with them through the paven highways of London the odour of Continental Ghettos, and bearing in their eyes, through all the shrewdness of their glances, the eternal mysticism of the Orient, where God was born. Hawkers and pedlars, tailors and cigar-makers, cobblers and furriers, glaziers and cap-makers – this was in sum their work: to pray much and to work long; to beg a little and to cheat a little; to eat not over-much and to "drink" scarce at all ... to keep the beard unshaven and the corners of the hair uncut; to know no work on Sabbath and no rest on week-day[8].

Small wonder if 'these humble products of a great and terrible past' transformed Whitechapel, Mile End and the old Irish Catholic enclave in Shadwell. By 1900 the Jews constituted over 95 per cent of the population in the Wentworth Street district of Spitalfields, in Hanbury Street, and in Goodman's Fields and over 75 per cent in a large area to the west of Cannon Street Road. 'East of Aldgate one walks into a foreign town', complained Major Evans Gordon, the MP for Stepney three years later[9].

The third of Jack the Ripper's victims was found in Hanbury Street, the fourth outside a Jewish Working Men's Club in Berner Street. Prejudice among cockney Catholics thereupon decided that the Ripper must be a 'Yid': the local newspaper reported how 'it was frequently asserted that no Englishman could have perpetrated such a horrible crime ... and forthwith the crowds began to threaten and abuse such of the unfortunate Hebrews as they found in the streets'. A police presence prevented serious rioting. But there remained a deep hostility towards the newcomers. Even Ben Tillett, in putting forward the dock labourers' case, complained of 'the influx of continental pauperism': the 'foreigners' who had 'come to London in large numbers' had, he maintained, aggravated 'the sweating system' which allowed 'the more grasping and shrewd' among them 'a life of comparative ease in superintending the work'[10]. In reality the Jewish workers were as hostile to the sweating system as Tillett's dockers and for five weeks in the autumn of 1889 machinists and pressers in the tailoring trade staged a successful strike to improve their hours of labour and system of payment. The East End Jewish socialists and trade unionists showed great independence of their English brother workers: at the end of the year an ambitious rally at Frederick Charrington's Great Assembly Hall in Mile End Road failed to bring about a federation of Jewish and non-Jewish unions in east London[11]. To many English and London-Irish workers the Jewish newcomers seemed to possess a ruthless and insatiable appetite for work. Significantly on two occasions in the last decade of the century the Trades Union Congress asked for restrictive legislation to keep the 'aliens' out.

Jewish immigrants were blamed for taking away jobs and for pushing up rents by accepting overcrowded conditions, thereby forcing native East Enders to move out. At the same time they were alleged to be rack-renting landlords. William Wilkins, whose book *The Alien Invasion* was published in the summer of 1892, claimed that Jews would accept sanitary standards 'which to the more highly developed Englishmen and Englishwomen mean disease and death'[12]. This nonsense won some popular backing and boosted support for the Association for Preventing the Immigration of Destitute Aliens, of which Wilkins had become founder-secretary in the previous year. More influential was the persistent campaign against the immigrant settlers waged by Major William Evans Gordon, who retired from the Indian Army in 1897 at the age of forty and took over the Conservative-Unionist campaign against 'destitute aliens' begun at Westminster ten years before by Captain Colomb, MP for Bromley and Bow. Evans Gordon contested Stepney unsuccessfully at a by-election in 1898, but his anti-alien views secured his return to Parliament in October 1900 and he served as Stepney's MP for seven years. Among Evans Gordon's supporters in his constituency, from 1900 onwards, there flourished the British Brothers League, the earliest Radical Right nationalist movement to cause trouble in the East End[13].

Evans Gordon was a xenophobe rather than an anti-semite. In January 1902 he painted an alarming picture of his constituency in the debate on the King's Speech: 'A storm is brewing which, if it be allowed to burst, will have deplorable results,' he warned the Commons. Yet, while he condemned the 'strangers from abroad' who made it impossible for 'an English working man in many parts of London to enjoy his day of rest', he also complained of 'schools crowded with foreign children' and, with sensational urgency, of 'a band of Italians, every one with a knife which he is too ready to use' who were 'at this moment causing great anxiety'[14]. Five other East End constituencies – St George's; Bethnal Green, South West; Shoreditch (Hoxton); Limehouse; Mile End – had returned Conservative MPs who were described as 'anti-aliens'; and this lobby was sufficiently powerful to secure the establishment in March 1902 of a Royal Commission on immigration. Major Evans Gordon sat on the Commission; so too, did Lord Rothschild, who was alarmed at the way in which the newcomers were pushing out long-established families from the traditional Jewish quarter in the East End.

The Commission's report, submitted in August 1903, urged a stricter regulation on immigrant settlement but not total exclusion. An Aliens

Bill, introduced in the following March, was withdrawn when the Liberal Opposition maintained that it was unduly severe: Churchill complained of 'a loathsome system of police interference' by which 'the simple immigrant, the political refugee, the helpless and the poor ... may be harassed and hustled at the pleasure of petty officials'. But in 1905 – the year Evans Gordon received a knighthood – a revised Aliens Bill was enacted which safeguarded the rights of political asylum but denied entry to 'undesirable immigrants' who had no 'decent means' of support. Statistics show thereafter a slight decline in the number of Jews entering the country. However, over the last eight years before the First World War at least 4000 Jews settled annually in Britain, many still choosing to live close to their point of disembarkation. By 1912 some 142,000 Jews were living in Whitechapel, Mile End, Poplar, Stepney and Hackney[15]. Thirty years before, Besant's *All Sorts and Conditions of Men* had provided a fictional social analysis of the East End without a single reference to Jews in all its three volumes.

'Paupers who fill the streets with profligacy and disorder' was how a leaflet produced by the Conservative Central Office for the 1905 Mile End by-election described the likely 'alien invasion' of the next few years, if immigration went unchecked[16]. The prejudice, although unjustified, is not entirely surprising, for modern Britain had become accustomed to emigration rather than to immigration. There is no doubt that the sudden arrival of so great an influx changed the character of English Jewry and the social composition of the old riverside hamlets.

Yet in retrospect it becomes clear that no group of East Enders over the centuries contributed so much to the life of the nation, not even the Huguenot refugees. They made possible the cheap clothing industry, a fifteen-year-old Montague Burton passing rapidly through Whitechapel in 1900 on his way from Lithuania to Leeds and the creation of the largest distributor of men's clothing in the world. They brought shrewd skills to the management of popular entertainment: Lew Winogradsky and Bernard Winogradsky who arrived in Brick Lane in 1912 from Odessa by way of Berlin were to become millionaire impresarios and, in 1976, life peers as Baron Grade and Baron Delfont of Bethnal Green. And they also brought the sharp commercial insight of the business tycoon: Charles Clore, two years older than Lord Grade, received his elementary education at the same elementary school in Rochelle Street, Arnold Circus, as the Winogradsky boys[17].

There was, too, a golden harvest of cultural and scientific genius in those last years of the long European Peace. As early as 1908 the twenty-year-old Selig Brodetsky was bracketed as a Senior Wrangler at Cambridge, and was soon recognised as an outstanding mathematician. Mark Gertler, born in Spitalfields of parents from Przemysl, secured in that same year a place at the Slade School of Art with the backing of William Rothenstein and the Jewish Educational Aid Society. Gertler, whose parents took him back briefly to Galicia before finally settling in Whitechapel in 1896, brought the lively realism of his working-class childhood to paintings which caught the eye with their fine draughtsmanship and bold use of colour; his most famous canvas, *The Merry-go-round* (completed in the autumn of 1916), is in the Tate Gallery. Isaac Rosenberg, whose family settled in Whitechapel in 1897 and who followed Gertler to the Slade, was by 1912 publishing starkly realistic poetry, far ahead of his time in form and content, but it was not until more than twenty years after his death in action on the Somme that the quality of his *Collected Poems* was fully appreciated. Gertler and Rosenberg had benefited both from the Whitechapel Library and from the art gallery next to it, which was opened in 1901, thanks to the initiative of the Barnetts; and a few years later the young Jacob Bronowski, newly arrived in England, found in that same Library the means of mastering the language in which he was to express with such clarity the philosophy of a scientific mind. And in June 1910 Solomon – a Whitechapel boy prodigy aged eight – made his public appearance as a pianist at Queen's Hall[18].

At the turn of the century the Jews' Free School in Spitalfields, founded as long ago as 1817, was the largest in the country, with some 4300 pupils and a teaching staff of more than seventy; discipline was good and the standard of achievement high. But conditions in the homes of these immigrant children remained deplorable and the environment uninspiring. Bud Flanagan, recalling the Hanbury Street of 1901 sixty years later, remembered 'a patchwork of small shops, pubs, church halls, Salvation Army hostels, doss houses, cap factories, and sweat shops'[19]. The anti-alien campaigners blamed the Jewish immigrants for overcrowded conditions and structural decay endemic to the neighbourhood long before the pogroms in Russia had provoked the great exodus. In reality, the newcomers cleaned up both Spitalfields and Mile End. A survey published in 1900 mentions Flower and Dean Street, Thrawl Street and Plough Street as having been 'vicious and semi-criminal' but now 'Jewish and respectable'. Even more striking was the change further north, when Jewish families – the Winogradskys among them – moved into the new LCC Boundary Street estate around Arnold Circus. There the Council flats were replacing notoriously lawless courts and alleys in Old and New Nichol Streets – the 'Nichol' area, transformed into the 'Jago' by Arthur Morrison for his famous fictional study of slum clearance, *A Child of the Jago* (1895). The immigrants' communal pride brought self-respect back to a district which, with the decay of the silk-weaving industry, had rapidly become 'a self-contained colony of criminal or semi-

criminal people', as an LCC report declared. Zangwill preferred to call
these colonies, more poetically, 'clotted spiders' webs'. While he was glad
of reformers' besom brooms, he warned his readers that 'the spiders have
scurried off into darker corners'[20].

Around the docks, two or three miles away, there were strange exotics
of a different kind: 'A large and motley crowd of labourers, to which
numerous dusky visages and foreign costumes impart a curious and
picturesque air', commented Baedeker's *London*. Their presence fired the
literary imagination of writers who, unlike Zangwill or Morrison, had
not themselves grown to manhood in the East End. Conan Doyle plunged
into this opium dream world in an early Sherlock Holmes adventure:
'The Man with the Twisted Lip' is a tale of addiction, dusky Malays and
terrifying Lascars attributed by Dr Watson to the month of June 1889
and set in a cavernous den behind wharves north and east of London
Bridge. A year later Oscar Wilde had his Dorian Gray go down to
Limehouse to replenish his opium. The shady mandarin reputation of
the riverside between Shadwell and the Isle of Dogs was by then well
established.

Was this notoriety justified? A few Chinese families had lived in
Limehouse before mid-century, having come apparently from the Straits
Settlements as seamen or ships' launderers. Shipowners who paid off an
overseas crew in London had an obligation to repatriate them, but it was
not always observed and many sought to settle in England. From 1857
onwards the Strangers' Home for Asiatics, Africans and South Sea Islanders in West India Dock Road had accommodated Lascars, Malays, Arabs
and blacks from Africa and the Caribbean so long as they had a prospect
of employment locally or on a ship. The Chinese, however, always kept
themselves apart from 'strangers' of other Asian or African lands. By
1890 the families of Chinese seamen from Shanghai were settled in
Pennyfields, Amoy Place and Ming Street while those from Canton and
southern China chose Gill Street and Limehouse Causeway, slightly
further to the west. Over the following twenty years the Chinese community grew rapidly, until by the time of George V's coronation in 1911
the district was reckoned as 'Chinatown': Pennyfields had its special
Chinese shops and clubs and a Christian mission to the Chinese Londoners; a Confucian temple 'on its last legs' at Ah Tack's lodging-house
in Limehouse Causeway could still intrigue a London journalist fifteen
years later[21].

It was tempting to weave tales of vicious gangs and opium dens into
the colourful texture of Limehouse life. Opium smoking in Chinatown
worried social missionaries, especially after the turn of the century. A
police raid on eighteen unlicensed lodging houses for seamen run by the
Chinese community in 1912 found traces of opium smoking in eleven of

Christ Church, Spitalfields. Hawksmoor's masterpiece, authorised by the New Churches Act of 1711, was built to satisfy the spiritual needs of a rapidly expanding East End.

The corner of Fournier Street and Brick Lane, showing the Spitalfields Great Synagogue, once a Huguenot chapel and now a mosque.

Boxing championship, 1788: Mendoza (right) puts Humphries on his guard.

Popular entertainment in Shoreditch High Street (1850s): Bianchi's Penny Gaff.

Shipping in the docks at the start of the recession of 1866. The photograph shows Trinity Wharf, Canning Town, with Blackwall Railway Terminus behind the trees and in front of shipping in the East India Dock. More masts up river to the left of the photograph show vessels in the West India Dock.

South-West India Dock in the 1870s, full of clipper ships and lighters.

*The first strike by unskilled women workers, Bow
1888: Bryant and May's match-girls protest
over a wage of no more than 4/- a week.*

*The fight for the dockers' tanner, August 1889: strikers prepare to haul a
fully rigged model ship to join their long procession up the Commercial Road.*

*St Anne's, Limehouse, floodlit in 1931, at the
end of the church's bicentennial year.
Hawksmoor's tower, at the head of Limehouse
Reach, was a landmark for vessels
sailing up river.*

*The past is a foreign country: Wellclose Square in the early 1890s.
A century later a primary school fills the centre of the square, which is
bounded by two blocks of flats. St Paul's mission house
and the tree remain.*

When Paul Martin photographed his 'Children of the Slums' in 1892 they were using a gas lamp as an improvised swing.

And so were the girls in front of a bomb-damaged house in 1950.

The children of east London at the turn of the century: (above) in a Whitechapel alley; and (below), two miles away, enjoying the see-saws and swings of Victoria Park, principal 'open space' for an overcrowded East End from 1845 onwards.

The Dominion Monarch *dwarfing a street in West Ham.*

The Blind Beggar, Whitechapel Road, shortly before the First World War. In 1966 George Cornell was shot in the saloon bar during a contest for gangland primacy. The brewery on the left was still in being then but a pub garden had replaced the drapery on the right.

Jellied eels on sale, Sclater Street market (1956).

Ben Tillett addressing striking dockers on Tower Hill in the abnormally hot summer of 1911.

Police escort perishable food supplies through Poplar on the fifth day of the Dock Strike, 1912.

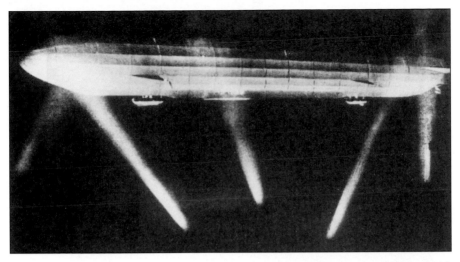

The menace from the skies: a German Zeppelin is caught by London searchlights, 1916.

Dornier-17s over Target Area A in the second wave of bombers on 7 September 1940. Fires burn along the Royal Docks and in Silvertown (bottom left). Prominent landmarks include West Ham Speedway Stadium (demolished c. 1973) and the line of the Northern Outfall Sewer (passing below rear Do-17's starboard wing-tip). A bomb seems recently to have fallen on Central Park Road. East Ham (top-right).

Hay carts and trams in Whitechapel, looking towards Aldgate (c. 1920). Whitechapel's hay market survived until 1928.

Poplar councillors on the march to the High Court, July 1921: The scene in East India Dock Road, with George Lansbury beneath the third banner, hat on the back of his head.

The police try to clear a path for Oswald Mosley during a provocative visit to Cable Street, October 1936.

Labour leaders from East End constituencies c. 1929: George Lansbury and Clement Attlee.

The Cunard White Star liner Mauretania *enters King
George V Dock August 1939, the largest
ship to use the Royals.*

*West India and Millwall Docks, looking across the North Quay from Poplar,
with two vessels in the centre moored at Canary Wharf.*

*Young Eastenders in 1954, out on the range
before their tea.*

Gangland bosses at home; Ronald and Reginald Kray, 1966.

Thames sailing barge and shipping in King George V Dock (c. 1952).

them. Although no evidence of organised crime emerged from such raids, a lingering suspicion of evil-doing kept the police on the alert. On several occasions in 1911–12 rumours that a mysterious and inscrutable 'Mr King' was peddling drugs among the Cantonese community sent Arthur Ward, a crime reporter from Birmingham in his late twenties, down to Limehouse Causeway and Pennyfields. And on one night Ward saw a tall, elegant Chinaman in evening dress leave a house in Gill Street and enter a waiting limousine. Perhaps he was Mr King, but from this brief sighting Ward's inventive imagination created the mysterious Dr Fu Manchu. Arthur Ward became Sax Rohmer and produced a succession of thrillers which from 1913 to 1957 made famous a Limehouse that might have been, but never was[22].

The mass immigration from Eastern Europe, together with the – numerically far smaller – settlement of Chinese families and others from overseas in Limehouse and Poplar, coincided in time with Britain's peak years of Empire. Even since 1878, when a music-hall song brought the word 'Jingo' into the English language, the stage had projected imperial pride with full-blooded vigour. Over the turn of the century an exuberant patriotism pervaded the East End. In Whitechapel and Stepney on the first Saturday night of January 1896 bricks were thrown through supposedly German shop windows and attacks made on German seamen at the news that their Kaiser had telegraphed his congratulations to President Kruger on capturing Dr Jameson's British raiding party in the Transvaal. Never before had there been anti-German demonstrations in any British town. But flag-waving was a popular gesture in the closing years of Victoria's reign, not least for those to whom the Union Jack retained a certain protective novelty. A death-or-glory stand against fanatical Arabs by Irish infantrymen singing 'Rule Britannia' provided the climax to *Tommy Atkins*, a box-office success in the winter season of 1895–6 for the Abrahams-Cohen partnership at the Pavilion Theatre. From the stage of this same theatre, in the Christmas pantomine of 1896, the sixty-four-year-old vocalist Albert Christian first brought down the house with his new and rousing patriotic ditty, *Soldiers of the Queen*[23]. Small wonder that the new, all-variety theatres were even named 'Empires': in the West End the curtain went up on the most famous of them all, at Leicester Square, as early as 1884; but East End audiences had to wait until the Boer War. The opening of the Hackney Empire on 9 December 1901 marked the coming of revitalised music-hall to a part of London where, for at least a quarter of a century, entertainers such as Marie Lloyd and Harry Champion could always be certain of good houses.

Some eighteen months earlier both capital and suburbs had celebrated the relief of Mafeking, where Colonel Baden-Powell and 700 men had withstood a Boer siege through 217 days of ingenious improvisation.

The news, which broke on the eve of a fine spring weekend, united rich and poor in a saturnalia of wild rejoicing; in the City itself gold sovereigns and silver coins were thrown among the crowds. By Monday *The Times* could attempt a sober assessment of this curious phenomenon. A reporter commented with mildly patronising surprise, on 'the extraordinary enthusiasm in East London': for there, 'Saturday was generally observed as a holiday'; 'The Whitechapel and Bow Roads were a mass of flags and bunting, while all the tramcars and omnibuses flew flags ...'; 'A large body of working men with flags and banners perambulated the Bow Road singing patriotic airs, while hundreds of cyclists wearing photographs of Colonel Baden-Powell formed into procession and paraded the principal thoroughfares of Poplar and Stepney'[24].

This column in *The Times* makes interesting reading on two counts: it shows how readily class fraternisation, present during the great Dockers' Strike, could be re-kindled at the end of the century; and it confirms that cycling, which flourished in southern suburbia, also enjoyed working-class popularity north of the Thames. But was the cycle parade a happy inspiration of the moment, or was it organised? How did hundreds of photographs of the hero of the moment come to be available for the cyclists to wear? It is tempting to speculate that, with the British Brothers League active in Stepney that summer, such a spontaneous chorus of patriotic pride may well have received political orchestration.

The census returns of 1901 show 42,032 'Russians and Poles' resident in the newly formed Borough of Stepney – a figure exceeded by only five towns in Russian Poland itself[25]. Inevitably, among these exiles were radicals whose principles inclined more naturally to anarchism than to a parliamentary form of social democracy. Foremost among them were Prince Peter Kropotkin, a veteran theoretician who hated all institutionalised government, and Rudolf Rocker, the non-Jewish German anarchist who edited the Yiddish *Arbeter Fraint* from what was virtually his libertarian commune off Stepney Green[26]. Other Russian and Polish socialists used Stepney as a launching pad for the revolution which they hoped would topple the Tsar and his fellow autocrats in Vienna and Berlin.

It was with the help of these immigrant socialists, and their contacts in the English Labour movement, that in 1907 Lenin – who four years earlier had delivered an anniversary oration for the Paris Commune at a hall in Jubilee Street – convened the Fifth Congress of the Russian Social Democratic Party. The main business of the Congress was transacted at the Brotherhood Chapel in Southgate Road, Islington, about two miles to the west of Victoria Park. But the preliminary meetings were held in the Jewish Socialist Club, at the corner of Fulbourne Street and Whitechapel Road and opposite the London Hospital; and it was in this improbable corner of the East End that Stalin – alias Koba-Ivanovich – first saw his rival of the 1920s, Leon Trotsky, a cartoonist's revolutionary incarnate. Across the road, in Fieldgate Street, there was – and is – a doss house where for some two weeks in May 1907 the future dictator of the Soviet Union and his Commissar for Foreign Affairs, Maxim Litvinov, found beds among the homeless ones who drifted in from Stepney's streets[27].

Lenin, Trotsky and Rosa Luxemburg, the doomed heroine of Germany's abortive revolution, all left London before midsummer in 1907, never to return. So, indeed, did Stalin; but a persistent legend – totally without foundation – has linked his name with 'Peter the Painter', the alleged burglar anarchist who, from 1911 onwards, stood second only to the Ripper among unidentified villains in East End folklore. Although the authorities had shown no interest in Lenin's Congress or the political activities of the recent immigrants, both the Metropolitan and City constabularies had been troubled throughout Edward VII's reign by an increasingly menacing crime wave in Whitechapel and Aldgate; they were particularly alarmed by gang warfare between a group of Bessarabian refugees and their rivals, who claimed to come from Odessa. But by the summer of 1910 violent crime seemed to be in decline.

Accordingly when, on Friday 16 December 1910; the City police were summoned to a flat in Exchange Buildings, Cutler Street, backing on to a jeweller's shop in Houndsditch they assumed that they were dealing with an attempted burglary. But six officers were fired on as they tried to enter the flat; three fell dead. Two men and a girl evaded capture and escaped through the back alleys of Whitechapel, carrying with them a mortally wounded comrade – and crossing into the jurisdiction of the Metropolitan police. News next morning that a wounded man had died at a house in Grove Street, Shadwell (now Golding Street), brought detectives to the tenements south of Commercial Road. The discovery of copies of the *Arbeter Fraint* and other radical literature at the Grove Street house convinced the police that anarchists were involved. By Monday *The Times*'s leading article was complaining that the district in which the three policemen were shot 'harbours some of the worst alien anarchists and criminals who seek our too hospitable shore'[28].

The famous sequel to the Houndsditch murders came fifteen days later. In the early hours of Tuesday, 3 January 1911, the police began to keep watch from a chemist's shop on 100 Sidney Street, a redbrick three-storey terrace house built ten years before; it was some 50 yards from Rudolf Rocker's Anarchist Club in Jubilee Street and was overshadowed by the cooling tower of Mann, Crossman & Paulin's Albion Brewery on the south side of Whitechapel Road. Soon after daylight shots were fired from the house wounding a police sergeant, standing beside the brewery wall. As no police revolver had the range of the Mauser pistols with which the fugitives had opened fire, a detachment of Scots Guards with rifles was sent from the Tower of London and, as a precaution, the Royal Horse Artillery were put on the alert in St John's Wood six miles away, eventually pulling two 13-pounders through the London lunch hour to the 'Battle of Stepney' in forty minutes. But their presence was not needed. At 10.15 twenty Guardsmen had arrived, keeping the house covered with their rifles; they were followed, at 11.50, by the Home Secretary, that veteran Hussar lieutenant, Winston Churchill. Also present by then were several dozen reporters and photographers, the earliest cinema newsreel camera, and hundreds of awed spectators[29].

Churchill stayed for three hours. He did not, as Liberal newspapers and the newsreel claimed, 'direct operations'; but he was, said *The Times*, 'full of resourceful suggestions'. Three hours was long enough for him to see the house in flames, with the fire brigade letting it burn until there could be no risk of further shooting from its gutted floors. The charred bodies of two Latvian refugees were taken to the mortuary. Of 'Peter the Painter' – described in the police report as 'believed to be Russian anarchist' – there was no sign. A medium built man, 'complexion sallow; skin clear; eyes dark; hair and medium moustache black', had disappeared. Perhaps he was the Latvian artist, Gederts Eliass. More probably he was Peter Piaktov, alias Schtern, a self-consciously handsome man, French rather than Slavonic in appearance. He may well have been a double agent; there are some grounds for suspecting that he was back in Russia before the Revolution, later serving in the Cheka, the earliest form of the Bolshevik secret police[30].

Yet although Peter's identity and fate are intriguing, the significance of Sidney Street lies in its consequences rather than the elusiveness of an individual. For the presence of the Home Secretary, the press, and the film camera – together with the unfamiliar crackle of shots echoing down Stepney streets and the clatter of gun teams across north-eastern London – made the battle of Stepney the news story of the winter. Rumour exaggerated the facts: even *The Times* invented a horde of Mausers and Brownings found beneath the debris of the gutted house[31]. Once more the East End's problems hit the headlines. Critics blamed the leniency of the Aliens Act for, as with the Ripper, it was emphasised that the shootings were not an 'English' crime. In those last suspicious years of a long peace it became harder for strangers to find sanctuary in Britain. The flames from that house in Sidney Street re-kindled embers of xenophobic prejudice well beyond the limits of the East End.

10

Peace and War

THE FIRST World War was to become the greatest agent of social fission in British history since the Reformation. In the crucible of battle, Edwardian and neo-Georgian Britain broke apart, releasing the energies which created a more egalitarian society and ultimately advanced the emancipation of women. Letters home from the Front, ribald songs, and war poems mingled a cynical realism with nostalgia for a lost golden age. Yet, however attractive 'dear old Blighty' might seem in retrospection, the last years of peace had in reality been pervaded by a short-tempered militancy, welling up from inner discontents; it is – if the jangled metaphor may be forgiven – as though the nerve cells of the body politic were misfiring on all cylinders. Suffragette militancy, the bitter constitutional conflict between Liberals and die-hard Lords, an unexpected backlash from Protestant Ulster, and the spread of syndicalism among trade unionists impatient with Fabian Socialism all seemed part of the general malaise of a society which even paid homage to violence and mechanical energy in the visual arts, music and literature. In the East End this mood was captured creatively by both Gertler and

Rosenberg; more immediately and dramatically it was expressed, between 1911 and 1914, by a passing enthusiasm for anarchistic ideals and a wave of strikes which brought dockers, seamen, railwaymen, tailors, and smaller bands of workers with local grievances out into the streets.

Concern over the inefficiency of the dock companies and the probable loss of trade by London to other seaports encouraged the Liberal Government in 1909 to set up the Port of London Authority, with control of the Thames and its docks from Teddington to the Nore, over 70 miles of waterway. Wage negotiations between Lord Devonport (the formidable PLA chairman), Ben Tillett and Harry Gosling, the watermen's leader, led to a promised increase of a penny an hour. But this offer was rejected by the dockers themselves, and a major dock strike followed in August 1911. Tillett again led some 100,000 men through the East End for meetings on Tower Hill and, as in 1889, it was a blazingly hot summer. This time there was little outside support for the strikers, nothing from overseas and no sympathy in the City. But trade was booming and a welcome negotiated settlement made the strike short-lived. Union membership trebled in the course of a year, and in the following spring the workers prepared for another round, seeking to end the PLA employment of non-union labour. This Dock Strike of 1912, marred by clashes with mounted police, is best remembered for Ben Tillett's rhetoric at a massed meeting on Tower Hill: 'Now repeat after me', he instructed the dockers, 'O God, strike Lord Devonport dead!'; and, like the chorus in a classical tragedy, they responded, 'He shall die! He shall die!'. But, in the short term, they were wrong; the Chairman of the PLA survived for a further twenty-two years; the strikers went back to work in August, after ten weeks of hardship. They faced a humiliating struggle to recover jobs lost to blackleg labour. 'Capitalism is capitalism as a tiger is a tiger; and both are savage and pitiless towards the weak,' Tillett reported back to his Union that autumn[1].

Other strikers had more success. Jewish tailoring unions, strongly influenced by Rocker and his *Arbeter Fraint* anarchists, came out in May 1912 and won improvements in the sweat shops of Mile End and Whitechapel. Stoppages by railwaymen and seamen lifted the status of their unions. On a much smaller scale was a communal effort on the Isle of Dogs in 1914, which secured better conditions for women workers at C. & E. Morton, the food-processing factory; their campaign recalled the Bow match girls' strike, but attracted far less publicity. At the same time, Sylvia Pankhurst founded her own radical East London Federation of Suffragettes, more left-wing than the mainstream movement inspired by her mother and her sister, Christabel. At first, in 1912, Sylvia Pankhurst had to overcome hostility and suspicion as an outside 'toff', but her magnetic personality soon drew crowds to open-air meetings in Victoria

Park. From her headquarters at 400 Old Ford Road, she led a movement
for women's enfranchisement which, she believed, necessarily implied a
further advance towards socialism. By November 1913 she had a
'People's Army' of 700 men and women organised to protect the Federation's meetings; and four months later she launched her own newspaper, the *Women's Dreadnought*[2].

It would be wrong to assume that the day-to-day existence of East
Enders in these last years of European peace was a grim struggle for
social recognition, punctuated by forays in an unending class war. Except
for the homeless ones, life was certainly better than twenty years before.
Even a visiting critic as acutely troubled as Jack London could note that
a 'fair measure of happiness reigned ... in little out-of-the-way streets',
where he found 'laughter and fun going on'[3]. There was certainly more
entertainment than at the time of the Mafeking hysteria. The first cinemas
in Old Ford Road and Mile End Road had begun to compete with the
music halls. Despite the temperance activities of Frederick Charrington
and the Salvation Army, public houses had increased in number, forty
in the Isle of Dogs alone. Some pubs had special opening hours, to suit
early morning workers; others were more clubbable, cultivating a robust
cheeriness, with bars painted in warm colours, orange and cream preferred; and some attracted custom from visiting seamen and natural
characters by the quirkish interests of the publican – thus Charlie
Brown's, by the gates of West India Dock (East), was a world-famous
curiosity bar.

The coming of tram-fares as low as a halfpenny a ride encouraged
an exodus to spectator sports on Saturday afternoons. Three professional
football clubs enjoyed a good following in the East End before the First
World War: Clapton Orient, which moved out to Brisbane Road, Leyton,
only in George VI's coronation year; Millwall, said originally to have
been the Mortons' factory side and known to have played on four pitches
in the Isle of Dogs before 1910, when they left the fields beside Millwall
Park viaduct to cross the river; and West Ham United, once the Thames
Ironworks side, which in 1904 moved from Canning Town to Upton
Park. Cricket lovers could, and did, make their way to Leyton, where
Essex had played first-class cricket since 1885 on a ground nearer to
Bow, Stepney and Poplar than was Lords; for the last four seasons before
the war the county was led by Clapton-born J(ohnny) W(on't) H(it)
T(oday) Douglas who, despite the nickname ingeniously contrived by his
Australian adversaries, recovered the Ashes from them in 1911–12 when
he took over the England captaincy. Many East Enders were boxing
enthusiasts, following in these years the fortunes of Ted ('Kid') Lewis,
from Aldgate, who after fighting his earliest bouts in Mile End Road
became world welterweight champion in 1915, and again from 1917 to

1919. There were plenty of clubs for those who wished to play football or cricket or to box or run, several of them sponsored by the charitable 'settlements'. Victoria Park and Mile End Park had so many cricket pitches that in the summers of 1913 and 1914 the local schools organised their own cricket league. While Victoria Park to the west of Grove Road was (in vintage Baedeker-ese) 'prettily laid out with walks, beds of flowers, and two sheets of water, on which swans may be seen disporting themselves', the Old Ford side of the Park was set apart for recreation, its 'bathing lakes' attracting thousands at summer weekends and bank holidays[4].

Jack London complained of smoke deposits in the air of the East End, which 'a poor workman ... breathes, and from which he never escapes'. Yet although little had been done to check pollution, families were less confined to what he called their 'out-of-the-way streets' than a quarter of a century before. Among the first charities established by Samuel and Henrietta Barnett was an organisation which ensured that children had opportunities to visit the countryside; pubs, churches, missions, street clubs and places of work ran outings, at least to Epping Forest, and often along the London, Tilbury & Southend line to the sea. People could get about more cheaply. Some forty bus routes served the East End, mainly red 'Generals' – belonging to the London General Omnibus Company – but 'Great Easterns', 'Union Jacks', 'Vanguards' and others, too. At Edward VII's accession there had been 3500 horse-buses in London; the first reliable petrol-buses went into service three years later (1904) and by 1908 a thousand of them were on the streets. When Edward VII died in 1910 the horse-bus had become a rarity: 'Generals' were mass-producing from their own works in Walthamstow 34-seater open-top B-type double-deckers, with a 28-hp engine. The East End was also criss-crossed by tram lines owned by the LCC, except beyond the Lea, where they were run by West Ham Corporation. It was easier, too, to cross the river, new links supplementing the first Wapping–Rotherhithe pedestrian tunnel of 1843, which some twenty years later was converted to carry trains between Shadwell and New Cross. While the City Corporation had completed Tower Bridge in 1894, the LCC went under the river: Black-wall, a road tunnel, was opened in 1897; Greenwich, a foot tunnel still attracting pedestrians from Island Gardens to south Greenwich, was completed in 1902; and a Rotherhithe road tunnel followed six years later.

Since 1871, when Sir John Lubbock MP successfully pioneered his Bank Holidays Act, family outings had become traditional on Easter Monday, Whitsun Monday and the first Monday in August. Some made their way to Hampstead Heath, Wanstead Flats or Epping Forest. Others were content with Victoria Park, which attracted over 300,000 visitors on 6 June 1892, when Whitsun was late and sunny. Excursions to Southend by trains from both Liverpool Street or Fenchurch Street were also popular; paddle-steamers plied down river, as far round the Essex coast as Clacton or Walton, and across the Estuary to Herne Bay and Margate. Newspaper advertisements tempted anyone enjoying passing opulence to something more ambitious. For, while special returns to Herne Bay cost 7s a head on 3 August 1914, any London excursionist with another 3s to spare was, from mid-July onwards, invited through newspaper advertisements to take an August Bank Holiday train and boat trip to Boulogne; at 11s 6d return, Calais was more expensive.

Did anyone go? Certainly within three weeks of that Bank Holiday Monday, 120,000 men had crossed to the French coast, many of them reservists from London's inner ring of suburbs, for Britain and Germany went to war at 11 p.m. on the Tuesday night, 4 August. Soon a commandeered bus was running from the army recruiting office, next to Poplar Recreation Ground, up East India Dock Road and on to the Tower, with 'To Berlin and Back Free' on its destination board. Any shop bearing a name which sounded Teutonic was a target for patriotic indignation; foreign bakeries seemed fair game for looting; and not even a chalked 'We are Russians' could safeguard windows from stone-throwing. Jewish refugees from Poland were subject to internment, in the first instance at Alexandra Palace or Olympia, if they could not prove that their place of origin lay within the frontiers of Russia, rather than in Austrian Galicia or Prussian Posen. Some of 5000 Belgian Jews who sought refuge in Britain in October 1914 were settled in Rothschild Buildings, Spitalfields; but they were far from popular: 'They looked down on us,' a resident recalled many years later, 'everything that anybody else did was below them'[5].

From the first weeks of the war Zeppelin raids on London were expected daily. An illustrated article on 'The Menace of the Zeppelins' appeared as early as 15 August; with a cruising speed of 54 mph one of these aerial battleships could cross from the Zeppelin sheds at Cologne to London's docks in six hours, it emphasised[6]. Street lamps were dimmed; lights were not allowed to show through curtains, a precaution which was met in the West End by the purchase of thicker draperies, but in the East End by turning down the gas or relying on a single candle. Kaiser William II was reluctant to authorise the bombardment of civilian targets in England; and vigilance weakened when, week after week, no Zeppelins appeared. Not until 12 February 1915 did the Kaiser sanction attacks on military objectives in London, including the docks. Preliminary raids were made on Southend and other towns in the Thames Estuary. No Zeppelin reached London until 10.45 p.m. on Monday, 31 May 1915, when Captain Linnartz in LZ38 found the blackout so ineffectual that he had little difficulty in spotting Commercial Road and headed for the docks[7].

German and British accounts of the raid differ considerably, as so often, over the following thirty years. Linnartz claimed to have struck a devastating blow, bringing his airship home through frenzied anti-aircraft fire and brave attacks by defending aircraft. In reality LZ38 was neither seen nor heard once Linnartz headed inland, and at 10,000 feet he was beyond the range of guns or night-flying pilots. Little damage was done. Of the 120 bombs dropped, 90 were incendiaries and the remainder hardly more than grenades. The first incendiaries fell on Stoke Newington and Dalston, Linnartz then changing course to drop both incendiaries and high explosive on Hoxton, Whitechapel and Stepney and, after turning northwards again, on Stratford and Leytonstone, too. Seven people were killed. There was no panic, but a mood of anger swept through the streets. Hatred of Germany, fanned by newspaper reports of the sinking of the *Lusitania* earlier in the month, erupted in savage attacks on foreign property, whether 'alien', 'allied' or 'neutral' (Scandinavian or Dutch, in particular). The Admiralty, responsible for protecting the metropolis from bombardment in the first eighteen months of the war, came in for popular criticism, at times caustically expressed.

There were four more night raids on London by Zeppelins in 1915 and another four in the following year; a last Zeppelin raid in October 1917 left the East End unscathed but caused heavy casualties elsewhere in the capital, particularly at Camberwell and Hither Green. The defences were so slow to improve that a parliamentary by-election in Mile End in the last week of January 1916 was dominated by the 'air issue', the war against the Zeppelins: the eccentric and intrepid flier, Noel Pemberton Billing, came within 400 votes of defeating a coalition government candidate backed by the party machines of both Conservatives and Liberals; Labour had not as yet contested the constituency[8]. Searchlight posts and anti-aircraft batteries were established in the winter of 1915–16, at first somewhat haphazardly. It was not until the small hours of 3 September 1916 – a night when, in their thirty-eighth bombing raid, fourteen German airships crossed the coast – that an enemy craft was destroyed, Lieutenant Leefe Robinson shooting down the newly commissioned SL11 in flames at Cuffley. Technically the airship was a wooden Schutte-Lanz rather than an aluminium Zeppelin; but the sight of what onlookers assumed to be a 'flaming Zepp.' boosted morale in north and east London, reviving a Mafeking mood of rejoicing. The fireball was clearly visible from the East End, even though Cuffley is almost twenty miles away. Within a month two more German airships were seen crashing in flames, both shot down by aircraft after being picked out in the beam of searchlights: Zeppelin L32 fell at Great Burstead, near

Billericay, on 24 September 1916; and eight nights later L31 plummeted to earth at Potters Bar, the most successful of the London raider commanders, Heinrich Mathy, dying that night with his crew.

Ultimately Zeppelins proved less of a menace to life in London than the 'England Squadron' of Gotha bombers which, from May 1917 to May 1918, were concentrated at two Belgian airfields near Ghent (Gand). Seventeen of these biplane Gothas flew in tight formation over the Essex countryside on the morning of 13 June 1917, dropping their first bombs on East Ham shortly before 11.30 and aiming for the Royal Albert Docks before heading for Liverpool Street Station, where they hit a train about to leave for Cambridge. Other bombs fell on Flower and Dean Street, the Minories and Fenchurch Street. In Spitalfields a bomb fragment broke a window of Commercial Street School. Rumours that the school was hit started a local panic, some parents scaling the walls in their haste to reach the children. Out of almost 900 boys and girls, 650 were kept at home that afternoon by mothers terrified at the prospect of daylight bombing[9].

By the early afternoon the parents may, too, have heard reports of the worst bombing tragedy of all in the East End during that war. For, only a few minutes after the false alarm at Commercial Street School, a 110-lb bomb hit the infants' class of Upper North Street School, Poplar, less than three miles away. At Poplar fifteen children were killed outright, three fatally injured and twenty-seven others maimed for life. Such a 'slaughter of innocents' was a horribly familiar aspect of warfare in towns and villages on the continent; but in London there had been nothing comparable for 900 years. Grief, shock and anger once more turned xenophobic. Since the bomb had fallen in daylight, it was assumed the school was itself a target. In reality, docks and railway lines were the England Squadron's main objective. Upper North Street School had the misfortune to stand barely half a mile from quayside warehouses and from a dockland railway siding. The seventeen Gothas killed 162 people that day, seriously injuring 432 others, nearly twice as many casualties as in any other raid on Britain by aircraft or airships during the First World War. Not one Gotha was destroyed on that Wednesday[10].

Morale, elated six months before by the apparent defeat of the Zeppelins, fell rapidly again. There was no systematic evacuation of children but the more fortunate boys and girls were sent away from the East End to friends or relations in the countryside; Lord Grade, for example, recalls how the Winogradsky brothers were moved out to Reigate after this first daylight raid[11]. The England Squadron returned to the capital again on 7 July, concentrating on the City, the West End and south of the Thames. But London's defences rapidly improved; and in three more daylight raids that summer the bombers failed to penetrate further inland than the Thames Estuary. East Enders on an excursion to their nearest seaside resort were among the casualties on 12 August when Southend was bombed in a Sunday evening attack by ten Gothas.

Interception by British fighter pilots led the Germans to change their bomber strategy a month later. London was attacked on seven nights at the end of September and the beginning of October 1917, a new and larger four-engined bomber, the Giant, joining the Gothas in the last three raids. Few bombs in these raids fell in the East End, but the nightly visitation aroused mounting apprehension; people trekked out to open spaces, even to Epping Forest, or sought shelter in the underground tunnels, especially the East London Line from Liverpool Street to New Cross which, at Whitechapel, Shadwell and Wapping was deeper than the District line. Irate station staff, bound by company regulations, were no more successful at excluding them than the keepers of Victoria Park. Air raid shelters were improvised in the basement of public buildings; East End families brought with them not only bedding, but pets as well. Hygienic conditions recalled Gavin's Bethnal Green of seventy years before.

In his *War Memoirs* the Prime Minister, Lloyd George, asserted that 'there was grave and growing panic amongst the population in the East End'. This was an exaggeration: an 'obstinate defiance of authority' would have been a more accurate phrase[12]. Yet there is no doubt that the fourth winter of war was hanging heavily on a people who in 1914 answered with alacrity Kitchener's original call to serve King and Country. Broken lives robbed parents of sons who had been their solace and support in all classes of society and left women at the head of families with large numbers of dependants to feed. For working women there was constant uncertainty over employment. A bad slump when the coming of war destroyed fashionable tailoring was soon countered by orders for more and more khaki, giving many women garment workers unprecedented take-home pay. Some women found employment in jobs previously reserved for men: on the buses and trams, in heavy engineering, in munition factories and at the docks. But many older East End occupations were hard hit: confectioners by the sugar shortage; bakers, butchers and fruiterers by the effects of blockade; smaller specialist trades by the cutting of links with the Continent.

Quite apart from the menace of Zeppelins and Gothas, everyday life became increasingly difficult as the war dragged on. An inadequate system of food distribution entailed dispiriting vigils in interminable queues while West End and City restaurants imposed an inequitable form of rationing by price. Sylvia Pankhurst, who in contrast to her mother and her sister Christabel remained opposed to the war effort, sought to counter the hardship around her in Old Ford Road by establishing a

'Price Cost Restaurant'. This idea was duly taken up by Lloyd George's Director-General of Food Production, who established four 'national kitchens' in the poorer parts of London: vegetable soup, fish pie and rice pudding was on sale for sixpence at Poplar on the day reporters visited it[13]. Allotments were encouraged in recreation grounds and neglected open spaces: on the Isle of Dogs even the notorious Mudchute – 30 acres of silt pumped from the docks in the last decades of the old century and left to form a health hazard hill on the far side of East Ferry Road – was 'civilised'; the allotments there flourished, for they possessed plenty of natural fertiliser. But wartime food directives could prove perverse, irksome and oppressive: in September 1917 a baker from Chapman Street, Shadwell, was imprisoned for three weeks for selling fresh bread; food regulations insisted that a loaf could not be sold until at least twelve hours after baking so that, by cutting thinner slices, the bread would go further[14].

East Enders long retained three vivid memories of the Great War: tinsel cigars falling to earth as flaming torches; Gothas, purposefully menacing in their compact formation; and that cold January Friday in 1917 when, around seven in the evening, the sky above Blackwall flashed bright as noon and all London was rocked by the Silvertown explosion. Brunner, Mond's works, to the south of Royal Victoria Docks in West Ham, had been producing munitions since the first months of the war, attracting many women workers who received good pay for a job recognised as socially noxious, their skins yellowed by the chemicals used in the plant. The factory was small, old-fashioned and, unlike more recent munition works, was sited in a heavily populated area. What mistake started the fire which ignited 50 tons of TNT on that fateful 19 January remains unclear, although the Ministry of Munitions accepted responsibility for a blast which killed sixty-nine people, seriously injured seventy-two others and left more than 300 men, women and children needing hospital treatment[15]. Homes were wrecked in North Woolwich Road and its adjoining side-streets, devastating more than a square mile on the north bank of the Thames and lifting roofs and breaking windows across the river, too; more damage was inflicted than in any air raid of that war. The cost of repairing such destruction was reckoned at £2.5 million, a huge sum in 1917, greater than was needed for a new battleship. While the personal tragedies of the explosion could be comprehended, it was difficult to appreciate the fear which the disaster spread in those closely packed streets of the eastern suburbs on both sides of the Lea. For what potentially disastrous explosives were being produced each night and day in other familiar factories along the Thames or in Bow or in Hackney Wick? The Germanic name 'Brunner, Mond' convinced Hun-haters that evil forces were at work among them.

Only once in the last two years of war did Zeppelins fly over London. L45 and L55 crossed the city late on 19 October 1917 without realising they were above their target for the capital was covered in mist, guns remained silent, searchlights did not open up; random bombs were dropped, none falling on the East End. Raids by Gothas and Giants continued until May 1918; by then London and its suburbs were protected by anti-aircraft batteries, barrage balloons and, north of the river, by six airfields in Essex from which Sopwith Camels would take off to intercept raiders. Air raid warnings were given by igniting the small cubicle fireworks known as maroons, normally fired from police stations. Sometimes, however, they were mistaken for bombs falling. So it was, on the night of Monday, 28 January 1918, when there were stampedes for safety both at an air raid shelter in the Bishopsgate goods depot in Shoreditch and at Mile End station on the District line; fourteen people were crushed to death or suffocated in the two incidents. The coroner was disgracefully unsympathetic. At an inquest on 1 February he pointed out that the dead were 'of foreign extraction': he insisted that, now they were in England, they should have accustomed themselves to behaving more like men and less like animals. At a second inquest, next day, he took up a police inspector's observation that many of the shelterers were young Russian Jews of military age: they ought to have been 'in the army', he commented[16].

Early on the Tuesday morning a lone five-engine Giant raider dropped a bomb six times as heavy as the one which had struck the school in Poplar, on Odhams Printing Works in Long Acre, trapping those who had sheltered in the basement, some of whom came from Hackney and the eastern suburbs. Thirty-eight of the sixty-seven people killed in that night's raids perished in Long Acre; remarkably, over 400 shelterers were rescued physically unharmed. The station stampedes and the Long Acre tragedy raised fresh fears over basement shelters, whether officially designated or improvised. Once again, in Mile End and Bethnal Green and Whitechapel, there was a further loss of confidence among a sorely tried section of the community. In a district so recently tinged with anarchism, special surveillance kept the Cabinet informed of what seemed to be happening, and much that was not. The Government remained uneasy. Fortunately on only five more nights of the war did the warning maroons send families scurrying for shelter.

Statistically the East End boroughs may seem to have been no more at risk in the First World War than several other towns of eastern Britain. There were fifty-three German airship raids on the United Kingdom; Zeppelins dropped their bombs as far north as Edinburgh and as far west as Bolton; and, in June 1915, good Yorkshire folk in Hull responded to a Zeppelin raid by heaving half a brick at 'German' windows as readily as the patriots of Poplar and Stepney. London was the objective on only twelve airship raids, some of which spared the eastern side of the metropolis entirely. The shorter range of Gothas and Giants did indeed mean that the twenty-seven mass bomber raids were concentrated on the capital and its suburbs, but the aircraft could not always penetrate inland and Chatham, Margate, Folkestone and Southend-on-Sea suffered heavily. Nevertheless the Kaiser's directives made the area around London's docks especially vulnerable. Since the total PLA bill for war damage to its properties between the Nore and Teddington was little more than £3000, it is clear that few bombs actually hit the docks[17]; but to have homes and places of work or instruction in the narrow roads and courts near to the docks – or near the railway lines which served them – was to live in fear of sudden death from the skies. Between 1915 and 1918 there was nowhere else in Britain where so many families, densely packed within a few square miles of sprawling streets, were so persistently exposed to enemy attack as in the East End of London.

11

The Lansbury
Years

ON THE last Friday morning in July 1921, 2000 workers set out on a five-mile march from Poplar Town Hall along radicalism's processional mall, towards Tower Hill and the City. To those who remembered the dock strikes it all looked familiar enough; cloth caps, dockers' banners, a drum-and-fife band at the head. This time, however, the procession had a different purpose and a different destination: 'Poplar Borough Council marching to the High Court and possibly to Prison to secure Equalisation of Rates for Poor Boroughs', proclaimed the leading banner. Behind it followed Poplar's mace-bearer and deputy mayor, wearing a chain of office. In the next file – his left arm steadying a raincoat thrown casually over the shoulder and his trilby resting, as ever, on the back of the head – came Poplar's former mayor, George Lansbury, 'uncrowned king of the East End'.

Apart from ten months in Queensland, Lansbury was an East Ender from 1868, when his parents brought their nine-year-old son from Greenwich to Bethnal Green, until his death in 1940, four months before the heavy bombing. He had worked as a coal-heaver and in a sawmill, learning his socialism from Hyndman and John Burns, and sitting in the Commons as Labour MP for Bow and Bromley from December 1910 until October 1912. The seat could have remained his far longer had he not resigned in order to force a by-election in the same constituency, which he fought and lost as a supporter of women's suffrage. For that same cause Lansbury had once already accepted imprisonment: six months in Pentonville for inciting men to 'stand shoulder to shoulder with the militant women' in their struggle for the vote. Like the suffragettes, he imposed upon himself the rigours of a hunger-and-thirst strike.

All that was eight years ago now, remote in a pre-war past. By 1921, over eight million women above the age of thirty had gone into polling booths for both local and parliamentary elections; and – what is more often forgotten – another six million new male voters, too, for the 1918 Representation of the People Act enfranchised virtually all men residing in a constituency, or occupying premises in it, for more than six months. Disappointingly, half the East End electorate did not bother to vote in the 1918 General Election: the Bow and Bromley seat was won by a Coalition Conservative, and South Poplar by a Coalition Liberal.

But when votes might decide purely local issues the turn-out was different; and in the LCC elections of 1919 Labour made striking gains, notably in Hackney, Bethnal Green, and Poplar. Social reformers came to dominate not only borough councils, but many of the Poor Law Boards of Guardians, who were responsible for the welfare of the old, the sick, the workless and the poor. Nevertheless Conservatives had the deciding voice both within Lloyd George's coalition cabinet and on the LCC, where the right-wing 'moderates' of the Municipal Reform Party held office until 1934. Complaints that wealthy boroughs, such as Kensington and Westminster, were not contributing a fair share towards relief in the poorer parts of the County of London made Poplar Council decline to hand over its quota to the LCC or supply certain sums due to central government, for the payment of the Metropolitan Police, for example. The borough councillors, knowing that almost a quarter of Poplar's people were living on the verge of destitution, fixed a low rate and allocated most of it to relieve their own poor. 'Poplar is paying £4500 a week in Out Relief', another banner in the procession proudly proclaimed on that Friday morning. But unilateral direct action of this kind brought the councillors into conflict with the law. This was why they were marching to the Law Courts and, as they assumed, to prison.

Yet that night all thirty rebel councillors returned to their homes. A rate strike, the Court held, was tantamount to anarchy: but the defiant rebels were allowed time in which to change their minds and levy the required rates as an alternative to imprisonment. The councillors were confident that publicity would bring victory to their cause. There were eleven Labour councils in London: why should not they follow Poplar's lead? Moreover Sir Alfred Mond, who as Minister of Health was cabinet spokesman on welfare, seemed eager to avoid a major confrontation in any East End borough – and small wonder, for Sir Alfred had been a director of Brunner, Mond & Co. for over twenty years before that unforgettable evening when Silvertown was devastated. But, though concessions were offered in the Commons, the councillors remained adamant. The men were locked up in Brixton and, on the first Monday afternoon in September, the five women councillors were arrested in the Town Hall. The car which was to take them to Holloway could move only at walking pace, for one in four adults in the borough had turned out to cheer Poplar's five heroines: Nellie Cressall, once a laundress in Whitechapel Road; George Lansbury's daughter-in-law, Minnie; Susan Lawrence, mathematics' graduate from Newnham, Cambridge; Jennie Mackay, a former militant suffragette; and Julia Scurr, who had served on Poplar's Board of Guardians for the past fifteen years[1].

The Borough of Poplar extended from the borders of Hackney Wick southwards to Cubitt Town and Millwall, and most of its citizens were tenants paying rent. Thousands supported their councillors by joining a Tenants' Reform League and threatening to pay no rents until the Government and LCC conceded equalisation of rates. Nevertheless 'Poplarism', as the right-wing press derisively named this defiance of central authority, had its critics even within the Labour Party. Ramsay MacDonald, who was about to resume the party leadership he lost in 1914, disliked Lansbury personally; and Herbert Morrison, the Mayor of neighbouring Hackney, disapproved of actions taken by a borough independent of the rulings of the London Labour Party, of which he was then secretary. But Bethnal Green proposed to follow Poplar's example; its Mayor was a member of both the Labour and Communist Parties. More unexpected was Stepney's support, for there the Mayor was an Oxonian barrister and war veteran who had known the gullies of Gallipoli and the trenches of France: 'I have always been a constitutionalist', Major Clement Attlee told Stepney Council, 'but the time has come when it is necessary to kick'[2].

Yet no kick was needed: a firm prod brought victory to Lansbury and his rebels. Mond and the LCC capitulated rather than risk Poplarism spreading elsewhere; there was, the cabinet was told, 'profound unrest and bitter feelings' in the East End[3]. After six weeks, the councillors were freed: a bill was drafted providing for the equalisation of the rates; and for several years Poplar and other boroughs on both sides of the Lea continued to spend money on relief far above the Government's official limits. But Neville Chamberlain, as Baldwin's Minister of Health from 1924 to 1929, had more success than Mond in bringing Labour boroughs to heel. By then, four of the imprisoned councillors could oppose the Conservatives within the House of Commons: Lansbury sat for Bow and Bromley from 1922 until his death; Susan Lawrence represented East Ham North in 1923–4 and again from 1926 to 1931; Samuel March sat for South Poplar from 1922 until 1931 when, on his death, he was succeeded in the seat by another imprisoned colleague, David Adams; and John Scurr was MP for Mile End from 1923 until 1932 when he, too, died. Like Lansbury and March, the Mayor of neighbouring Stepney was also returned to the Commons in 1922, as MP for Limehouse. Attlee still held the seat in 1945 when he formed the first socialist government with a clear majority. Poplar's act of defiance, although largely forgotten for the next half-century, provided London Labour with its most fruitful seedbed.

Far better remembered were the nine days of the General Strike in May 1926: they brought tense hours to the East End, with steel-helmeted troops ensuring the safe unloading of food supplies while loyal Trade Unionists watched, angrily impotent, from outside the dock gates. But the General Strike was a one-act drama in the history of the nation as a whole, not specifically a London affair. There were a succession of short strikes in the mid-1920s on the buses and the trams, in the docks, and in Covent Garden market; many were unofficial and came as part of a power struggle over the creation of larger unions, especially Ernest Bevin's new Transport & General Workers' Union[4]. Few of these strikes brought benefit to those who lived in the five eastern Metropolitan Boroughs (Shoreditch, Hackney, Bethnal Green, Stepney and Poplar) or in West Ham, which was rapidly becoming an annexe of the East End.

Loss of prestige by the Unions did not lessen support for Lansbury's style of socialism. The veteran campaigner was too much of a rev-olutionary evangelist to accept the pragmatic policies of MacDonald, Bevin and Morrison, markedly different though these were from each other. He was content to go on living in great simplicity in Bow Road. From February 1925 to July 1927 he edited *Lansbury's Labour Weekly* which, at least in its first year, enjoyed a good circulation within the East End and far beyond it, too. Except for the electors of Bethnal Green (South West) – who returned a Harrovian Liberal, Sir Percy Harris, as MP from 1922 to 1945 – Labour was in the ascendant throughout the 1920s on the LCC and in 'London over the water' (i.e. across the River Lea) where West Ham, a County Borough since 1889, was controlled by socialist councillors even before the turn of the century. Their successors had responded to the Silvertown disaster with ready understanding of the need for prompt municipal assistance; and in 1926 West Ham's Poor Law Guardians were suspended from office for their generosity in giving relief to the sick, destitute and unemployed. It is not surprising if east

London's voters remained overwhelmingly left-wing in sympathy until 1978, when seven wards in Bow rediscovered Liberalism.

The most revolutionary social change for East Enders between the wars was the development of municipal housing. For this initiative they could thank Dr Christopher Addison, the only person to sit in the first peacetime cabinets after both world wars and then a Liberal MP for Hoxton. As Minister of Health in 1919 Addison was responsible for the earliest Government funds to help local councils build housing estates. A year later George Lansbury laid the first turf of Poplar Council's miniature garden city, the Chapel House Estate, at the southern tip of the Isle of Dogs. But of even greater significance were the LCC's 'cottage' estates in outer suburbia; for one of these – Becontree – became the first outpost of County Hall empire in rural Essex. Such colonisation was soon to change the approach map from the Thames Estuary beyond recognition; in time it would leave the concept of the 'East End' virtually boundless.

Becontree, some ten miles from Whitechapel, was once marshland belonging to Barking Abbey, flat and frequently flooded: 'enclosed heath', a visitor commented in the 1870s, noting, 'a collection of mean houses, with a beer-shop and Wesleyan chapel'[5]. Work began on houses there in 1920; by the time Labour gained control of the LCC in 1934 the Becontree estate had become the largest single municipal development in the world, greater in extent than the famous socialist housing complex in Heiligenstadt, bombarded that year in Austria's brief civil war. In all, some 35,000 houses went up in Becontree, spreading the workers over four square miles of orderly, two-storey, neo-Georgian 'cottages' rather than concentrating them in barrack-like blocks of flats, as in Vienna and so many other Continental cities. Electric services on the District line, steam trains on the London, Tilbury & Southend route (by then part of the LMS – London, Midland & Scottish – network), and good bus services encouraged cheap-day commuting for those wishing to retain their jobs in the East End itself. But many families sought work locally, for in 1931 the Ford Motor Company began producing cars at their Dagenham Thames-side plant, only a few miles from Becontree. Some east London pharmaceutical and chemical industries also moved out to Dagenham. The combined effects of the Becontree estate, and the new industrial zones, was to relieve the over-population of the East End, at its peak in the first decade of the century.

Despite these opportunities to follow a different way of life from the earlier generation, much in inter-war London recalled the conditions exposed in the 1880s by Sims, Mearns and Charles Booth: over-crowding; sweat-shop factories in small basements; and, for dockers and porters alike, all the uncertainties of a casual labour system. Bethnal Green,

Poplar and Stepney remained the three metropolitan boroughs in which poverty was most concentrated in particular areas of destitution. Fortunate families, those with money to go out late on Saturday night and buy meat at knock-down prices in the markets, would carry their Sunday dinners through the streets to be cooked cheaply in the ovens of local bakeries. With the most generous of borough councils fighting to raise outdoor relief for a man, woman and two children to £2 a week, the struggle for existence was as harsh as ever. Edgar Lansbury – George's son, later Poplar's Mayor and father of that distinguished actress, Angela Lansbury – remarked of his own Borough in the summer of 1922 that 'People who can afford to live out of it wouldn't be found dead in it'[6].

The battle for improved housing continued into the next decade. 'Up with Houses, Down with the Slums', was a popular slogan which helped win the LCC for Labour in 1934. But by then the council was concentrating not so much on houses as on homes. It was forced to build blocks of flats in the old, familiar streets rather than look for new Becontrees – not least because of opposition from local authorities in Essex (and Hertfordshire, Surrey and Kent, too). The flats were provided with bathrooms and electric light. But within the inner East End the Waterlows and the Peabody Buildings of the 1860s were solid enough to survive; fewer flats went up there than nearer the Lea. Despite Herbert Morrison's 1934 ideal of creating 'A Healthy London', the first post-war survey of Bethnal Green showed that less than one in ten homes possessed a bathroom[7].

Technically, in the 1930s the East End did not become a 'depressed area'. For while unemployment reached 66 per cent up in Jarrow, it never rose above 15 per cent in the Tower Hamlets. But these figures are misleading. Joe Jacobs, whose immigrant father had died young from the terrible conditions in a Whitechapel sweat shop, has left a moving account of life in Whitechapel between the wars. As a tailor's assistant, aged twenty-seven in 1930, Jacobs was 'seldom out of work for more than 7–8 weeks at any one time', but friends of his who were unskilled labourers went jobless for months and months on end[8]. Public works' projects provided some employment during the Depression, notably on the Essex bank of the River Lea in Bow Creek where the hundred-year-old iron bridge was replaced and new embankments constructed. But, in general, the gradual trade revival brought relief more slowly to east London than to the north or west of the capital: enterprising businessmen preferred to build new factories where road and rail links with the rest of the United Kingdom were better than along the Essex border. There was a marked contrast in character between two complementary arterial roads of the inter-war years: for, while Western Avenue (A40) was lined with factories from its inner starting point at Acton out to

Perivale and Greenford, Eastern Avenue (A12) was a residential route, with over three miles of houses from its innermost point at Wanstead before the first, small factories were sited at Newbury Park. When in 1933 Hoover opened its Perivale factory in Western Avenue, job-seekers were attracted from as far away as Bow and Aldgate, some cycling there and back each day and thus covering more than 200 miles a week[9].

Economic recession intensified the frustrations caused by the casual nature of dock labourers' employment, and Bevin, who had succeeded Tillett as the dockers' principal leader, campaigned vigorously in favour of 'de-casualisation'. But MacDonald's two minority Labour Governments – ten months in 1924, twenty-six months in 1929–31 – were powerless to change the system. The last word remained with the PLA who, although accepting casualisation, had throughout the 1920s sought to expand the network of docks and thus create new jobs. With the return of peace in 1918 seaborne trade began booming again and by 1930 the Port of London's incoming tonnage was 56 per cent up on the 1913 figures[10]. Much of this success was due to the PLA's determination to complete the construction of a new 'Royal' dock, first proposed in that hot-tempered summer of 1911 but on which all work had stopped on the outbreak of war.

On 8 July 1921 King George V opened the dock, which was named after him. As his yacht sailed down river a huge banner the length of a cricket pitch spelt out a riverside borough's loyal greeting: 'Poplar's Message to the King: Work or Maintenance for the Unemployed'. But the new dock lay beyond Poplar and, indeed, outside the LCC area entirely; it was sited in East Ham, to the south of the Royal Albert Dock, with Beckton's gasholders in brooding proximity. It had three miles of quays, and seven long jetties on the south side, with enough clearance to accommodate huge liners; the berthing of so large a vessel as the 35,655 ton *Mauretania* in August 1939 was an exciting event long remembered by youngsters on both banks of the Thames[11]. There were two major contrasts with earlier enterprises: the project received government sponsorship; and great care was taken to provide new homes for families displaced by the construction work in the neighbourhood with which they were familiar. The PLA set aside 9·5 acres between the dock and the Woolwich Free Ferry. Here they built over two hundred houses, each with a small garden and the chance of allotments close at hand. Rhea Street, Winifred Street, Auberon Street and Fernhill Street looked neat and trim when seen across warehouse roofs from the ships moored along the quayside. They were more pleasant to the eye than the streets around the older docks up river.

For at least the past hundred years East Enders ambitious to climb the social ladder had tended to move away from inner London and settle in the new suburbs. Few emigrated south of the river for, except perhaps to the people of Millwall and Cubitt Town, the Thames remained a social Rubicon, which was not to be crossed lightly or wantonly. Railways had, since their inception, served as pathfinders: the Great Eastern (especially the Loughton branch in 1856 and the Chingford branch in 1873); the Tilbury line and the District; and the 'Hampstead Tube', which in 1902 was opened as far as Golders Green and Archway by Lloyd George. This northwards thrust of the Underground system may well have contributed to the relative failure of the Great Eastern's Barkingside and Fairlop extension which, although opened as early as 1903, never attracted suburban settlement on the scale of the Loughton or Chingford lines, even in the inter-war years. The outward spread of new Jewish communities may be traced from the dates in which permanent synagogues were established: northwards to Dalston, 1885; Stoke Newington, 1903; Finsbury Park, 1912; Stamford Hill, 1915; north-westwards to St John's Wood, 1882; Hampstead, 1892; Golders Green, 1922; and north-eastwards to Leytonstone about 1900–1; Walthamstow, 1902; and Gants Hill, not until the eve of the Second World War. But there remained some older and prospering Jewish immigrant families who had travelled far enough. They were content to stay in the East End, at least until the racial rowdiness of the 1930s menaced their lives with the threat of new-style pogroms.

Most east London homes were rented, sometimes from the council but often from landlords who had themselves moved out to the suburbs. Between 1925 and 1938 many families became 'plotlanders' in rural Essex. Local newspapers would carry advertisements for strips of field offered for sale by farmers or enterprising middlemen for as little as £5 or £8 a plot. If someone in the family could earn extra money – the wife working in the evenings in a shop or charring for example – the husband would go down to the advertised site on his first free Saturday or Sunday, buy a plot, stake his claim, and mark it off with posts and barbed wire. He would then be entitled to put up a tent, shanty or even build his own bungalow; and there the family would come for weekends and holiday breaks[12]. The delights of the Laindon Hills and the headwaters of the Crouch, and the curiously Netherlandish challenge of life on Canvey Island, became a welcome escape from a dreary, weekday existence. By the eve of the Second World War the plotlanders had discovered the coast beyond Clacton, and some even joined south Londoners on the edge of Kent and Sussex. Their tents and shanties held promise of a wider experience than any traditional outings could offer.

But, despite the novel attraction of plotland ownership, most families found escape by taking excursions, as they had before the coming of the First World War. A day trip to Southend-on-Sea, in full pursuit of

peppermint rock and a muddy tide, remained a special delight. The
Kursaal survived throughout the first half of the century as a high-
spirited Edwardian pleasure park unmatched in London, east or west.
The iron pier, completed in the same year as the Eiffel Tower, provided
a far-flung promenade $1\frac{1}{3}$ miles out into the estuary for those who, by
foot or electric tramway, sought the salt tang of deeper waters. After
dusk each summer in the 1930s the pier and the Esplanade from
Southchurch to Westcliff were transformed, as if by pantomime magic.
Festooned alleys of coloured globes linked palmists' tents, jellied eel or
Leigh cockle stalls and the smaller amusement arcades, while the electric
glow of a sylvan fairyland came from the cliffside shrubberies. Saturday
evenings and Bank Holidays were especially lively. Resorts further north
might be proud of their 'illuminations', but in this East-End-by-the-
Sea London's day-trippers were content to enjoy, monosyllabically, the
'lights'.

Back home, some 35–40 miles up river, Saturday nights were often
as noisy, but far less fun. By Silver Jubilee year (1935) there were over
fifty cinemas in the East End, forcing several of the best known music-
halls to close. Entertainers who had come originally from Whitechapel
or Stepney – among them the band-leader Ambrose, the comedian Issy
Bonn and the violinist Albert Sandler – were by now national stars of
the stage, the gramophone record and the radio. Social life remained
centred on public houses. Joe Jacobs recalls Stepney's Drunkart, a conveyance locked up in a special shed behind the urinal at the junction of
Philpot Street and Commercial Road and fetched out by the police to
trundle street drunks unceremoniously to their cells. He also writes of
the *Shpieler*, the gambling dens of the Whitechapel underworld, where
hard-earned wage packets could be emptied as speedily as in the most
tempting of pubs[13]. There were, however, healthier pursuits: George
Lansbury, who received great publicity for the determined campaign
which he waged to secure the opening of the Serpentine to mixed bathing
in June 1930, had earlier encouraged the building of a proper lido in
Victoria Park; and there were more football pitches on Hackney Marshes
than on any other expanse of fields in the country. Boxing remained
popular. There were arenas at the Premierland, off Commercial Road,
and the Wonderland in Mile End Road. A Poplar lad, Teddy Baldock,
became bantamweight champion of the world in May 1927 when he
defeated Archie Bell at the Albert Hall; a fleet of fifty-two hired buses
brought Baldock's fans from Poplar to Kensington Gore that night for
the title fight.

The most famous of modern Jewish boxers, Aldgate's 'Kid' Lewis, was
back in the public eye by the autumn of 1931, although in an unfamiliar
and unfelicitous rôle. In February 1931 disillusionment with the cautious

domestic policy of MacDonald's second Labour government induced one
of its ablest members, Sir Oswald Mosley, to establish a radical New Party.
Although Mosley seems, from the start, to have admired the Fascist ideal
of strong leadership and orderly discipline, his New Party was never a
racialist movement and he attracted young men impatient with the old
order. Mosley welcomed support from the former welterweight champion
of the world: he invited Lewis to train his personal bodyguard (nicknamed
the 'biff boys' by the press) and secured his nomination as New Party
parliamentary candidate for Stepney, assigning the eminent poet and
essayist Sacheverell Sitwell to serve as Lewis's intellectual minder. All
twenty-four New Party candidates were defeated in the General Election
of October 1931, but none fared so badly as the unfortunate 'Kid' Lewis.
From his native East Enders he attracted only 157 votes[14].

Many of the New Party's founding fathers cut their contacts with
Mosley when, in 1932, he sought to turn it into the BUF (British Union
of Fascists). Sadly, Lewis stayed on. He may well have failed to understand
the splinter loyalties of right radical politics. Moreover it could be argued
that Mussolini was still, at that time, contemptuous of Nazi racial theories
and counted on support from several influential Italian Jews. But,
although Mosley continued to look to Mussolini for funds as well as the
inspirational theatricality of his movement, the BUF appropriated Hitler's
anti-semitism from 1934 onwards[15]. By then there was no longer a place
for Aldgate's ex-welterweight champion among the biff boys of Chelsea.

As yet the East End had not become a battleground between Fascism
and its enemies. But hostility to the Jewish community as an alien
intrusion and as alleged exploiters of sweated labour had remained a
latent political force since the days of the British Brothers League, before
the First World War. Demagogic attacks on outsiders who were taking
work from British hands were sure of a good response, especially from the
Anglo-Irish Catholics of St George's-in-the-East and Shadwell. Mosley's
most effective lieutenants in the East End were Mick Clarke and Owen
Burke, both of whom were (like Tillett) of Irish origin. The first BUF
branch in east London was established at Bow in the autumn of 1934,
with Bethnal Green coming a little later, Shoreditch in 1935 and Limehouse in July 1936. Throughout the remaining years before the heavy
wartime bombing there were three localised pockets of BUF loyalty: in
Bethnal Green, along the western section of Roman Road, then known
as Green Street; in Duckett Street, Stepney, leading from the south side
of Mile End Road almost to St Dunstan's Church; and, further south, in
Salmon Lane, the oldest route from Limehouse to the centre of medieval
Stepney[16]. These districts were too remote from each other to become
strongholds of armed defiance, but they were potential sally-points along
the outer ring of a compact and predominantly left-wing area; for Step-

ney's Communists had gained a considerable following in the Tenants' Defence League, led by their young and gifted spokesman, Phil Piratin. Mosley concentrated the BUF's efforts in the East End, not simply because of its large Jewish community, but because he counted on support from convinced anti-Communists. He believed that to them a uniformed blackshirt legion would represent the continuation of policing by other means[17].

The para-military character of Mosley's movement had disturbed Lord Trenchard, the Metropolitan Commissioner of Police, in the autumn of 1934, even before BUF strategy turned to east London. He wished to have the Fascist movement banned. So, too, did his successor, Sir Philip Game, two years later. Lower ranks in the police force may have shown a greater indulgence towards the BUF, but the constant attacks on Jews personally and on their property in Shoreditch, Bethnal Green and Stepney during the spring and summer of 1936 were all meticulously noted and analysed by the authorities[18]. When Mosley, strutting in a new uniform complete with shining jackboots, addressed 5000 followers in Victoria Park in July 1936 there was rioting; both Fascists and non-Fascists needed hospital treatment. His announcement that in October he would lead his blackshirts on a route march through the East End, making four speeches on the way, should have induced Sir John Simon, the Home Secretary, to impose an immediate ban on so provocative a gathering. That was the wish of Attlee and Herbert Morrison who led a deputation to Simon.[19] They should have known better: 'Simon has sat on the fence so long that the iron has entered into his soul,' Lloyd George once remarked; and over that first weekend in October, the Home Secretary retired to the country. He left Sir Philip Game to keep order in the capital. Into the East End were drafted 6000 foot constables and all the mounted police. For the first time a rotating-wing aircraft, an autogyro equipped with radio, stood by, ready to hover over London's streets[20].

There followed, on 4 October 1936, one of those occasions which pass into East End folklore. A magnificent mural, painted in 1982–3 on the old town hall in Cable Street, commemorates what happened that Sunday. Since the Home Secretary would not ban Mosley's parade, the police assumed responsibility for enabling the march to move unrestricted through the streets. But by mid-afternoon 100,000 opponents of Fascism were concentrated in Whitechapel, between Gardiner's Corner (the inter-section of Whitechapel Road and Commercial Road) and the junction of Cable Street with Cannon Street Road. A force of over 2000 blackshirts was inspected by their leader at Royal Mint Street. Before they could march off, the police found their route blocked in Cable Street by an overturned lorry, with the bricks it was carrying serving as an improvised barricade. The 'Battle of Cable Street' was a defensive operation aimed at preventing the police from clearing away the barricade to let the BUF through. Much of the resistance came from Wapping dockers; it was so resolute that Sir Philip Game contacted the Home Secretary by telephone. At last Simon authorised an order to Mosley calling off the march. The BUF headed back towards its headquarters in Chelsea, a pipe band at its head.

Throughout Stepney the Jewish People's Council against Fascism and Anti-Semitism, the International Labour Defence, local workers for the Labour Party, the ILP and the Communist Party jointly celebrated their victory over the blackshirts. The newspapers that weekend carried reports of a bloodbath in Toledo, where Nationalist troops had recently relieved their beleaguered garrison in the Alcazar; and feelings over the Spanish Civil War ran so high, that some people in Stepney saw in the discomfiture of Mosley a defiance of Franco. But it was rash of the anti-Fascists to convene a victory rally at the following weekend. For, while it was in progress, 100 youths smashed shops along Mile End Road and attacked anyone they believed to be Jewish. A barber was thrown through a plate-glass window and a four year-old Jewish girl picked up and hurled after him[21]. By good fortune, no lives were lost in any of these riots.

From New Year's Day in 1937 a Public Order Act banned political uniforms and tightened the law on the marches and the use of insulting language. Never again was there so serious a confrontation as in October 1936. The BUF, however, retained a considerable following in the East End. In March 1937 they contested the LCC elections for the first time, polling 23 per cent in Bethnal Green North-East, 19 per cent in Limehouse and 14 per cent in Shoreditch (where one candidate was William Joyce, subsequently nicknamed 'Lord Haw-Haw' for his arrogant wartime broadcasts from Berlin)[22]. But, while no Fascist was elected to the LCC, in Stepney the Communists secured their first success, with the return of Phil Piratin.

Among such hot-headed militancy there were few opportunities for an elderly Christian Socialist, who abhorred violence from Right or from Left, to assert himself. But, from his home at 39 Bow Road, George Lansbury remained active. In 1935, after four years leading the Labour Party and the Opposition in the Commons, he returned to the back-benches and agreed to serve once more as Mayor of Poplar, 1936–7. But his main concern was to promote international peace. For this cause he travelled thousands of miles from his East End constituency: to Roosevelt in Washington, Hitler in Berlin, Benes in Prague, Schuschnigg in Vienna, Horthy in Budapest, Prince Paul in Belgrade, King Carol in Bucharest, and King Boris of Bulgaria in the Ritz, Piccadilly. His travels convinced him that world statesmen everywhere shared his desire to avoid another war[23].

Yet it was Lansbury's misfortune to see his hopes dashed month by month in those last years of armed truce. By the time he met Prince-Regent Paul, Chancellor Schuschnigg was in a Nazi concentration camp. The sandbags went up around Poplar Town Hall during the Munich Crisis of September 1938, the council workmen digging protective slip trenches across the recreation ground beside East India Dock Road. A year later people noted the strange silence in East End streets: children were no longer playing hopscotch, football, knock-down ginger, wall-stump cricket or tin can tommy; for they had gone with their schools to the countryside, fearing bombing raids more terrible than anything inflicted by the Zeppelins and Gothas of the earlier war. But that experience, at least, George Lansbury was spared. He died on 7 May 1940, three days before war came in earnest to western Europe. By the end of the year nothing remained of Lansbury's Bow Road home, except a doorway leading on to rubble.

12

Target Area A

GREAT Britain officially went to war with Hitler's Germany at 11 a.m. on 3 September 1939. Exactly twenty-eight minutes later the first air raid warning ululated over east London, a sound repeated on 1223 occasions before the last alert on 29 March 1945, an average of one wail each forty hours. On that Sunday morning the sirens sounded (with slight variations in timing) across all southern England, linking evacuated children with distant parents in shared apprehension. Not that there was any cause for alarm; an unidentified aircraft on a lone cross-Channel flight was sufficient to alert a vigilant and untried civil defence system. So it was, too, at 2.45 on Monday morning, when the sirens sounded again in the East End. A second error in identification sent people groping down to basements and cellars or stumbling out to slit-trenches in the unfamiliar blackout. For the past two years – ever since October 1937, when the King's speech at the opening of Parliament gave priority to an Air Raid Precautions Bill – Londoners expected the coming of war to be followed by days and nights of aerial bombardment, an ordeal already suffered by the people of Madrid, Malaga and Barcelona. But these fears proved groundless. The Germans were anxious to prevent retaliation on their own cities by the RAF. Not a bomb fell on English soil in the following eight months, nor on metropolitan London for almost a year[1].

This long period of deceptive calm, with no major attacks along the Western Front and little activity in the winter skies, was dubbed by American newspapermen the 'phoney war', an epithet which won widespread acceptance. In many London districts, these months of inactivity bred resentment, not so much at wartime restraints, as at administrative muddle and confusion. The blackout, for example, caused so many road accidents that it had to be modified as early as October 1939. Food rationing was promised but long postponed, prompting complaints that the Government had given so much notice of its intention that the wealthy were able to hoard supplies, particularly of sugar. London's riverside communities were, however, kept more conscious of the war, for U-boat attacks on merchant vessels had begun on its first day. During September and October 1939, magnetic mines in British coastal waters accounted for over 60,000 tons of shipping, much of it sunk in the Thames estuary and the approaches to the Nore.

The greatest outward change to life in east London during those first months was the closing of all state schools. Not, however, for long. Almost half of London's children had said goodbye to their parents in the last days of peace and accepted evacuation with their schools, but by January 1940 one in three were back home again, swelling classroom numbers in the skeleton schools which were allowed to re-open in the ninth week of the war[2]. In the East End the proportion was even higher, largely because the children had not been moved so far from their homes and could be visited by parents on a cheap day rail ticket. Some, rather strangely, had been taken to towns on the east coast, well within range of German bombers. Others were settled in Hertfordshire, close to key factories which were natural targets in any strategic air offensive. It was reasonable for a parent to fetch home their child from so risky a sanctuary. There were cases of unhappy children seeking to make their own way back to dockland on foot from the more distant reception areas, including Dorset and Oxfordshire. Many mothers of children under five who had been evacuated with their infants returned to their East End homes before the end of October. When, in March 1940, the Ministry of Information began a publicity campaign to encourage parents to accept a revised scheme for evacuation, it was received with cynical indifference. Although there was a small flow of evacuees to the western counties of England in June 1940, over half a million children of school age were still living in London when the heavy bombing began that autumn. East End families continued to mistrust all evacuation plans[3].

In 1939 many people did not feel so strongly committed to fighting against Germany as they had in 1914. Mosley spoke at a successful BUF rally in Bethnal Green eleven weeks after Hitler's invasion of Poland; and when a by-election was held in the West Ham (Silvertown) constituency on 22 February 1940, two of the three candidates – the Communist, Harry Pollitt, and the Fascist, Moran – opposed the war. Pollitt and Moran were both able to campaign in the constituency, but little more than a third of the electorate went to the polls on that Thursday, and they gave Labour a majority of 13,377; of the anti-war candidates, Pollitt received 966 votes and Moran 151. The second wartime by-election in east London came sixteen weeks later, two days before German troops entered Paris, and was a contest for Lansbury's old seat of Poplar (Bow and Bromley). By then, although the BUF was not yet a proscribed organisation, its leaders had been interned; an anti-war Communist challenged the Coalition. She received, however, only 586 votes, the people of Poplar preferring Alderman Charles Key, a councillor for twenty-one years and former Labour Mayor; he arrived in the Commons with a safe 11,000 majority. Fortunately for Poplar, Key had already built up an efficient team of ARP wardens. Within seven months he was appointed London's joint regional commissioner, with special responsibility for shelters[4].

The decisive phase of the Battle of Britain antedated the offensive against the capital. As early as 10 July the Luftwaffe launched attacks on shipping, airfields, coastal towns, and strategic railway-junctions as a prelude to invasion. Hitler still forbade the bombing of London for fear of retaliation on Berlin, a city unscathed by war since the campaigns of Napoleon. Not until 24 August did the first bombs fall on the East End – in Stepney and Bethnal Green – and on the City and outer suburbs. These bombs were dropped by single aircraft, in error: their pilots were looking for the oil depot at Thameshaven, 10 miles down river; they seem to have mistaken dockland for Tilbury. As Hitler had feared, this unintentional bombing of the London area prompted Churchill at once to urge the Chief of Air Staff to hit the Germans hard, in their capital. More than forty British bombers reached Berlin on 25 August and an even larger force three nights later. The anger of the Berliners caused the Luftwaffe to change its bombing strategy, giving the airfields a respite and bringing in additional bombers for the long postponed assault on London. An operational directive drawn up by the Luftwaffe early in September 1940 proposed night and day attacks until the docks and all power supplies were destroyed: 'The city is divided into two target areas: Target Area A comprises East London with its extensive dock installations, while Target Area B covers West London'. This strange geographical division lumped together the City, Whitehall, the 'diplomatic quarter', and Battersea Power Station as part of the same, strategically inferior, region[5].

The assault on Target Area A began shortly after half-past four on 7 September, a gloriously sunny Saturday afternoon, ideal for cricket or (as several thousand East Enders thought) for watching an improvised West Ham United take on Spurs at Upton Park. Soon after the sirens sounded, more than 150 Heinkel and Dornier bombers, flying more than 3 miles up in the sky and above a protective shield of Messerschmitt fighters, could be seen following the line of the Thames up to Beckton Gas Works and Woolwich. They were followed by a second formation of more than 170 bombers, some of which sought targets in Area B. But it was dockland that bore the brunt of the attack. High-explosives and incendiaries rained down on wharves and quays along both sides of the river, and on the roads and railways which supplied them. Industry and domesticity had become so closely integrated in the East End that the long-terraced houses and blocks of flats were swept away in the bombing. From East Ham to Bethnal Green, homes close to the docks or to the railway lines were especially vulnerable in this first daylight attack. Worst hit were Silvertown and Canning Town[6].

On that Saturday evening the 'All Clear' sounded about half past six. But the raid had started fires which were still burning intensely when the night bombing began, less than two hours later. Wave after wave of bombers pounded east London until shortly before half-past four on Sunday morning. By midnight nine major fires were burning in the East End and West Ham. A stretch of riverside south of the Royal docks was virtually flattened; it included the part of west Silvertown devastated by the Brunner, Mond explosion in 1917. The heavy bombing was resumed by more than 200 planes at 7.30 on the Sunday evening and continued for fifty-seven consecutive nights. The nightly Blitz was maintained, with brief respites, until the second weekend in May 1941. The Luftwaffe's bombers then turned eastwards to support Hitler's surprise invasion of the Soviet Union.

The Blitz destroyed or damaged 3·5 million homes in metropolitan London and killed over 15,000 men, women and children. Although the South Bank boroughs from Greenwich to Southwark also suffered heavily, no area was attacked so systematically as the East End and its trans-Lea dependencies. Raids on 15–16 October and 15–16 November in 1940 and 19–20 March and 19–20 April in 1941 concentrated particularly on east London, while every part of the metropolis was hard hit on the final night of the Blitz, the raid which began late on Saturday 10 May 1941. But in retrospect it is clear that the key Battle of the East End – the straddling of Target Area A – was fought in September 1940, before Hitler authorised the extension of the raids to what he described as the 'residential areas' of London.

Over 1400 incendiary canisters fell on dockland in the second week of September and almost a thousand tons of high-explosive. Unexploded bombs (UXBs) caused streets to be roped off and forced thousands of families to leave their homes and seek refuge in packed rest centres: about one in ten of the UXBs were duds, but some had delayed action fuses. Fires cut off some communities completely: an improvised river rescue service helped many Silvertown refugees on the first night of bombing; and on Monday, 9 September, the Town Clerk of Stepney arranged for a thousand homeless shelterers to be evacuated by river-steamer from the Wapping waterfront and taken up-river to the supposed safety of Richmond. Much depended on such moments of local initiative and enterprise.

Poplar was fortunate in the leadership given by Alderman Key, MP, his deputy and chief ARP warden, Alderman Smith (whose bravery was recognised by the award of the George Cross), and the Rector of Poplar, the Revd Mark Hodson (who, in 1961, became Bishop of Hereford). But the emergency machinery of some other boroughs faltered under the strain. It had been assumed that municipal rest centres would house victims of the bombing for only a few hours, until they could be moved out to unscathed areas. Council schools, often more than fifty years old and short of lavatories or washing facilities, provided temporary accommodation. Most, however, had no shelters and were themselves vulnerable. So, indeed, were some of the allegedly safer suburban sanctuaries. A family whose dockland home was badly damaged in West Ham found itself trying to sleep out the following night's air raid in the stalls of the Majestic Cinema at Woodford, a likely target for any bombs straddling either the railway on its eastern flank or the arterial road on its northern[7].

But however alarming the risk might seem in Woodford or Chingford or Finchley, these evacuees were the fortunate ones. After the devastation of the first weekend's bombing in West Ham, several hundred families were temporarily housed in South Hallsville Road School, Canning Town, equidistant from a huge power station by Bow Creek and the Royal Victoria Dock. Some spent Saturday, Sunday and Monday nights there, waiting for buses which, they were assured on the Sunday, would take them to less exposed districts in the suburbs. A convoy of buses was, indeed, organised to evacuate these refugees before dusk on Monday, 9 September. But the convoy never arrived. What went wrong is still not clear, almost half a century later. The buses appear to have gone, in the first instance, to Camden Town in mistake for Canning Town. They were then hampered in their journey eastwards by blocked roads and diversions. Long before the buses reached the Lea on Tuesday morning the Luftwaffe returned: at 3.50 a.m. South Hallsville Road School received a direct hit; and some 400 people perished in the rubble. No other bomb which fell on Britain carried away so many lives[8].

Rumour magnified even this terrible tragedy, as well as inflating or inventing other incidents. Morale was at rock bottom on that Wednesday. Bombing had breached the northern outfall sewer, contaminating the River Lea and leading to panic demands in West Ham for transport to evacuate the whole borough. The muddle and confusion encouraged an impatient hostility towards all authority. At first, many East End families had bought tickets on the District line or the tube and trekked west to shelters across the capital. Why, it was now asked, should they be denied overnight refuge in their local tube stations or in the unused tunnels east of Liverpool Street? On the fifth night of the Blitz officialdom was defied and the tubes invaded; angry East Enders brought blankets and pillows down to the platforms and refused to move out again. A count taken fifteen days later showed that on Friday, 27 September, the London tube system was providing shelter for 177,000 people[9].

Shortage of adequate shelters in east London caused widespread social resentment. The mild nights of a warm September induced some 5000 people to travel out to Epping and camp in the forest and fields of Churchill's constituency; he was not, at that moment, a leader for whom they held great regard. Local reports exaggerated their anger, but they were certainly more spirited than the refugees who blocked the French roads four months before[10]. There was a widespread conviction – not unknown in 1917 – that the burden of the war effort fell more heavily on some shoulders than on others. While 1400 people were packed into the trench shelters of Victoria Park, with water seeping up through the duckboards, hotels in the West End could offer wealthy visitors safe dormitory accommodation in their basements.

A protest was duly made. The Savoy Hotel was only three miles from the 'Tilbury', an underground goods yard off Commercial Road where thousands sought cover every night. In the second week of the Blitz two leading Communists from Stepney – Phil Piratin and 'Tubby' Rosen – led a hundred East Enders into the Savoy to seek shelter. An 'All Clear' saved the hotel management from taking a decision over so vexing an issue; but Piratin, Rosen and their supporters had made their point. Writers hostile to the Left have scoffed at the episode – and thereby missed its double significance. The intrusion of East End Reds into the Savoy sent a shiver of apprehension through the Establishment, identifiable in the diaries of the time[11]. Thereafter government inspectors and rep-resentatives of charitable societies regularly visited the East End shelters, hoping to improve conditions. And the Piratin–Rosen campaign was not forgotten five years later. When, in the General Election of 1945, Mile End returned Piratin as the only Communist MP for an English con-stituency, the voters were moved by local sentiment rather than by admiration for their Soviet ally, as outside commentators assumed.

Even before the march on the Savoy, the higher civil servants and their ministers were anxious about morale in east London. 'In dockside areas the population is showing visible signs of its nerve cracking from constant ordeals,' a government intelligence report noted less than 48 hours after the bombing began. When the War Cabinet met next day – Tuesday, 10 September – Churchill turned for enlightenment to Sir John Anderson, the Home Secretary, who had already sounded out Herbert Morrison (then Minister of Supply) because of his understanding of London's needs and the mood of its people. Anderson was reassuring; there had been a failure of nerve in the administration of certain boroughs, but he could see no sign of panic – as, indeed, Churchill had himself realised when touring Stepney and Poplar on the Sunday afternoon[12]. The Minister of Health travelled out to West Ham on Wednesday. Later in the week it was reported that when the AA-guns mounted a steady defensive barrage, morale generally was lifted. Concern over the East End was noted by neutral diplomats, including the Americans. Tales of panic-stricken East Enders threatening Churchill with social upheaval eventually filtered back to Berlin, by way of the German Embassy in Washington[13].

The devastation grew worse in late September and October with the introduction of mines dropped by parachute. These instruments of destruction, first used on east London's streets early in the morning of 19 September, generally exploded at rooftop level and caused more widespread blast damage than conventional bombs. Many failed to explode and had to be dismantled by naval specialists from the Directorate of Torpedoes and Mining. The parachute missiles, sometimes caught in trees or draped over lamp-standards or telephone poles, closed more streets than the UXBs. Some mines fell in the Thames, temporarily closing the port for mine-sweeping operations. The bombing did not cripple the docks nor destroy the railway routes into Liverpool Street or Fenchurch Street. A third of the PLA's warehouses were destroyed: the north quay of the West India Import Dock was heavily hit; so, too, were St Katharine's Docks and the neighbouring wharves in Wapping. Rum barrels exploding on the West India quayside spread fire to other warehouses. On another night a warden crossing Bow Bridge noticed that the River Lea was burning with a blue flame, and realised that the local gin factory had been hit. In Woolwich Reach the Thames itself was ablaze with liquid sugar from a Silvertown refinery. Yet, remarkably, the Port of London was not totally crippled by the raids. Nor, indeed was the work of London as a whole[14].

The will of the East Enders never broke under the strain of bombardment, as some outsiders who did not understand them had anticipated. Once bombs began to fall on the wealthier parts of London, with

even the King at Buckingham Palace singled out for attack, the earliest
sufferers from the raids found satisfaction in 'again being united in our
cause'[15]. Moreover, after the first days of administrative chaos, they could
no longer feel that 'Hitler has it in for us, and no one up West cares a
damn'. Although many improvised shelters continued to be health
hazards, particularly during the long winter nights, belated efforts were
made to encourage a community spirit, especially in the tunnels of the
uncompleted Central line extension. The tube trains that now run
through Bethnal Green to surface at Stratford cover tracks which, at the
height of the Blitz, were home for 10,000 people. Bunks were fitted beside
the station platforms, above what was to become the track itself. To the
consternation of the authorities, some families remained below ground
for weeks at a time; but most people continued to go to work by day.
There was impromptu entertainment even at the Tilbury, where singing
was allowed until 10 p.m. in the main section and until midnight in the
outer annexe. Eventually, LCC evening classes were held in some tube
shelters; and at Bethnal Green station, a special branch of the public
library was opened, with 4000 books for the shelterers to borrow. Since
it was good to feel alive after a night of bombs and parachute mines, the
shared experience of common suffering tended to break down barriers of
reserve between traditionally exclusive groups within the community.
'This is the Jews' War' ran graffiti scrawled by some unrepentant
Mosleyites on ruined walls in the old BUF enclaves; but fortunately,
in this Second World War, such asinine incitement provoked no response.

Three massive raids in March, April and May of 1941 inflicted more
damage on homes and historic landmarks than the initial assault in
the previous autumn. Hawksmoor's St George's-in-the-East, fortunate to
survive the September attacks on the London docks, was gutted and
St Anne's, Limehouse, badly damaged. But, once again, the bombing
linked the different parts of the metropolis: when, at five minutes to two
in the morning of 11 May, three bombs hit the Houses of Parliament,
fire crews were already at the British Museum and working hard to
contain blazes in Bethnal Green Road and the Royal Albert Dock, while
there was also a major alert at Poplar, where twelve barges were blazing
beside what is now Heron Wharf, and a serious incident upstream at
St Katharine's Dock where the walls of a warehouse, shorn up after
earlier raids, had now collapsed. And those early hours of that last
Sunday morning of the Blitz brought death and destruction across the
river, too: notably to Southwark and Wandsworth, and especially in
the closely packed streets of Rotherhithe, the riverside village for nine
centuries complementary to Wapping, north of the Thames. By next day
the wind had carried charred invoices from one East End fire as far as

Ilford, where the cricket ground in Valentine's Park looked as if there had been a leaflet raid[16].

The East End suffered again on 27–28 July 1941, from a short raid by light fighter-bombers who mainly dropped incendiaries. But over the following eighteen months no attacks were concentrated on targets in east or central London; and in 1942 – the year of the so-called 'Baedeker' raids on Exeter, Bath, York,.Canterbury and other cathedral cities – the civilian deaths on ARP casualty lists within the metropolitan area fell to twenty-seven[17]. The respite from Luftwaffe raids gave the authorities an opportunity to find alternative housing for families already bombed out and, at the same time, to establish a better system of relief in anticipation of a second Blitzkrieg. During the worst months there had been difficulties with borough councils who did not understand the need for organising a re-housing department or who remained obstinately suspicious of Whitehall intervention: Stepney and West Ham were the chief offenders. There were also problems of local sovereignty over homeless families sent from one borough to another. Mistrust of LCC penetration, engendered by the 'cottage estate' colonisation of the inter-war years, led to such friction in parts of Essex that thousands of homeless people were subsequently moved yet again, to outer Middlesex or Hertfordshire[18].

Some derelict streets in Stepney and the Isle of Dogs became battle training areas for the Home Guard. But elsewhere people began to cultivate the waste spaces, creating allotments. Social life revived: for those unwilling to travel to the blacked-out West End, there were still some local places of entertainment: the People's Palace; a few of the old music halls; cinemas; and dance-halls. 'Double summer time' – when, from 1941 onwards, the clocks in May, June, July and August remained two hours ahead of GMT – gave long, light evenings which encouraged recreation after work, not simply at the weekends. Supplies of beer tended to be erratic and the quality of the brew fell below pre-war standards, but pub-going remained popular. Some pubs were, accidentally, democratised: local folk went into saloon bars – originally priced up to cater for toffs and swells 'doing the East End' – because wartime economy made it impossible to keep all the public bars open. Working-class culture was never self-consciously constrained during the war: jazz and the big bands were popular with young factory workers, but so, too, was the aesthetic escapism of classical music, drama and ballet. LCC sponsorship of 'Stay at home and Play at home' holidays led to a growth of open-air theatre in the parks. There were swimming galas, fêtes, Punch-and-Judy shows and, for those who were slightly older, fun dancing – the Conga, the Lambeth Walk, Boomps-a-daisy, and the Palais Glide – and carefree singsongs (from music hall favourites such as *My Old Man Said Follow the Van* down to the imported nonsense hit of 1943–4, *Mairzy Dotes And*

Dozey Dotes). But here, too, cultural frontiers were sometimes unexpectedly crossed. Thus for a week in August 1942, and again eleven months later, the Sadler's Wells Ballet performed in Victoria Park; in the warm evenings, an appreciative audience could see Fonteyn and Helpmann dance – for sixpence.

East End factories which had escaped total destruction in the Blitz concentrated on the demands of war. Despite the memory of the Silvertown disaster of 1917, chemical firms in Hackney, Stratford Marshes and Canning Town were engaged in munition work; and, at Bow, Bryant & May's factory – beside the main railway to the east coast – produced safety fuses, as well as its familiar safety matches, and demolition charges, too. Corvettes, destroyers and at least one light cruiser were repaired in the dry docks on the Isle of Dogs and North Woolwich. In 1943 the East India Dock at Blackwall was dammed and dried out so as to become one of several construction sites for the floating breakwaters eventually used to create the artificial Mulberry harbour on D-Day; other caissons were built across the river in the Surrey docks and downstream at Tilbury. Although their purpose was unclear, the presence of these strange creations could not be concealed. Small wonder that the Luftwaffe resumed air attacks on the capital in January 1943, with the docks as a particular target.

German propaganda maintained, however, that these raids were in revenge for attacks on Berlin and that mightier blows would follow. Accordingly, as a precaution, many East End families began to return to the deep shelters, a nightly habit abandoned during the lull of the previous year – significantly the Borough of Bethnal Green had closed its underground branch library at the end of the first week in February 1942. When, on 3 March 1943, the BBC reported a 300-bomber raid by the RAF on Berlin, it was assumed that the Luftwaffe would strike back and when darkness fell there was a steady trek to the shelters. As soon as the siren sounded, in the early evening, more people hurried down. Some 500 yards from Bethnal Green tube station a new battery of anti-aircraft rocket projectors opened up, with an unfamiliar 'whoosh', which sounded as if bombs were falling. Latecomers rushed down the nineteen steps from the street to the subway entrance at Bethnal Green, from which over-zealous shelterers on earlier nights had removed lamp bulbs for fear that they infringed the blackout. On the sixteenth or seventeenth step a woman stumbled; would-be shelterers fell over her and were crushed against a wall, where the steps turned to enter the main booking hall. In the panic, twenty-seven men, eighty-four women and sixty-two children were asphyxiated or crushed to death and another sixty taken to hospital, seriously injured. On that terrible night for Bethnal Green no bombs fell anywhere in the East End[19].

Herbert Morrison, by now Home Secretary, successfully concealed the cause of the tragedy; any hint of a panic stampede would have been interpreted as evidence of low morale. Fortunately the Germans did not launch a sustained air offensive in that spring of 1943, as the cabinet feared. Crush barriers and other safeguards were introduced into many deep shelters later in the year. At the same time, more families received the indoor steel table shelters; these were named 'Morrisons' after the Home Secretary and were first issued in the winter of 1941–2 to replace the outdoor corrugated 'Andersons' of 1938–9, which had proved cold, damp and unpopular. Thus when the 'Little Blitz' came – a series of four raids on London in March 1944 – the East End boroughs were all better prepared to meet the challenge than in 1940. But the brunt of these attacks was borne this time by other London districts.

A week after the allied invasion of Normandy in June 1944, London was attacked by the Vergeltungswaffen-1, the earliest of Germany's threatened 'weapons of reprisal'. These V-1s were pilotless jet-propelled aircraft fired from launching-sites near the Channel coast and originally targeted on London's docks; they soon became known as 'buzz bombs', 'doodlebugs' or, officially, 'flying bombs'. The first V-1 to cause casualties fell at the junction of Antill Road and Grove Road in Bow, close to the railway into Liverpool Street, shortly before half-past four in the morning of 13 June. It was followed by a sustained attack and, for a fortnight, casualties in Greater London as a whole were heavier than in September 1940, with more people injured but fewer killed outright; the destruction was even more widespread, about 20,000 houses damaged each day, particularly in Kent and south of the Thames[20]. Hopes that the Allied armies would soon overrun the V-1 launching-sites boosted morale (as also did the knowledge that you had eleven seconds in which to dive for cover when you heard the engine cut out). The cabinet, aware that rocket missiles (V-2s) might soon follow the flying bombs, discussed the V-weapon threat on 27 June. Ministers were uneasy and encouraged fresh evacuation of families, with free railway warrants. There was no great exodus of schools as on the eve of war. Some pupils found their summer term ending early. Education committees and head teachers hoped the bombardment would cease before they returned in the autumn.

Sure enough, on 7 September Duncan Sandys, the junior government minister responsible for co-ordinating defence against V-weapons, felt able to summon a press conference and announce that, 'except possibly for a few last shots', the Battle of London was over; Montgomery's troops had occupied all the areas from which attacks could be launched against the capital[21]. Yet, at 6.40 on the following evening, two explosions were heard in east London so clearly that one seemed like an echo of the other: 'Thunder, no doubt', many thought. But by next morning rumours had begun to circulate: in west London a gas main was said to have blown up in Staveley Road, Chiswick; and a few seconds later another 'gas main' exploded, out at Epping. The government kept silent; they did not want the Germans to know that their V-2 rockets were on target.

Over the next few days, the incidence of explosions became too frequent to sustain the gas main theory. Some people thought the missiles were flying bombs with engines that cut off earlier; others believed London was under shellfire. There was no panic and no evacuation. Once again, it was assumed that the victorious advance of Montgomery's army would soon bring an end to the ordeal. Not a single rocket landed on London or its suburbs during the battle of Arnhem (17–26 September). Unfortunately the failure of the British Second Army to consolidate its position along the lower Rhine at Arnhem enabled the V-2 launching area to remain in German occupation for another six months.

On 10 November, exactly nine weeks after the flying gas mains of Chiswick and Epping, Churchill confirmed to Parliament that England was under missile attack, although he minimised its importance[22]. Blast damage from the V-2s was more confined in area than from the V-1s, but the rockets caused heavier casualties as there could be no warning of their coming. The worst single incident occurred south of the Thames, when a rocket fell on Woolworth's shop at New Cross on the last Saturday morning in November. Since the missiles were launched from the Netherlands, mostly from sites near The Hague, they more frequently fell to the east of the capital; more rockets exploded in Ilford than in any other borough, with Barking, Dagenham, East Ham, West Ham and Walthamstow suffering heavily, too. The most sustained rocket bombardment came as late in the war as 13–14 February 1945 when fourteen rockets hit London in fifteen hours, one of them causing twenty-eight deaths in West Ham[23]. On that same night and day British and American bombers razed the city of Dresden, in two ghastly raids killing twelve times as many civilians as perished in the Greater London area during nine months of V-1 and V-2 attacks.

Mercifully, within another twelve weeks, all bombardments were to end in Europe. But not before Target Area A suffered one final tragedy. On 27 March the last V-2 rocket to fall on metropolitan London struck Hughes Mansions in Vallance Road, Bethnal Green, wrecking sixty out of ninety-three flats in the block and killing 134 people, as well as seriously injuring more than forty. Rescuers were still at work in Vallance Road when, two days later, London's 2420th flying-bomb made the sirens sound for the last time.

On VE-Day (Tuesday, 8 May 1945) there were celebrations throughout London, with dancing in public places and, over the next few days, street parties and bonfires. The King and Queen and the two Princesses were cheered as they made a State Drive through the East End and into metropolitan Essex, across ravaged wasteland and shorn-up terraced streets. People accepted that there was a war to win in the Far East, for many had sons or brothers serving in Burma; but the strain of battle was over and there was a widespread desire to live peacefully within a more equitable society. East London could never be the same again: old landmarks had gone; thousands of houses were still awaiting repair; between a third and half the population had moved away, with many of the young content to settle in the outer suburbs or the home counties. But the older generation of inveterate East Enders were nostalgically parochial; two social researchers – writing soon after the end of the war – reported how, in Bethnal Green, 'many stories were told of families who would rather camp in the kitchens of their uninhabitable blitzed houses or sleep in public shelters than accept accommodation in another area of the borough'[24]. Such families were determined to bring back to their own districts in Bethnal Green or Stepney or Hackney an improved model of a familiar way of life. They were socially conservative in their habits and conservatively socialist in their politics. It is hardly surprising that when, two months after VE-Day, they had an opportunity to vote at the first General Election in nine years, two-thirds of the East Enders followed the invitation of a campaign poster and 'looked to the future with labour'. The novelty in this General Election was that, for the first time, a majority of the British people thought as the East Enders did, and gave their support to an experiment in democratic socialism.

13

Labouring On

T HE Attlee Governments, the first in which Labour enjoyed a parliamentary majority, possess a psychological symbolism which leaves
their record prone to attack. The Right complains of shackles on individual enterprise; the militant Left mocks a revolution stopped at the first
quarter-turn towards socialism. But during these years $4\frac{1}{2}$ million men
and women were demobilised, fairly and in an orderly manner; there
was no significant fall in employment, and no upheaval more menacing
than an organised squat. By 1949 Britain's exports were 55 per cent up
on the 1938 figures, a rapid recovery unmatched elsewhere in Europe.
Coal, gas, steel, electricity and the railways were taken into public
ownership, holding out a prospect (unrealised) of working-class participation in the control of industry. Rationing and food subsidies were
continued, ensuring distribution according to need, rather than income.
A reformed national insurance scheme abolished the 'means test' while
from the first Monday in July 1948, a National Health Service gave
promise of social welfare from the cradle to the grave; deprived families
in east London, and the poorer districts of other cities, could count on

free medical, dental and optical care. No government has understood the East End so well as Attlee's. Small wonder that when, in August 1946, James Griffiths as Minister of National Insurance wished to observe the social services in action, he chose to visit a post office off Commercial Road to greet the first recipients of family allowances.

Yet, perhaps because six cabinet members had experience of London's problems, there were several times when the Government and local leaders found themselves in conflict. Attlee's own familiarity with Stepney politics made him fully alive to the menace of Communist militancy. He was ready to tolerate organised squats by the homeless – as when, in September 1946, the Communists encouraged the occupation of empty mansions in Kensington and Bloomsbury so as to hustle government planners into making positive decisions over housing. But Attlee knew his dockland too well to allow 'Communist hypocrites' (as he termed them) to close the Port of London. In the summer of 1948, and again late in the following spring, he threatened to move troops into the London docks rather than see the economy wrecked by a Communist-inspired strike. His resolute stand kept the port together, shaping it to handle, in the early 1950s, an unprecedented trade boom.

For to say that London's docks never flourished again after the Blitz, or that they were bled white by thirty-seven strikes in the ten years following VE-Day, is to minimise a notable achievement by management and workers. The Thames recovered trade lost, before and during the War, to the Mersey and the Clyde. Only the East India Export Dock, damaged during the construction of the Mulberry harbours, was abandoned and sold; the Brunswick Power Station, built on the site, revived a name familiar in eighteenth-century Blackwall but virtually forgotten after 1862 when the old Mast House was demolished. So long as London continued to send abroad the high-quality goods of Britain's renascent engineering industries and to receive a third of the exports from all the Commonwealth countries, nothing could challenge the claim of the PLA to govern the greatest port in the world. Many ships were loaded and unloaded at Tilbury rather than in the up-river docks. But, even so, as late as 1958 the quays and wharves from Tower Bridge eastwards to the three 'Royals' handled the greatest volume of trade over any twelve months in their history[1].

This trade boom did not reach its peak until after 1951, when Labour was back in Opposition. In the immediate post-war years there was widespread frustration, some of it intensified by the exceptional severity of the weather in the early months of 1947. No one, in 1945, anticipated six years of austerity; sterling's new dependence on the dollar bred a fear of inflation which, in its turn, caused a continuance of tight restraints throughout the Attlee Governments. Worst hit in east London, as in other bombed cities, was the housing programme.

As early as 1941 the LCC (by then Labour controlled for seven years) had commissioned Professor Patrick Abercrombie to prepare a County of London Plan: he was to provide, not merely for re-building after the Blitz, but for logical re-siting which would get rid of 'depressed housing', create urban parkland, and allow traffic to move freely along purpose-designed roads. A second Abercrombie survey (government-sponsored on this occasion) produced in 1944 a Greater London Plan which covered a far larger area. It recommended a ring of eight new satellite towns, from 15 to 30 miles out in the Home Counties, where 300,000 Londoners should be encouraged to settle. Despite the constraints of austerity, attempts were made to implement both the County of London Plan and the Greater London Plan: the LCC in 1947 included Poplar and Stepney among its Comprehensive Development Areas, later adding part of Bethnal Green, too; and the Ministry of Town & Country Planning listed fourteen new towns for Britain as a whole, including two in Essex (Basildon and Harlow) which would relieve congestion in east and north-east London. As a stop-gap measure, 125,000 prefabricated houses were manufactured, for quick assembly on bombed sites. These 'rabbit hutches' – as they were dubbed by the Minister of Health, Aneurin Bevan – were meant to give only temporary accommodation. Some provide it still, more than forty years later.

The prefabs were not unpopular with small families; they offered the privacy of detached cottage bungalows. But Labour's show-piece was the 'Exhibition of Live Architecture' which was to serve as an adjunct to the Festival of Britain of 1951 and as the model for the Stepney/Poplar Comprehensive Development Area to ensure that 'the East End will at last be a worthy place in which to live, work and play'. There would, it was hoped, eventually be sixty new schools in the Area, with 218 acres of parkland between Regent's Canal and Burdett Road. Only nine schools were, in fact, built in the ten years after the war and only 12 acres were added to the existing 42 acres of Mile End Park; but this disappointing record was the fault of Government restrictions in the 1950s rather than of failings by the LCC or the local Borough Councils. The 'Exhibition of Live Architecture' had held promise of 'a new town in the East End'. The bomb-damaged Victorian terrace houses between East India Dock Road and Limehouse Cut were swept away in 1948–9; blocks of flats – mostly of three storeys and spaciously designed – went up over the following two years, together with shops, new churches and schools, two small parks, and what is generally called 'Chrisp Street Market', with a pagoda-style clock tower at its centre. The estate was named in honour of George Lansbury; the first family moved into a council flat on St Valentine's Day in 1951; and during that summer buses ferried visitors from the Festival of Britain down Commercial Road to admire 'Live Architecture'. Sadly, however, by Christmas less than 1200 homes were ready for occupation. At that pace it would have taken thirty years to satisfy the pressing housing needs of east London[2].

Progress was slow, too, in setting up the new towns[3]. Harlow had a population of under 6000 when Attlee left office and did not reach the 'designated' total of 80,000 until the early 1970s, while Basildon did not formally become a town until 1955. Meanwhile the LCC encouraged families to settle on new housing estates in Essex, on the edge of what had once been the royal forest lands of Hainault and Epping. Some moved to Harold Hill, to the east of Romford, or the familiar prototype council dormitory at Becontree.

Except perhaps for Harold Hill, public transport services between the migrants to Essex and their families left in east London were good and, during those years of high employment, the fares were relatively cheap. Yet wives complained that, whatever their husbands might be earning, they at least were kept too short of money to 'go visiting relations'. There was, certainly, a deep sense of deprivation among those who remained in the old East End, where loyalty to childhood friendships persisted and where the bonds of kinship had been astonishingly close. A pioneer study by Michael Young and Peter Willmott, in which between 1953 and 1955 they interviewed about 1 person in every 54 within Bethnal Green, emphasised the extent to which families held together through three generations by the mother–daughter relationship found the cord of kinship broken by this move out to new estates[4].

Wartime upheaval and the planning policies of the LCC left the East End streets emptier than in earlier years. The population, falling steadily since Edwardian times, dropped drastically over the middle decades of the century. The statistics for Bethnal Green reflect the general trend: a population of around 130,000 in 1901 had fallen to 108,000 thirty years later; on the eve of war in 1939 it was 90,130, falling to 47,330 in 1941, after the Blitz; it then rose to 60,580 in 1948 and dropped to 58,000 in 1951 and 53,860 in 1955, with the LCC's encouragement of migration to the new estates. The 1981 Census returns showed a population of about 30,000 for the same area, by then part of the London Borough of Tower Hamlets. Those families still in Bethnal Green when the Census was taken enjoyed a higher standard of life: in 1951 only 21 per cent had baths of their own and 37 per cent were expected to share their WC; by 1981 95 per cent had baths or showers and only one in a hundred had to share a WC[5]. The long battle for improved sanitation seemed won.

Families whose homes faced demolition as part of the post-war municipal improvement were never compelled to move out of their old borough. The LCC might offer them a home in the country or elsewhere in London, but if they applied to their own council they would be found a flat reasonably close to their old home. Some women, who were strongly opposed to leaving 'dear old Bethnal Green', admitted to Young and Willmott that they did not like visiting relatives on the new estates 'out in the country', one explaining that 'it disheartens you to see them nice places and come back to this dump'[6]. Not so much was done to improve these 'dumps' as had been anticipated immediately after the war. For the Lansbury estate, which should have set a pattern for development throughout the bombed areas of the East End, became unique. Modern theories of architecture, influenced by Le Corbusier, favoured an upward thrust of concrete; your street would be stood on its end, rising to the sky. Blocks of flats, more than twenty storeys high, would offer spacious homes in an uncluttered setting, thus ending the curse of urban congestion. Successive governments welcomed high flats as using up less land in expensive areas; in 1956 and 1957 the Metropolitan Boroughs could count on receiving larger subsidies if they built higher flats[7]. By 1962 tall blocks were beginning to break the London skyline, sweeping away prefabs and many decaying slums as well.

Tower blocks were soon to provide a backcloth for the streets and squares of the Lansbury estate. Others dwarfed the surviving two-up and two-down terraced houses between Roman Road and Old Ford Road. But the most concentrated cluster lay east of the Lea. More than a quarter of the high-rise blocks in the metropolis went up in West Ham or East Ham: 125 of them were scattered through Newham – as, in 1965, the combined borough was unimaginatively named. It was assumed that well-designed tower blocks, with efficient lifts, roomy and well-appointed flats, and splendid views would create a sense of liberated spaciousness in contrast to claustrophobic back-to-back cottages in garbage-filled streets or the ageing tenements of the Victorian philanthropists. This expectation, like so many others in the false dawn of a welfare state, proved no more than a high-minded illusion. Lifts broke down; families felt isolated; and lack of playing-areas for children left them more boxed in than their parents had been during those years when front doors opened on to streets and courtyards. In May 1968 a section of new flats at Ronan Point, near the Royal Albert Dock in Newham, collapsed after a gas explosion, killing five people. That tragedy marked the end of tower block skyscraping. No more were commissioned by the Greater London Council. But it was not the end of high-rise living. Twenty years later thousands of families were still in flats twenty storeys above the ground; and tower blocks, opened as showpieces of municipal splendour, survive as patched-up relics of a lost illusion[8].

The East Enders are disinclined to accept illusions, and during the

1950s there was a healthy realism on both sides of the Lea, once the glamorised excitement of the Coronation passed into rain-dampened memory. The Coronation Year of 1953 saw, fittingly enough, the re-opening of a Theatre Royal in Stratford. But on this occasion it was under the radical management of Joan Littlewood; her Theatre Workshop was to give east London over the border its most socially stimulating cycle of plays in modern memory, although for its first years the seats remained distressingly empty[9]. There was a new interest, too, in East End creative writing: Wolf Mankowitz's success with *A Kid for Two Farthings* in 1955 was followed four years later by Bernard Kops's *The Hamlet of Stepney Green*; and when, also in 1959, the Theatre Workshop presented Frank Norman's *Fings Ain't Wot They Used T'Be* at Stratford, it was in a sense complementing Arnold Wesker's *Chicken Soup with Barley* which, a year earlier, had carried Chelsea audiences through two decades of Sarah Kahn's battles for a generous-hearted Whitechapel communism.

In the 1960s the fringe of east London began to attract many more visitors, British and foreign, and there were districts which acquired a superficial lustre from a romanticised past and present. At times the East End turned upon the world a Janus face, which it has never entirely lost. As early as August 1963 Ian Nairn, writing in the *Daily Telegraph*, could condemn the Spitalfields area as 'London's worst slum'[10], forgotten and neglected; and yet around the corner from Spitalfields that month – and in many others – 'furriners' were flocking to Petticoat Lane market as the Sunday sight of the City, avidly hunting for bargains. The more daring visitor might make an even cheaper acquisition from costers along Wentworth Street or Whitechapel Waste.

Some tourist delights were gone. There were no paddle-steamer trips down the Thames and no tramcars: although they survived south of the Thames until 1953, the last tram in east London finally rattled to its depot on the eve of the Blitz; and by 1960–1 even the tram's hermaphrodite successor, the trolley-bus, was off the roads. Chinese families still lived in Limehouse but 'Chinatown', as a centre of night life, had moved closer to Soho. Bloom's, the famous kosher restaurant, remained in Whitechapel High Street; but from 1963 onwards it had a branch, too, in Golders Green Road. Once again, as between the wars, the riverside pubs attracted visitors from other parts of London and from abroad. They could find a fast fading glory at Charlie Browns's but, in the swinging sixties, it was fashionable to go down to the old Newcastle Arms at the south-eastern tip of the Isle of Dogs for, re-named the Waterman's Arms by its landlord Dan Farson, it became a celebrity spot. Along the banks of the Lower Pool two historic pubs, three-quarters of a mile apart, competed for tourists: the Prospect of Whitby, at the eastern end of Wapping Wall, was already a notorious tavern more than 200 years old in the late

1770s, when it acquired the name of a vessel which lay moored off it; and the Town of Ramsgate, further upstream, once held in its cellars felons awaiting transportation to Australia, but it preferred to recall links with the Ramsgate fishermen who had landed their catch close by. Downstream from the Prospect of Whitby, along Narrow Street and backing on to Limehouse Reach, the Grapes stood propped up by a half terrace of smart 're-habs' amid a wasteland of refuse dumps, council flats and wharves for barge repair. Admirers of Charles Dickens's novels came out there, if they could find the way, because he had known the district well and the Grapes was almost certainly a model for the Six Jolly Fellowship Porters in *Our Mutual Friend*. A century after its publication fashionable critics were discovering in this somewhat neglected chronicle of waterside villainy a relevant social realism.

But there were newer attractions to visit as well, among them some east London drinking clubs far smarter than the locals of earlier years. At least one club was to acquire a dubious fame. In the first week of March 1962 the cockney comedy film, *Sparrows Can't Sing*, had its première at the Empire Cinema, Bow Road, with Princess Margaret and Lord Snowdon as principal guests. Later that night, after the royal car headed back to Kensington, a party was held at the neighbouring Kentucky Club, which was beginning to attract the social élite from up West. None of the outsiders, and no more than a few Club members, seems to have realised that its proprietors, who were generous patrons of local hospitals, boys' clubs and other good causes, were also masterminds of organised crime. The Kray Twins remain the most notorious gangsters to have carved out for themselves a dominion beyond the law in the streets of the East End[11].

Reginald and Ronald Kray were born in Bethnal Green in October 1933; they used as their earliest headquarters their parents' home at 178 Vallance Road, to the north of the railway bridge and of the Hughes Mansions flats destroyed by the last V-2. But their field operations were at first based on a billiard hall in what had been the Regal Cinema, Eric Street, close to Mile End station; and, in the early fifties, it was from there that they struggled for supremacy with gangs from Tottenham Court Road, Upton Park and, most persistently, from Watney Street in Wapping. Ronald Kray was gaoled for three years in November 1956 for causing grievous bodily harm; in his absence his brother opened a smart drinking-club in Bow Road, a forerunner of the Kentucky Club. Reginald Kray was territorially ambitious; he demanded and secured protection money from Mayfair clubs. By the summer of 1959, when Ronald Kray was back in his old haunts, the twins had hopes of controlling London.

This spread of organised crime, with extortion rackets, blackmail and illicit gambling, led Scotland Yard in 1964 to seek ways of breaking both the Krays and their chief rivals south of the Thames, the Richardson brothers. But the public did not become alarmed at the extent of gang-warfare until after 6 March 1966; for on that Sunday evening Ronald Kray went into the saloon bar of the Blind Beggar at the eastern end of Whitechapel Road, and shot dead George Cornell, a Richardson muscle man. Even so, it was not until the small hours of 9 May 1968 that Inspector Read and an armed squad of police broke down the door of Braithwaite House, Shoreditch, to take the Kray Twins, and others in their 'Firm', into custody. After the Old Bailey's longest criminal trial, on 8 March 1969 Mr Justice Melford Stephenson sentenced the Krays to life imprisonment, which he recommended 'should be not less than thirty years'. The most determined attempt to establish a Chicago-style crime syndicate in the East End had been exposed and broken before it could acquire the power to hold to ransom the government of London itself[12].

That authority remained with the Labour Party, at least up to the year the Krays began their life sentences. For Labour retained a majority on the LCC from 1934 until 1965 when it was superseded by the Greater London Council, a body with responsibility for local affairs in an area five times as large. Even during the GLC's 21-year lifespan, the Council was under Labour control for three periods (1965–9, 1973–7, 1981–6) and Labour's hold on the East End borough councils was hardly loosened. Electoral campaigns were, however, uniformly dull; the greatest political interest in east London streets from 1948 onwards was aroused not so much by the traditional political parties as by an unexpected resilience of Fascism. Mosley re-constituted his pre-war BUF as the Union Movement in the winter of 1947–8 and set up headquarters at Ridley Road, Dalston. From there the UM looked southwards, to the BUF stamping-grounds in Hackney, Shoreditch and Bethnal Green. As early as May 1949 the UM was contesting wards in all three of those boroughs; by 1953 it was publishing its own periodical called, significantly, *East London Blackshirt*; and a year later Mosley was leading 'East Enders through their own streets' in a provocative demonstration against the 'coloured invasion' rather than against the BUF's traditional enemies. The movement soon spread to dockland, Mosley addressing a rally at Limehouse Town Hall in the second week of March 1956, while two months later the UM contested two wards in Stepney as well as the local elections in the three neighbouring boroughs[13].

The Union Movement achieved even less electoral success than the pre-war BUF. When Mosley stood as UM candidate for Shoreditch & Finsbury in the 1966 General Election only 1126 voters in an electorate of 45,883 constituents gave him their support. Over the years 1974–81, the UM's avowedly non-Fascist Right Radical successor, the National Front, fared slightly better at the polls: over the inner East End – Bethnal

Green, Hackney, Stepney, Bow, Shoreditch and Poplar – the National
Front reached a peak of success in the GLC election of May 1977 with
17·4 per cent of the vote; but, after two years of Tory government led by
Margaret Thatcher, this fell to 3·7 per cent in the GLC election of May
1981, when the strongest National Front backing in London was in
Newham South, and then only a mere 6·3 per cent of the votes[14]. Yet
both the Union Movement and the National Front have considerable
significance anti-socially if not electorally: their demagogic concentration
on racism encouraged anti-coloured hostility in popular consciousness.
It was in December 1969 that the media reported the first skinhead
violence – dubbed, even then, 'Paki-bashing'; and the news stories came
from parts of Spitalfields and Whitechapel where, a third of a century
back in time, blackshirt thugs were beating up the Jews. These attacks
grew in intensity in the following decade, the violence in Brick Lane in
1978 causing especial concern to the local Trades Council[15]. Most of the
victims were Bangladeshi, who formed a compact community in the
Middlesex Street, Princelet Street and Old Montague Street district. They
lived in overcrowded poverty in the same streets as the 'strange exotics'
of an earlier immigration; some even worked in the same sweatshops. It
was their misfortune, too, to suffer from the familiar prejudice of older
residents against the alien newcomers in their midst.

Many Bangladeshi came originally in the 1960s as Bengali Pakistan
seamen from Chittagong, Chalna or the upriver towns, leaving their
vessels during the political tension with the authorities in Karachi over
autonomy. Subsequently they brought their families over to England,
distant relatives and friends hastening to London ahead of the tighter
immigration laws imposed both by the Conservatives under Macmillan
and Heath and by Labour under Wilson. The pathfinders among these
Bangladeshi proved to be the last of London's seaborne immigrants,
settling naturally within a few miles of their port of disembarkation, as
Huguenots and East European Jews had done before them. For, within a
few years, cheaper air travel was providing newcomers with a different
point of arrival. Later immigrants from the Indian sub-continent settled
near the airport of London Heathrow, notably in Southall. It is significant
that in the winter of 1969–70, while the authorities in Tower Hamlets
were seeking to contain a 'Paki-bashing' onslaught around Whitechapel,
some districts in west London, as close to Heathrow as Spitalfields to
dockland, were facing for the first time the problems of chronic racial
unrest.

By this winter of 1969–70 it was clear that the docks on which much
of the East End had depended for trade and industry for so long were
virtually doomed. They became victims of Commonwealth emancipation,
their trade falling away when newly independent countries in Africa and

Asia found greater profit in direct commercial links with the United States, Germany, Japan and the Soviet Union than in the maintenance of a post-imperial relationship with Britain. At the same time the integration of the EEC and the growth of Europort at Rotterdam imposed a form of competition which exposed the vulnerability of up-river quays in what was, by continental reckoning, an offshore island. Nevertheless the decline of the docks was extremely rapid. Newspapers barely commented on what was happening and, when they did so, it was to expose a militant unionism among the dockers. It is still fashionable to emphasise the folly with which in 1967 5000 members of the Transport & General Workers' Union came out in protest at modernisation, a stoppage called by local Communists against the advice of the TGWU's own leaders. But, however poor labour relations may have been, this saddest of London's dock strikes was a consequence, rather than a cause, of the riverside revolution.

At first the inner docks had adjusted themselves well to the post-war need for mechanisation: fork-lift trucks were used in the East India Dock in 1946 and within five years spread throughout the port; new and spacious transit sheds, with pre-stressed concrete frames, were commissioned in the early 1950s for the London Docks and ten years later for the Millwall and Royal Docks; and the PLA re-designed the wine vaults at the London Docks so that they could hold large tanks of liquor rather than the traditional casks. But, while the spread of a railway system had helped the port's growth in the nineteenth century, the development of road transport was a heavy blow to docks which could be reached only through the congested roads of an inner city. With the coming of roll on/roll off vessels and of standardised containers in the mid-sixties, Tilbury alone had room for expansion and improved access roads, its docks capable of competing with the purpose-built new terminals at Felixstowe and Harwich. The PLA accordingly invested more than £30 million pounds in modernising the down-river docks. Container ships began to use Tilbury for crossings to Europe in January 1968 and by midsummer there was a regular transatlantic service. Despite a harmful strike of dockers who feared the spread of mechanisation, by the summer of 1970 Tilbury was handling 150,000 containers a year[16].

The success of these modern methods downstream emphasised the contrast with port facilities up-river. Increased competition from the airways led to the re-deployment of liners as cruise ships and thus took them away for ever from the Royal Docks. At the same time, cargo ships were becoming so big that they could navigate a crowded tidal river only slowly and with nerve-racking caution. There were several mishaps in the early 1960s: one ship on a maiden voyage rammed the outer lock gates when leaving the West India Dock and then scraped the jetty; another vessel damaged the Shadwell entrance to the London docks in

June 1963; and a flared bow caught a quayside crane and sent it crashing through the roof of a warehouse[17]. Yet attempts were made to modernise the older docks by widening their entrances: and a new western lock for the Royal Victoria Dock was opened as late as 1967, after four years of difficult engineering work[18]. But by then shipping companies were already leaving the docks; a berth in the Royal Victoria Dock constructed for the United States Line when trade was still booming in 1958 was in use for barely seven years. There seemed no point in bringing a vessel slowly up river when time and fuel could be saved by a quick turn-around at Tilbury. Much of the money spent on updating the 'Royals' was wasted.

By concentrating resources at Tilbury, the PLA inevitably struck a blow at other industries in the East End; for trade followed the Red Ensign down river and out of London. Before the Second World War the bulk-handling of grain had been pioneered on the Isle of Dogs: modern granaries were completed on the south side of the Royal Victoria Dock; and in 1935 the white 'organ pipes' of McDougall's silos went up beside the Millwall Dock, where they remained as a familiar sight from the river for the next half century. But at Tilbury a new grain terminal made it possible for cargoes to be discharged from bulk carriers by suction, either into one of three private flour mills or into a silo building which could store up to 100,000 tons. McDougall's had no further use for their Millwall silos, and jobs were lost in Cubitt Town. The coming of fewer ships up-river hit famous firms such as Green & Siley Weir or Badger's and the London Graving Dock which had concentrated on ship-repairs after the collapse of the Thames shipbuilding industry. For every docker made redundant by the riverside revolution, three workers in dock-related industries lost their jobs.

Yet it was not only the move to Tilbury that spread unemployment through the area. Tate & Lyle, founded originally as two separate Silvertown firms dating from 1871 and 1881, had become by 1947 the biggest sugar refiners in the world[19]: they were a paternalistic company, creating not only social and sporting clubs for their employees, but a riverside park in the middle of the industrial estates overlooking Bugsby's Reach. A new and magnificent Portland stone building was completed in 1950 at Plaistow Wharf; but within fifteen years there was no longer any need for Caribbean sugar to be refined in Silvertown on its way out to old imperial dependencies and in 1967 drastic cuts were made in the work force. But the plant was kept in being and in the mid-1990s still employed over a thousand workers. Confectioners, food processors and biscuit manufacturers similarly 'rationalised' their resources. By the beginning of the 1970s, 10,000 workers were on the dole in the docklands north and south of the river, a part of London which had enjoyed full employment twenty years before. At the start of the following decade, with the coming of the Conservative counter-revolution led by Margaret Thatcher, the jobless total for the same area had increased eight times over[20].

The first of the docks to close were the remaining East India quays, in 1967; but already by then it was known that the London and St Katharine's Docks were running at a heavy loss, and in January 1968 the PLA confirmed that they would be shut down over the following two years. The authority sold St Katharine's Dock to the Greater London Council in 1969, the year the Council passed from Labour to Conservative control, for £1,500,000 – a bargain price 13 per cent lower than the original cost in George IV's reign. The GLC, in consultation with the London Borough of Tower Hamlets, then invited plans from developers. They hoped to preserve some historic warehouses, create a marina and provide council housing and popular amenities.

Taylor Woodrow were granted a 125-year lease. They exercised their artistic sensitivities by making St Katharine's Dock a tourists' delight, with carefully sited trees and bollards, a modern sundial and a statue of a girl with a dolphin. The Italianate Ivory House, built during the Crimean War, was restored and given a frontage of chic shops and a clocktower, while an eighteenth-century warehouse became the Dickens Inn. Overlooking the Yacht Haven and what was to become (in 1979) the Historic Ship Collection of the Maritime Trust, the developers built an impressive World Trade Centre. And between the dock and the Thames stood the Tower Hotel which, when it opened in 1973, was the third largest in London. Nothing like this St Katharine's Dock Development had been seen before in the East End. Yet among those people who recognised in it a blueprint for the docklands some felt uneasy; for it was socially disturbing that when the Tower Hotel was offering its first visitors their choice from 826 bedrooms, the housing list of Tower Hamlets Council should show 6000 names awaiting a home[21].

14

Transformation Scene?

T HE warehouses of Wapping might be emptying fast, but in 1969–70 there was still hope that the docks on the Isle of Dogs and the Royals could be saved. All that was needed, optimists maintained, was for the PLA and the Union leaders to sit down together, agree on a policy of modernisation, and ensure that Britain joined the EEC with a speedy, mechanised system functioning along the capital's up-river quays. In 1971 the PLA came out of the red for the first time since 1966; a year later the Authority's profit was well over £1¼ million. But the dockers remained extremely suspicious of fork-lift trucks or palletisation and of shipowners who talked glibly of applying bulk-load principles to the carrying of cargoes. They were trade unionists loyal to their own traditions, some of which were narrowly local in application, but they were willing to act nationally in support of Union members whom they considered to be victimised.

The doubts of the dock workers increased after the Conservatives won the General Election of June 1970 and sought to 'impose the rule of law' on Union activities through an Industrial Relations Court. The

Government soon found itself in conflict, not so much with leading national Trade Unionists, as with highly articulate spokesmen for local groups with particular grievances. In the summer of 1972 the growth of container traffic induced London's dockers to declare 'black' all vehicles using the Midland Cold Storage Depot at Stratford; and when the Industrial Relations Court ordered an end to this blacking, five shop stewards refused to obey the ruling and were gaoled in Pentonville for contempt. There followed London's last great demonstration of dock solidarity, with mass meetings in Victoria Park and banner-carrying processions to Tower Hill. A national strike of 170,000 dockers put pressure on the Government, and the Pentonville Five were released.

At this point management and labour came together. With some difficulty, the dockers were persuaded to accept a report prepared jointly by Jack Jones, the TGWU leader, and Lord Aldington, the PLA Chairman, which sought to allay redundancy fears. But the combination of Union militancy and traffic congestion in Bow, Poplar and Stratford had already influenced the London Docklands Study Team, set up twelve months previously by the Heath Government. The LDST was convinced of a need to close the West India and Millwall Docks in the late 1970s and the Royal Victoria Dock in the early 1980s, but it thought that the Royal Albert Dock and the King George V Dock might survive until 1988 or 1989, provided that new relief roads around east London could improve the flow of container lorries into the surviving dockland centres.

In retrospect, it seems as if every electoral buffeting of the 1960s and 1970s led to the creation of yet another brains trust of expert advisers. With the return to power of Labour (under Wilson from March 1974 until April 1976 and then, until May 1979, under Callaghan) a Docklands Joint Committee replaced the Study Team. It was instructed to consult the public over the future of east London on both banks of the river and then lay down guidelines for decision makers in the London Boroughs of Tower Hamlets, Newham, Greenwich and Southwark. The committee's Strategic Plan of July 1976 was an ambitious undertaking; it examined ways of retaining local trades, building small factories in new industrial parks, constructing relief roads, meeting the need for local housing estates, safeguarding recreational facilities and increasing the number of schools. It also proposed to ensure that the whole of the riverside was made more attractive, with pedestrians able to walk along the riverbank from the Tower down to the Isle of Dogs, and beyond. The Strategic Plan recognised that the old upriver docks and their dependent industries belonged to the past. But it emphasised the need for continuity, and believed that, in some form or other, cargo-handling had a future, either in modernised wharves or in part of the Royal docks. 'The Docklands Joint Committee wish to see a flourishing and viable port in east

London,' the Strategic Plan declared unequivocably[1].

A progress report, published by the GLC two years later, listed new factories in Silvertown and Beckton, where a smart housing estate was expected to provide homes for workers in the local 'industrial park'; but the report showed a certain reticence over plans to revive the port[2]. And this silence was hardly surprising. For by 1978 – with Labour out of office on the GLC, although not in Parliament – the PLA's finances were again badly in the red and the Authority duly announced the imminent closing of the up-river docks. It was hoped, the PLA indicated, to keep London alive as a port by concentrating on Tilbury. So it was that in November 1981 all commercial shipping operations came to an end in the Royal docks, although funnels and masts remained part of the east London scene for another two or three years; at the height of the New Depression in 1984 there were still vessels laid up alongside the idle quays[3].

The closure of the Royals, an event scarcely noticed by the national press, was seen as the passing of an era throughout the East End, not simply in Newham. It emphasised a deterioration in the standard of working-class life which had first become apparent in the early 1970s with the decline of communal ties. Blocks of new flats began to show structural faults: they let in the rain; their heating systems failed; their drains were easily blocked. Early in 1979 – before Mrs Thatcher's first electoral triumph – a team from the Institute of Community Studies prepared a *Report from Hackney*, sampling and analysing the frustrations of 929 residents in the Borough. When the Report was published in 1981, its four authors declared that 32 per cent of the families interviewed were below the poverty line – 'as far as we know the highest [percentage] ever shown by any study made in this country up to now, and that was before the recession began to bite'. Two-thirds of the residents thought that Hackney had deteriorated since becoming, in 1965, a Metropolitan Borough: they complained of violence to individuals, vandalism, poor housing (some flats were plagued by brown ants, who liked the hot-air ducts of the central-heating systems), dirtiness in the streets, the tolerance by young parents of the bad behaviour of their children, and the challenge to old habits presented by new immigrants. Most council estates lost their caretakers/wardens as early as 1972, when runaway inflation imposed a tightening of municipal belts. But the greatest complaint was at the loss of any sense of 'neighbourhood'; despite a fall in numbers, Hackney had become so impersonal a borough that families felt isolated within the community[4]. A survey of housing problems of the younger generation in Bethnal Green, made in 1981, also emphasised social loneliness. The researcher, Anthea Holme, commented particularly on the loosening of that 'mother-daughter bond', which Young and Willmott had emphasised in their famous analysis of kinship and community during the mid-fifties. By the early 1980s far fewer East End families had relatives living close at hand[5].

The free enterprise principles of Thatcherism left little money available for easing housing problems. Nor indeed was it possible to maintain municipal services at an appropriate level for such a socially inequable community. Fortunately, old traditions of voluntary work survived in the inner East End. Even during those years when the welfare state provided adequate basic benefits, deprived families could develop still further their spiritual and material well-being with help from the Victorian and Edwardian foundations: Clement Attlee lived long enough to welcome the expansion of Toynbee Hall[6]; and many other settlements and clubs continued to flourish, although in the 1970s municipal egalitarian sentiment turned against 'missionising' public school philanthropy. Social counsel was provided, too, by the Bernhard Baron Settlement, that distinctive liberal Jewish club for young people established in Berner Street (a road now re-named to honour the Settlement's inspiring leader, Sir Basil Henriques). And, like Toynbee Hall, the Salvation Army's havens of refuge have also expanded; the new Booth House resembles a temperance hotel rather than a mission hostel. The Children's Country Holidays Fund, founded in Whitechapel by Samuel Barnett in 1884, was in 1988 still taking 3000 inner city schoolchildren away each summer for a fortnight of fresh air and green fields[7].

The changing demands of the post-war world led to new foundations with a different emphasis from their predecessors: in Whitechapel Road was built a mosque with two minarets, so that the Bangladeshi and other Islamic settlers could find their own cultural and spiritual centre; and in East India Dock Road what was once a seamen's hostel, and later a convent, became Pope John House, with a fine, modern Roman Catholic church across the road. In Canning Town a Mayflower Family Centre was set up in 1958 by the Revd David Sheppard, the former Sussex and England cricket captain, who seventeen years later became diocesan bishop in another deprived dockland city, Liverpool[8]. Individual churchmen fought social evils within their own parishes, as in the days of Lowder and Headlam. Father John Groser – a majestic priest, who played the part of Becket in Hoellering's 1951 film of *Murder in the Cathedral* – vigorously sought justice for his Stepney parishioners after the Second World War, just as in the 1920s and 1930s, when he presided over the Stepney Tenants Defence League[9]. By 1966, when John Groser died, 'Father Joe' (Williamson), an East Ender by birth, was leading campaigns against the most recent and most blatant forms of vice; and in 1968 Trevor Huddleston – already famous as a crusader against apartheid – came back to London as suffragan Bishop of Stepney, for ten years offering wise counsel on immigration and passionately championing the underprivileged.

Father Groser's last years of active ministry were spent as Master of the Royal Foundation of St Katharine. For, by one of history's pleasanter ironies, the Foundation, exiled to Regent's Park by the dock builders in 1825, returned in 1948 to a bombed site off Butcher Row, Stepney. Medieval relics and a pulpit from the old church near the Tower survive in the new chapel, which also contains a magnificent teak crucifix designed by Fr Groser's son, and a pear wood cross made for Hoellering's film. In the year St Katharine's Dock closed, St Katharine's Foundation was charged with new vitality; for in 1968 care of the Royal Foundation was entrusted jointly to the Community of the Resurrection – of whose London house Bishop Huddleston had once been Prior – and the Deaconess Community of St Andrew. During the socially perplexing years of economic recession in the 1970s and 1980s, the brotherhood and sisterhood of St Katharine's could undertake welfare work in the local community, while fulfilling the remaining injunctions of the Foundation's medieval charter: to keep their liturgical observances; to foster education; and to provide hospitality and spiritual refreshment for strangers. Nowhere else in east London can there be so fascinating an example of active continuity and renewal through eight centuries of social change[10].

By contrast, the volatility of modern politics has made experiments in local government short-lived. East London socialists – and others in the Labour Party – were always convinced that the old LCC was dismantled by the Tories for political purposes. But the Greater London Council, which came into being on All Fools Day in 1965, was also in its turn to fall foul of Conservative Government. From 1981 onwards the Council sought to revitalise London's ailing industries by socialist planning, while spending public money on housing, education and transport and in improving the well-being of men and women who were socially or racially underprivileged. The GLC survived just long enough to celebrate its twenty-first birthday. For the clash between radical policies in County Hall and the good housekeeping precepts of Downing Street was resolved by Mrs Thatcher in 1986 with devastating finality. After what Edward Heath condemned as 'a bad bill ... the negation of democracy', the people of London were denied all further opportunities to vote on metropolitan affairs, and the GLC was sent about its non-business[11]. The three East End boroughs were left in being, chastened and rate-capped.

Yet, although specifically socialist planning might be discredited, the Thatcher administration showed a natural predilection for forward-looking commercial enterprise. In the spring of 1981 the government created the London Docklands Development Corporation to supervise the regeneration of eight square miles of London's docklands, on both sides of the Thames. A year later, in April 1982, Sir Geoffrey Howe as Chancellor of the Exchequer announced the creation of London's first 'Enterprise Zone', an area covering much of the Isle of Dogs. To this favoured enclave of the East End it was hoped to attract new businesses by assurances that, for ten years, no rates would be levied on commercial or industrial premises and all capital investment within the zone might be offset against tax; for the whole 5000 acres of redundant dockland was to become 'the Metropolitan Water City of the Twenty-First Century'.

By the following autumn the stage of riverside east London was cleared for the greatest transformation scene in Europe since Baron Haussmann remodelled Napoleon III's Paris. Public attention was given, in the first place, to the Isle of Dogs: there was more space on the Island for development than further west; and the great bend of the Thames, with Greenwich across the river, made the site as fine a source of architectural inspiration as anywhere in Britain. When, on 22 September 1983, Princess Alexandra opened the red-brick roads of the Enterprise Zone, the names chosen for the new streets between the old West India Dock South and the Millwall Outer Dock had pleasant associations with an earlier past: Mastmaker Road and Lightermans Road in tribute to old crafts; Canary Wharf, to recall shipments of bananas and other fruit from sunnier islands; Marsh Wall, a name carried by the western embankment when the Island was still open pastures; Millharbour and Limeharbour, also looking back to the pre-steam age; Crossharbour, as a statement of fact; and Heron Wharf, like Canary Wharf an old name revived, but recalling the screaming wading-birds who nested in these creeks and marshes when there were still Cistercians in Stratford Langthorne and nuns at Bromley St Leonard[12].

On these delightfully named streets and quays the LDDC encouraged speculative property developers to project the most concentrated aggregation of buildings in the capital. Although the LDDC agreed to use the Docklands Strategic Plan of July 1976 as a starting point[13], it was hard to identify any grand design. At first the LDDC seemed to resemble a jumbo-sized estate agent with some 12 million square feet of office floorspace to lease or sell. Everything about the project conjured up superlatives. In March 1988 the Canadian developers Olympia and York were able to submit plans for Canary Wharf, at the centre of the old West India Docks, which envisaged office blocks accommodating 60,000 people. They proposed the construction of a waterside frontage of ten-storeyed neo-classical solidity, greater in extent than any previous office building development in Europe. Dominating Canary Wharf – and, indeed, Docklands – would be a 46-storey light-reflecting prism with a pyramid top, over 800 feet high. This skyscraper, the first to be built in Britain, was designed by the Argentinian-American architect Cesar Pelli

and was intended to be the tallest building in Europe, a third as high
again as the National Westminster Bank tower at Bishopsgate; smaller
towers, linked by colonnades, were to flank the skyscraper[14]. Before the
end of the century, Canary Wharf and its neighbouring quays would be
accepted as the out-of-town campus of the City of London, much as La
Défense became for Paris in the boom years of the Fifth Republic.

Throughout the Thatcher era construction work in Docklands went
forward at an extraordinary pace. Traditionalist exteriors served as outer
vests for steel-framed interiors erected by the fastest of building methods.
In 1991, just ten years after the LDDC came into being, the first tenants
moved into the skyscraper at One Canada Square. Progress did not,
however, continue to run on smoothly and unimpaired. During 1992 the
uncertainties of computerised capitalism threatened to delay development, checking that flow of direct or indirect public subsidy which was, it
seemed, essential to the restructuring of any enterprise zone. The original zonal concessions came to an end in that year and Olympia and York,
the principal developers of Canary Wharf, went into administration.
Moreover, the sheer dominance of the new Docklands on the London
skyline attracted unwanted attention from terrorists. Widespread
damage was caused by an IRA bomb which exploded at South Quay on
the evening of 9 February 1996, one hour after the ending of an eigh-
teen-month ceasefire; two people were killed and there were over a
hundred injuries, many caused by flying glass. South Quay Plaza suffered
extensively. By the late spring the more distant damage had been
repaired, and it was possible to enjoy the vista which the planners had
intended: glimpses of a broad expanse of river, neatly trimmed young
trees, and in Cabot Square a fountain giving a sense of spaciousness.

Ever since the wartime bombing of Target Area A, there had been a
succession of artistic impressions of a future London, offering neatly bal-
anced dreams of leisure parks, riverside walks, smokeless factories and
tidy housing estates. Much was achieved in the landscaped squares of
badly bombed Poplar under the Attlee government, but nothing that
came off the post-war drawing-board ever matched this redevelopment of
the West India Docks thirty years later. Yet the project aroused sharp criticism, both architectural and social; for while in the 1950s the twenty-
five floors of the Lansbury district's Balfron Towers helped meet Poplar's
housing needs, the forty-eight floors of One Canada Square seemed to
offer little to native East Enders. In a well-reasoned essay Bill Risebero, an
architect teaching urban studies at the University of East London, has
condemned 'the office city . . . south-east from Limehouse' as 'relentlessly
commercial and alien'. 'There is a sense in which the implanted Canary
Wharf is colonial,' Risebero argued, voicing widespread doubts over the
merits of the transformation[15]. Critics complained that the building pro-

jects gave free rein to developers' architects instead of forming part of a carefully designed and landscaped city. A jumble of stylistic changes still occasionally irritates perceptive eyes.

The task confronting the LDDC was formidable: the administration of an empire which, north of the Thames, extended from Wapping as far east as Gallions Reach. While hardening its heart against old-fashioned planning restraints, the Corporation soon recognised that particular areas had distinctive architectural identities and that the key to good living in others lay in imaginative landscaping. The derelict marshland around Beckton, so recently the largest gasworks in Europe, was developed with particular care: an accumulation of waste material from purification processes served as a base for the creation of 'Beckton Alps', the only hill in Newham and which provided east London with a dry ski-slope; a bridleway and cycle track cross Beckton heading eastwards towards Dagenham; and shortly before the LDDC handed responsibility back to Newham, a Docklands Equestrian Centre was opened, to the north of Alpine Way. Further west, in the densely built-up stretches of riverside, some of the new glass and stone offices affect a lightweight intimacy in happy contrast to the down-at-heels grandeur left behind in the City; and, between the Thames and Westferry Road, the craggy broken-ness of The Cascades seen from a fast ferry unexpectedly gives the river a cliff-face[16].

For seventeen years the Corporation had responsibility for bringing together commercial premises, shopping centres, parkland, recreational facilities and homes in a new suburb upon which it hoped to foster communal identity and purposeful pride. By March 1998, when the LDDC was disbanded and its last 'possessions' (the Royal Docks) reverted to local authority control, 24,000 new homes had been created, 55 miles of new road were in being, and 28 new schools or educational institutions and 5 health centres had opened. Sometimes the Corporation's planners showed a greater sensitivity towards the past than had their immediate predecessors, notably over Limehouse. There was an obvious need for better access from the Isle of Dogs to the City. The LDDC rejected earlier proposals for a surface express-way, recognising fears that it would have destroyed the last traces of the historic riverside hamlet. Instead, between 1989 and 1993, the Limehouse Link, a sunken road partially tunnelled and with underground sliproads to Canary Wharf and Westferry Road, was constructed at enormous expense. Inevitably, however, the project led to social upheaval. Between five and six hundred households were uprooted, to be rehoused by the LDDC on the Isle of Dogs a mile and a half to the south, in Timber Wharves Village, newly built on land where timber had been stacked when the Millwall Docks were flourishing.

The earliest and least socially exclusive of LDDC housing estates was completed in 1982 at East Beckton; 'Barristers, dustmen rub shoulders in new Beckton homes' ran an intriguing headline in the July 1983 issue of the Corporation's *Docklands News*, a house paper prone to moments of patronising condescension[17]. The LDDC continued to seek to keep home prices down; in July 1985 *Docklands News* reported that the most expensive house in Beckton was on the market at £70,500, and the majority of Corporation homes were far less costly. By then a penthouse flat in Wapping (not subject to LDDC control) already cost £325,000. But three years earlier – in 1982 – there had still been houses on sale in the district at around £20,000. By May 1998, a few weeks after the disbandment of the LDDC, *The Times* could report that one- or two-bedroom flats in Wapping were on offer at £110,000. Riverside 'urban village' apartments in fashionable blocks on the Isle of Dogs ranged in price from £198,000 for one room to £2,137,000 for four rooms. The word 'dockers' was by then being used to describe, not workers loading or unloading ships' cargoes, but affluent home dwellers gentrifying Docklands[18].

Long before the LDDC came into being it was clear that the highly congested area north of the Thames needed a new east London railway. In the 1970s the Docklands Joint Committee envisaged a tube extension, an expensive undertaking in such a marshy district, as the tunnelling of the Central Line had already shown. The LDDC rejected this proposal in favour of a computer-operated Docklands Light Railway (DLR). Seven and a half miles of the £77 million project were opened by Queen Elizabeth II on 30 July 1987, although teething troubles in the system meant that it was another month before the first passengers could travel between Tower Gateway, Island Gardens (the southern extremity of the Isle of Dogs) and Stratford. The DLR was extended westwards to Bank (in the City of London) in 1991 and three years later another ten stations were opened eastwards to Beckton. Hopes of extending the DLR southwards under the river from Mudchute and Island Gardens to Greenwich should be fulfilled before the end of the century. An extension of the underground Jubilee Line from Green Park to Stratford by way of Waterloo, Greenwich and the Isle of Dogs was due to open in 1998, but completion was delayed by technical problems and strained labour relations[19].

The eastward progress of the DLR, and improved express road links with the M11 and M25, finally determined the siting of a short take-off and landing airport (Stolport) for rapid business travel to the nearer European capitals and within the United Kingdom. An aircraft had made an experimental landing on Heron Wharf on 30 June 1983, but with land prices leaping above £2 million an acre in the Enterprise Zone, it made sense to place the Stolport north of the Royal Docks. The London City Airport was officially opened by the Queen on 5 November 1987, although by then commercial services had been using the Stolport for ten days. Worries over air safety led to the suspension of flights to Paris for three weeks but by the end of January 1988 compact and quiet aircraft were using the Stolport regularly. Business executives were promised a speedy check-in – and no tourists to clutter up the departure lounge[20].

The commerce and industry of the regenerated dockland were far removed from the traditional occupations of east London. It is true that the first major enterprise to move from the City was connected with the oldest of all seagoing callings: a new Billingsgate fish market opened on a 13-acre site beside the West India Dock on 19 January 1982, three days after the old Billingsgate Market in Lower Thames Street ceased trading. But thereafter the emphasis was on high technology and finance. In November 1983 Limehouse Productions Studio came into operation on Canary Wharf, south of new Billingsgate, in what had been Shed 30, a post-war warehouse opened as late as 1950 at a time when the cargo ships were still coming regularly to the dock from the Caribbean; Limehouse Productions brought a touch of television glamour to a bleak and windswept site, but the studios survived for only four years. In May 1984, six months after the studios opened, the multinational Samas Office Systems moved into the Enterprise Zone and thereafter the main demand was for air-conditioned offices rather than converted warehouses. The service industries which came into the area required high financial and business skills and, despite the LDDC's hope of creating jobs for East Enders, unemployment continued to rise. Although the Corporation spent more than £30 million between 1988 and 1993 on training projects 'better geared to the needs of local people', the problem plagued the LDDC for the remaining years of its mandate. In 1997 the administration of Wapping, Limehouse and the Isle of Dogs was returned to Tower Hamlets, a local authority with one of the highest rates of unemployment among working men in the country.

The early spaciousness of the empty Docklands appealed to Press magnates eager to centralise production and expand. By the autumn of 1987 no less than five newspaper groups had established their headquarters in Docklands, the *Daily Telegraph* using the prototype of a 24-knot catamaran riverbus service to take employees speedily to and from their old offices in Fleet Street[21]. But it was the move of Rupert Murdoch's printing plant out of central London which focused nationwide attention on Wapping during much of the sixth and seventh years of the Thatcher era. Unlike earlier unrest in the traditionally turbulent riverside hamlets, the 'Murdoch troubles' were not local in origin. The industrial dispute, which first hit the headlines early in 1986, arose from Rupert Murdoch's dismissal of 5,000 employees who refused to sign a no-strike deal ahead of the move to new premises, off Virginia Street, south of The Highway.

Few of News International's employees seem to have come from the old East End; this was not the high-walled Wapping of the fight for the 'docker's tanner'; the narrow streets and derelict warehouses provided stage and backcloth for a modern melodrama of confrontation, with performers coming in from elsewhere – at least until the end of July 1986, when a High Court order banned any further mass picketing.

Members of the National Graphical Association (NGA) and the Society of General and Allied Trades (SOGAT) continued to defy News International from 26 January 1986 until the first week in February 1987. When SOGAT refused to accept a court order to call off a boycott of Murdoch's newspapers, the Union's assets were seized on 10 February 1986. Angry demonstrations the next weekend led to intervention by the police, in riot gear. There was renewed violence at the beginning of May, with 150 demonstrators and 175 police reportedly injured during the clashes; and at a demonstration marking the first anniversary of the dispute more than 160 police and 300 protesters were hurt. Victory lay, in the end, with the 'bosses'; it generally did during the Thatcher era. 'Fortress Wapping', as the News International works is widely called, remains architecturally uninspiring. By contrast, only a few hundred yards to the south-east, imaginative landscaping has created a delightful tree-lined canalside walkway beside John Rennie's quay wall for the London Docks, which was completed in the year of Trafalgar.

The LDDC was by no means indifferent to the cultural, recreational and educational well-being of the community. In earlier centuries the City Livery Companies, as privileged monopolistic corporations, undertook extensive charitable and educational activities: thus the Brewers', Coopers' and Drapers' Companies were all trustees of schools founded in the East End, and the Drapers' Company also contributed substantial funds to the institutions in Mile End Road which, in 1934, were recognised as Queen Mary College, a part of London University. A contemporary privileged corporation such as the LDDC also accepts paternalistic responsibilities, although as a sponsor rather than a long-term trustee. Among grants authorised in the first two years of the LDDC's existence were over £200,000 towards cleaning up and restoring St George's-in-the-East, a slightly larger sum for neighbouring St Paul's Church, £17,000 to the new Half Moon Theatre in Mile End Road, and £22,000 for a new nature park attached to St Luke's Primary School in the Isle of Dogs. Interest was later shown in several museums, notably at North Woolwich railway station and at St Mark's Church, Silvertown, and in a museum for Docklands on the North Quay of the West India Docks. Not all the projects were fulfilled, and some found their purpose considerably modified. Sadly the imaginatively designed Half Moon Theatre (which was funded by the outgoing GLC and the Arts Council, as well as by the

LDDC) was sold; it never became the community playhouse envisaged by its architect, Florian Beigel[22]. In the summer of 1985 the LDDC converted the former Fred Olsen shed for bananas into a sports stadium. The Olsen building, on the east side of Millwall Dock, had only been completed seventeen years previously. The stadium was opened as the London Arena in 1989, to serve both as a concert-hall, capable of seating more than 12,000 people, and as the home for the only professional ice-hockey team in the metropolis. *Docklands News* emphasised the Corporation's ecological commitment and its interest in three urban farms – at Stepney Green, Mudchute on the Island, and Manor Way, Beckton. 'Lambing time down on Mudchute Farm' ran a picture caption in the very first issue; and this arcadian theme returned often enough in later issues to suggest a rather older soap opera than *EastEnders*[23].

Despite the LDDC's encouragement of leisure activities for all and the provision of some relatively low-cost housing, it remains hard to refute accusations that the great transformation down-river has revived social divisiveness. Anyone who attempts to walk some of the 180-mile-long Thames path will find that the need to protect property has, in places, barred public access along what the LDDC hoped would be a right-of-way. The spread of luxury apartments stirred resentment between many old East End families and the new arrivals. In the late 1980s 'Toffs Out', 'Yuppies to Chelsea' and, more alarmingly, 'Boil a Trendy' could be seen scrawled on railway embankment walls which had once carried Fascist slogans and anti-Semitic obscenities. There is no doubt that the development of Docklands has brightened east London, at least to tourist eyes, but it has brought once more into sharp focus the contrasts which Disraeli noted in the 1840s and which the exiled Lenin decried sixty years later: 'Ilyich', Lenin's widow recalled in her memoirs, 'would mutter through clenched teeth, and in English: "Two nations!"'[24]

Around the north-eastern fringe of Tower Hamlets, and in the west of neighbouring Hackney, the restored social barriers are less exclusive. In Bow, for example, gentrification seems to have crept back naturally to Tredegar Square and its offshoots, an 'up-market' district in Victorian times. Train travellers from Liverpool Street, heading towards Chelmsford or Southend, pass one of the subtlest of recent social changes: Bryant and May's works in Fairfield Road, in mid-Victorian times the biggest factory in the East End and the setting for the heroic match-girls' strike of 1888, survives as 'The Bow Quarter'. Most of the old factory is now a select apartment block, neat and trim, with curtained windows looking out across smokeless railway tracks. Through ornate and firmly secured gates an onlooker can admire in the forecourt a fountain playing beneath a small flowering cherry tree: here, a century and a quarter ago, the yellow phosphorus fumes of match manufacturing poisoned what was then the factory yard; 'luminous vomit gathered in the gutters when the girls finished work', the social historian Jane Cox reminds us[25]. Yet, though Bow Road to the east of St Mary's Church is grey and grimy, and the men's lavatory to which Gladstone's statued hand helpfully showed the way is now padlocked, the streets north of the main road remain today as pleasantly residential as any in the East End, even if the western end of Cable Street and the old dockmasters' houses by Wapping Pier are more excitingly sited.

But in historic Spitalfields, the traditional heart of the East End, there remain enough contrasts for a visitor to pick out three or even four nations and not simply the conventional distinction between the rich and the poor. Four weeks before the Queen opened the Docklands Light Railway in the summer of 1987, her eldest son led a group of prominent businessmen on an East End trip to urge private capital to help alleviate urban blight and poverty. There were, at the time of the Prince's initiative, 16,000 unemployed and 1,300 people listed as homeless in Tower Hamlets. Alan Hamilton in *The Times* described how Prince Charles handed over a cheque for £50,000 from Lloyd's of London to the Tower Hamlets Centre for Small Businesses and took his eminent companions to Brick Lane. There, *The Times* reported next day, 'The Prince of Wales peered into the Stygian gloom of a tiny sweatshop where up to 10 Bengalis hunch over ancient sewing machines under a rotten, leaking roof, making up leather garments for the rag trade. Only four were at work yesterday: business has been bad since the rain got in and spoiled the coats.' The Prince is said to have commented, 'This is terrible. All we manage to do is to recreate the conditions they left behind in the sub-continent. This is not acceptable: we must do something.' Five months later the Prince made a 'secret visit' to see for himself a derelict estate in Limehouse[26]. It was just over a century since concern over London's slums prompted his great-great grandfather to join a Royal Commission on the Housing of the Working Class.

Little betterment of working conditions seems to have been made in the ten years after Prince Charles's visit to Brick Lane. For when the national minimum wage was introduced in the spring of 1999 it was reported that earnings in the sweatshops of Tower Hamlets were far lower than in the country as a whole. On the other hand, race relations between the Bangladeshi immigrants and other community groups greatly improved in the two decades following the Brick Lane riots.

As early as the summer of 1987 the borough councillors of Tower Hamlets were looking to the redevelopment of the best-known site in Spitalfields as a means of regenerating the inner East End. But they had no wish to find their authority diminished by another government-sponsored corporation, as in the docklands. In Bethnal Green the 1982 borough council elections were a notable success for the Alliance and, in particular, for the 'Liberal Focus' movement, which placed emphasis on decentralised politics[27]. By 1986–7 the local Neighbourhood Committee consisted of six Liberals and three Labour members, people who knew well the streets and stones of an area steeped, not only in history, but in the litigious peculiarities which accompany a tumultuous past. For, while Tower Hamlets remained the planning authority, the eleven acres of Spitalfields Market were owned by the City of London, whose Markets Authority was required to ensure that Londoners had an efficient wholesale fruit and vegetable emporium on a site acceptable to existing market tenants. Moreover any redevelopment of Spitalfields needed parliamentary sanction, for the market was set up in 1682 by licence from the Crown.

Rival contenders produced a succession of development plans between the spring of 1986 and the autumn of 1987, modifying them to meet objections either from local groups or from the Corporation of London. In the last week of October 1987 the City finally approved a plan, already accepted locally. The Spitalfields Development Group (SDG) – a consortium of London & Edinburgh Trust, Balfour Beatty and Country and District Properties – was authorised to move the market to Temple Mills, a railway marshalling yard between Hackney and Leyton. By 1992 the move was completed, although the covered market building – dating from the 1860s and modernised in the 1920s – remains standing, with its future still uncertain. In May 1988 the SDG had won parliamentary approval for proposals to raise on the old site and its immediate vicinity 80,000 square feet of shops, one million gross square feet of office accommodation and 230 'residential units'. The project's supporters were confident that redevelopment would inject capital into the area, arrest the creeping paralysis of urban decay, and carry a regenerated Spitalfields into the twenty-first century. Perhaps it will[28].

Much progress was made during the late 1990s. The SDG gave financial backing to many community projects, including an archaeological unit excavating Roman remains in Spitalfields. But market fluctuations meant that transformation here was less extensive than the planners had hoped. To an outside observer construction work seemed to move at foxtrot pace ('slow, slow, quick, quick, slow'). Meanwhile the building operations had one fortunate consequence – they opened up a fine vista of Christ Church, Spitalfields, allowing Nicholas Hawksmoor's masterpiece to be seen as he intended. This is appropriate, for as a centre of Christian witness Christ Church flourishes once again, after thirty years – from 1957 to 1987 – in which no services were held there. Yet it is a significant commentary on life in Tower Hamlets during the last months of the century that the church crypt continues to be needed as a nightly shelter for the homeless. Fewer drop-outs linger in neighbouring 'Itchy Park' gardens. Sadly, today's sprawlers are from a much younger generation than ten years ago.

A new east London is coming into being from Bishopsgate down to Beckton. It may well break down the vestigial frontiers of the old East End: the thriving ex-LDDC colony across the river at Bermondsey and Rotherhithe now shares development with Docklands as the 'Thames Gateway'; and the SDG always envisaged links between Spitalfields and the honeycomb squares of Broadgate, the huge City complex which envelops Liverpool Street Station. Yet even though there are more East Enders nowadays in Essex or Hertfordshire than in Stepney or Bow, familiar sights remain, some as a reproach rather than in happy nostalgia: the pathos of puzzled immigrants; the jollity of pubs; costers and customers bargaining along Whitechapel Waste and, on Sundays, amid the flower market of Columbia Road or among the stalls of Brick Lane; and those rickety barrows on which precariously perched furniture is street-handled through far too much traffic. Although since 1984 improbably flanked by a mosque, there is still in Whitechapel Road a bell foundry, as there has been in east London since the King returned in triumph from Agincourt. There are still breweries, as in Pepys's time; and the art gallery which the Barnetts founded; and Victoria Park, more litter-strewn than in earlier years, but retaining that open-air junk-stall appeal it acquired when a discarded Chinese pagoda was erected on the boating-lake island, back in Chartist days.

For the supreme delight of the East End remains its quality as an ever-changing curiosity shop, fascinating as a microcosm of London's past. It is kept in being by a people who are too astute to cling to yesterday and too sharp-witted to accept unquestioningly today's fashionable blandishments. With the prospect in the summer of 2000 of a metropolitan Mayor and a statutory Greater London Authority, they hope still to shape for themselves the pattern of their tomorrow.

Notes on Sources

1 CREAM AND GOOD CHERRIES

This chapter owes much to Millicent Rose's *The East End of London* (London, 1951) and to the sections on the religious houses of eastern Middlesex in Volume 1 of the *Victoria County History of Middlesex* (London, 1971), particularly the entry on St Leonard's, Bromley by Bow (pp. 156–9) by H. P. King.

1   J. Stow, *Survey of London*, ed. C. L. Kingsford (Oxford, 1908), I, p. 128; Goodman reference, p. 126.
2   For Pepys I have used the definitive edition of the diary, edited by R. Latham & W. Matthews (published in eleven volumes, London, 1980–3). For Dutch gunfire reference, 8 June 1667, VIII, p. 249; for the Great Fire see entries for Sept. 1666, op. cit., VII passim; for cream and cherries, see entry for 11 June 1664, op. cit., V, p. 120.
3   Figures taken from statistical tables in the valuable chapter by M. J. Power, 'East London Housing in the 17th Century' in P. Clark & P. Slack (eds.) *Crisis and Order in British Towns* (London, 1972), p. 243.
4   K. G. T. McDonnell, *Mediaeval London Suburbs* (London and Chichester, 1978), p. 100.
5   Latham and Matthews' edition of Pepys Diary: 'Royal Oak', II, p. 14 and VI, p. 36; East India Company's storehouse, V, p. 202; George Margett, V, p. 265; hot Saturday in 1663, IV, p. 268; stoves, VI, p. 34; Wapping carpenter, IV, p. 232.
6   M. Power, 'Shadwell: The Development of a London Suburban Community in the Seventeenth Century', *The London Journal*, IV (1978), no. 1, pp. 29–48, taverns listed and identified on the map on p. 37 of this fascinating article.
7   J. N. P. Watson, *Captain-General and Rebel Chief* (London, 1979), pp. 146, 153, 154; Pepys references in this paragraph and the next from diary entry for 19 Dec. 1666, Latham and Matthews, op. cit. VII, p. 416.

2 SUBURBS – OR POWDER KEGS OF REVOLT?

1   J. Strype, *A Survey of the Cities of London and Westminster* (1720 edition), I, p. 1, II, pt. 4, p. 87; on population statistics, see George Rudé, *Hanoverian London* (London, 1971), pp. 4–10, hereafter cited as HL, and an article by E. A. Wrigley, 'A Simple Model of London's Importance in Changing English Society and Economy', in *Past and Present*, no. 37, 1967.

2 See Daniel Defoe, *A Tour Through the Whole Island of Great Britain*, I, pp. 314,
   XX. *The Diary of Dudley Ryder* (London, 1939) was edited by W. Matthews,
   with an informative introductory note on the Hackney of Ryder's youth.
   See also M. Rose, *The East End of London* (London 1951), pp. 111–16.
3 Defoe, op. cit., XXX. For the Huguenots and the Spitalfields silk industry,
   see F. Warner, *The Silk Industry of the United Kingdom* (London, 1921),
   chapters 1 and 2.
4 HL., pp. 185–6. For the Calico Act, see D. B. Horn and M. Ransome, *English
   Historical Documents, 1714–1783* (London, 1957), vol. X, pp. 456–8.
5 On the Fifty New Churches Act see John Summerson, *Georgian London* (rev.
   edn. Pelican Books, Harmondsworth, 1969), Chapter 6. For the collapse of
   St Leonard's, Shoreditch, J. Bird & P. Norman (eds.) *Survey of London*, vol.
   VIII (London, 1922), p. 96.
6 Summerson, op. cit., pp. 86–8; F. Sheppard (ed.) *Survey of London*, vol.
   XXVII (London, 1957), pp. 148–77.
7 Ibid., p. 209.
8 M. Dorothy George, *London Life in the Eighteenth Century* (London, 1925),
   p. 75.
9 Rose, op. cit., p. 56; Summerson, op. cit., pp. 44–51.
10 HL, pp. 187–90; *Gentleman's Magazine*, 1736, p. 422; *General Williamson's
   Diary* (Camden Society, 3rd Series, vol. XXII, London, 1912).
11 HL, pp. 196–7.
12 Dr Rudé is the foremost modern authority on Wilkes. His summary in HL,
   pp. 164–74 and 211–26, may be amplified by his *Wilkes and Liberty* (Oxford,
   1962), notably pp. 28–8, 50–60, 173, 181–3. See also E. P. Thompson,
   The Making of the English Working Class (rev. edn. Harmondsworth, 1980)
   pp. 75–8.
13 HL, p. 167. The outer fabric of the Three Tuns Tavern survives, as 1 Wilkes
   Street, on the corner of Fournier Street; Sheppard (ed.), *Survey of London*,
   vol. XXVII, p. 211.
14 *Annual Register* 1769 (London, 1769), p. 159.
15 See J. H. Clapham, 'The Spitalfields Acts, 1773–1824', *Economic Journal*
   (1916), vol. XXVI.
16 HL, pp. 178–9 and 224–6; Thompson, op. cit. 77–8; C. Hibbert, *King Mob*
   (London, 1958).
17 Thompson, op. cit, pp. 186 and 289; J. Steven Watson, *The Reign of George
   III* (Oxford, 1966), p. 585.

3 LIFE AND LEISURE

1 Letter from R. P. Hare to Sir R. Brocas, 1730, in M. Dorothy George, *London
   Life in the Eighteenth Century* (London, 1925, hereafter cited as *Lond. Lif.*),
   pp. 289, 395.
2 Cited from *Tribune*, 23 September 1795 by E. P. Thompson, *The Making of
   the English Working Class* (Harmondsworth, 1980), p. 157.
3 *Public Advertiser*, 7 February 1758, cited *Lond. Lif.* p. 326.
4 George Rudé, *Hanoverian London* (London, 1971, hereafter cited as HL),

p. 93; C. R. Elrington (ed.), *Victoria County History of Middlesex* (Oxford, 1985), vol. VIII, p. 174.

5   W. B. Boulton, *The Amusements of Old London* (London, 1901), vol. II, pp. 64–8. See also M. Rose, *The East End of London* (London, 1951), pp. 226–7.

6   James Thorne, *Handbook to the Environs of London* (Reprint of 1876 edn. by Godfrey Cave Associates, London, 1983) pp. 24–5; W. R. Powell (ed.), *Victoria County History of Essex* (Oxford, 1966), Vol. VI, p. 218.

7   F. Sheppard (ed.) *Survey of London*, vol. XXVII (London, 1957), p. 139.

8   For the Madrigal Society see S. Sadie (ed.) *New Grove Dictionary of Music and Musicians* (London, 1986), vol. XI, p. 194.

9   See the following entries in the *New Grove* (cited above): for John James, article by Susi Jeans, vol. IX, p. 471; for Prelleur, article by P. Pratt, vol. XV, pp. 209–10; for Hawkins, article by P. Scholes, vol. VIII, pp. 323–5. See also Rose, op. cit., pp. 91–4 and 96; and *London Daily Post and General Advertiser*, 21 August, 1739.

10 Rose, op. cit., pp. 97–9; W. R. Chetwood, *A General History of the Stage* (*more particularly the Irish Theatre*), Dublin, 1749), p. 169.

11 Chetwood, op. cit., p. 160; D. M. Little and G. M. Kahrl, *The Letters of David Garrick* (Oxford, 1963), vol. 1, pp. 31–2, 39; G. W. Stone and G. M. Kahrl, *David Garrick, A Critical Biography* (Southern Illinois University Press, 1979), p. 541.

12 Chetwood, op. cit., p. 160.

13 Rose, op. cit., pp. 99–100.

14 W. H. Reid, *The Rise and Dissolution of the Infidel Societies of the Metropolis* (London, 1800), pp. 44–90; HL, p. 110.

15 N. Curnock (ed.) *John Wesley's Journal Abridged* (London, 1949): not suffered to conclude sermon (18 February, 1739), p. 64; Whitechapel cows (12 September 1742), p. 135; 1800 people at Spitalfields (11 September 1755), p. 271; world not to end that night (28 February 1763), p. 299.

16 HL, pp. 110–11 and 113.

17 *Lond. Lif.*, pp. 125–32; HL, pp. 7–8.

18 *Lond. Lif.* p. 128.

19 P. Magriel (ed.), *Memoirs of Daniel Mendoza* (London, 1951), p. 16.

20 Ibid., p. 108. Other references in Mendoza's *Memoirs*: Odiham, pp. 36 and 38; Stilton, p. 59; Doncaster, p. 65; meeting with George III pp. 82–3.

4   THE COMING OF THE DOCKS AND RAILWAYS

1   T. Smollett, *The Expedition of Humphrey Clinker* (ed. L. M. Knapp, Oxford, 1966), pp. 91–2; up river shipping estimate based on figures in G. Jackson, *The History and Archaeology of Ports* (Tadworth, 1983), pp. 55. See also R. C. Jarvis, 'Eighteenth-Century London Shipping' in A. J. Hollaender and W. Kellaway (eds.), *Studies in London History* (London, 1969), pp. 403–25.

2   P. Colquhoun, *A Treatise on the Commerce and Police of the River Thames* (London, 1800), p. 80.

3   Jackson, op. cit., p. 54.

4 Ibid., p. 56; John Pudney, *London's Docks* (London, 1975), pp. 24–6.
5 J. L. Howgego, 'Docks on the North Bank', *East London Papers*, X (1967), no. 2, pp. 75–108 (especially for these paragraphs, pp. 77–84).
6 Colquhoun, op. cit., pp. 59–81; W. M. Stern, 'The First London Dock Boom and the Growth of the West India Docks', *Economica*, XIX (1952), pp. 59–77.
7 *Gentleman's Magazine*, LXXVI (ii), Aug. 1806, pp. 724–6; Pudney, op. cit., pp. 51–2, citing the *Globe*.
8 *Gentelman's Magazine*, LXXV (i), Feb. 1805, pp. 176–7.
9 Pudney, op. cit., pp. 33–52; G. Pattison, 'The East India Dock Company, 1803–38', *East London Papers*, VII (1964), no. 1, pp. 31–40.
10 K. Baedeker, *Handbook to London and its Environs* (1906 edn., Leipzig), p. 141.
11 M. Rose, *The East End of London* (London, 1951), p. 124.
12 Jackson, op. cit., pp. 61–2.
13 Pudney, op. cit., pp. 64–7; *Gentleman's Magazine*, XXVI (i) Feb. 1826, pp. 105–6.
14 *The Times*, 27 Oct. 1828; C. Jamieson *History of the Royal Hospital of St Katharine* (London, 1952), ch. 10, passim.
15 *Gentleman's Magazine*, XCVI (i), Jan. 1826, pp. 9–10.
16 *The Times*, 27 Oct. 1828.
17 Howgego, loc. cit., p. 93.
18 See the article by W. M. Stern, 'Isle of Dogs Canal', *Economic History Review*, 2nd Series, IV (1952), no. 3, pp. 359–67.
19 *The Times*, 15 Dec. 1836. For railway development in general, E. Course, *London's Railways* (London, 1962); A. A. Jackson, *London's Local Railways* (Newton Abbot, 1978), a very detailed study.
20 F. Sheppard, *London, 1808–1870: The Infernal Wen* (London, 1971), pp. 144, 152–3; Course, op. cit., p. 144.
21 Ibid, pp. 117–9; Sheppard, op. cit., pp. 128–9.
22 M. Robbins, *The North London Railway* (London, 1966).
23 H. J. Dyos, 'Railways and Housing in Victorian London', *Journal of Transport History* (1955), II pp. 11–21, 90–100.
24 W. H. Fairbairn, 'Poplar and Bromley 1852–64', *East London Papers*, V (1962), no. 1, p. 37.

5 CRIME AND CHOLERA

1 David Hughson, *Walks through London* (London, 1817), I, p. 27.
2 F. Sheppard, *London 1808–1870: The Infernal Wen* (London, 1971), pp. 30–40; cited below as Sheppard, *Wen*.
3 *Annual Register, 1818*, pp. 266–7; Ibid, *1826*, pp. 140–1.
4 Ibid., *1811*, pp. 138–9 and 141–2; *Collected Works of T. de Quincey* (London, 1890), XIII, pp. 74–118.
5 Emma Brownlow, *Slight Reminiscences of a Septuagenarian* (London, 1867), pp. 30–1; *The Times*, 28, 29 December 1813.
6 For soup kitchens, see F. Sheppard (ed.), LCC *Survey of London*, vol. XXVII

(Athlone Press, London, 1957), p. 126; for the mendicity report and other details see K. Leech, 'The Decay of Spitalfields', *East London Papers*, VII, no. 2 (1964), pp. 57–62.

7   The Nova Scotia Gardens murder occupies many columns of *The Times* for November 1831.

8   Contemporary account: Anon (? W. B. Gurney), *The Trials at Large of Joseph Merceron, Esq.* (W. Wright, London, 1819). Detailed narrative in S. and B. Webb, *English Local Government; The Parish and the County* (London, 1906), pp. 79–90.

9   A. J. Robinson and D. H. B. Chesshyre, *The Green* (Tower Hamlets Library, London, 1986); H. J. Dyos, 'The Slums of Victorian London', *Victorian Studies*, vol. XI, no. 1 (1957), pp. 7–30.

10 On the cholera epidemics see Norman Longmate, *King Cholera: The Biography of a Disease* (London, 1966); S. E. Finer, *The Life and Times of Sir Edwin Chadwick* (London, 1952); R. A. Lewis, *Edwin Chadwick and the Public Health Movement, 1831–1854* (London, 1952); A. S. Wohl, *Endangered Lives: Public Health in Victorian Britain* (London, 1983).

11 *Report of the Select Committee on the Health of Towns 1840*, Parliamentary Papers, XI, pp. 3 and 7.

12 C. Dickens, *Sketches by Boz*, penultimate paragraph of Chapter 21 has the description of the Ratcliff Highway; Mrs Lewes, *Dr Southwood Smith* (London, 1887), p. 104; Chadwick's report for House of Lords, *Report on the Sanitary Condition of the Labouring Population of Great Britain, 1842*, Parliamentary Papers, XXVI.

13 Ashley's diary, printed in Edwin Hoder, *Shaftesbury* (London, 1886), I, p. 361.

14 L.C.C. *Survey*, cited above, XXVII, p. 8.

15 H. Gavin, *Sanitary Rambling, Being Sketches and Illustrations of Bethnal Green* (London, 1848), pp. 32–40, 66–92, 98–103. See also the reassessment of Gavin's book by R. S. Roberts, *East London Papers*, vol. 8, no. 2 (1965), pp. 110–18.

16 Sheppard, *Wen*, p. 272.

17 Roberts, loc. cit., p. 117; Longmate, op. cit., pp. 182–3.

18 *The Times*, 3 July 1858.

19 See the interesting article on water supply in B. Weinreb and C. Hibbert, *The London Encylopaedia* (Macmillan, London, 1983), p. 931.

20 Longmate, op. cit., pp. 216–20; Sheppard, *Wen*, pp. 253–96.

21 For prayer, see *The Times*, 5 July 1849. On inquiries about East London Water Company, See J. Simon, *Public Health Reports* (London, 1887), II, pp. 287–90 and 407–8.

6 THE PROBLEMS OF FREER TRADE

1   A. K. Sabin, *The Silk Weavers of Spitalfields and Bethnal Green* (London, 1931), pp. 14–15.

2 Gordon Jackson, *The History and Archaeology of Ports* (Tadworth, 1983), pp. 80–1.
3 F. Engels, *The Condition of the Working Class in England* (ed. E. Hobsbawn, London, 1986), pp. 117–18.
4 *Reynolds News*, 25 February 1855, cited by G. Stedman Jones, *Outcast London* (Oxford, 1971), p. 45.
5 Ibid., p. 46, citing *Morning Star*, 18 January 1861.
6 Gordon Jackson, op. cit., pp. 81–2.
7 See: S. Pollard, 'The Decline of Shipbuilding on the Thames', *Econ. Hist. Rev.*, 2nd Series, vol. 3 (1950), pp. 72–89; Eve Hostellter, 'Shipbuilding and Related Industries on the Isle of Dogs', *Dockland* (North-East London Polytechnic, 1986), pp. 137–44; T. Wright, *Some Habits and Customs of the Working Classes* (London, 1867), p. 250–2.
8 G. S. Jones, op. cit., pp. 46, 102.
9 F. Sheppard, *London 1808–1870* (London, 1971), pp. 77–80.
10 Pollard, loc. cit., pp. 81–2.
11 F. W. Galton, *Workers on their Industries* (London, 1895), p. 58.
12 M. Rose, *The East End of London* (London, 1951), pp. 156–8.
13 G. S. Jones, op. cit., pp. 27–30.
14 For Beck and Beckton, see S. Everard, *The History of the Gas Light and Coke Company, 1812–1949* (London, 1949), especially pp. 220–47, 382, 411.
15 James Thorne, *Handbook to the Environs of London* (1873 edn. reprinted, Chichester, 1986), p. 683.
16 Rose, op. cit., p. 143; G. S. Jones, op. cit., pp. 85–6; for Batgers, see W. G. Crory, *East London Industries* (London, 1876), pp. 198–200; C. Kerrigan, *History of Tower Hamlets* (London, 1982), pp. 32–7.
17 *Pall Mall Gazette*, 30 August 1877, cited Jones, op. cit., p. 91.
18 G. S. Jones, op. cit., pp. 106–19.
19 H. Pelling, *History of British Trade Unionism* (4th edn., London, 1987), pp. 42–3, 54; on Newton, J. M. Bellamy and J. Saville, *Dictionary of Labour Biography* (London, 1974), II, pp. 270–6; Wright, op. cit. pp. 45–66.
20 J. Lovell, *Stevedores and Dockers* (London, 1972), pp. 60–2; G. S. Jones, op. cit., p. 144.

7 CHURCH AND CHARITY

1 David Goodway, *London Chartism, 1838–1848* (Cambridge, 1982), pp. 83–5, 119–22, 126–7, 273.
2 K. S. Inglis, *Churches and the Working Classes in Victorian England* (London, 1963), pp. 5–6.
3 Report of the House of Lords on *The Deficiency of Means of Spiritual Instruction and Places of Divine Worship etc.* (Parliamentary Papers, 1857–8), IX, pp. 42–7, cited below as PP; *Gentleman's Magazine*, 1840, vol. XIV, pp. 307–8; B. F. L. Clarke, *Church Builders of the Nineteenth Century* (London 1938), pp. 26–7.
4 J. Hollingshead, *Ragged London in 1861* (Everyman Classics, London, 1986), pp. 37 and 40.

5   Goodway, op. cit., pp. 80–91, 95, 139, 264.
6   M. H. Port, *Six Hundred New Churches* (Oxford, 1961), pp. 128–9; PP. p. 132;
    T. Okey, *A Basketful of Memories* (London, 1930), p. 9.
7   F. Engels, *The Condition of the Working Class in England* (ed. E. Hobsbawn,
    London, 1986), pp. 118, 139–408.
8   Owen Chadwick, *The Victorian Church* (London, 1966), I, p. 328; J. R. H.
    Moorman, *A History of the Church in England* (London, rev. edn., 1976),
    p. 360; Hollingshead, op. cit., p. 43.
9   The best modern account is in Chadwick, op. cit., I, pp. 495–501.
10 Extract from the *Church Times* of January 1888 reprinted in the issue of 15
    January 1988.
11 See C. Masterman, *The Heart of the Empire* (London, 1901), p. 29.
12 H. Mayhew, *London Labour and the London Poor* (London, 1851), I, p. 88.
    See also Sheridan Gilley's study, 'Catholic Faith of the Irish Slums' in Dyos
    and Wolff (eds.), *The Victorian City* (London and Boston, Mass., 1973), II,
    pp. 837–53.
13 See A. S. Wohl, *The Eternal Slum* (London, 1977), Chapter 6.
14 D. Owen, *English Philanthropy 1660–1960* (London, 1965) pp. 374–81;
    W. Stern, 'The Baroness's Market; The History of a Noble Failure', *Guildhall
    Miscellany* II (London, 1960–68), pp. 353–5.
15 Wohl, op. cit., pp. 166 and 179–99.
16 For the Salvation Army, see E. Bishop, *Blood and Fire* (London, 1964). On
    Barnardo, see A. E. Williams, *Barnardo of Stepney* (London, 1943) and on
    Charrington, see G. Thorne, *The Great Acceptance* (London, 1912). In general
    see Chapter 3 of W. J. Fishman, *The Streets of East London* (London, 1987).
17 H. O. Barnett, *Canon Barnett: His Life, Work and Friends* (London, 1918), I,
    p. 68; T. Okey, op. cit., p. 36.
18 Wohl, op. cit., pp. 98–105.
19 Ibid., pp. 130–8.
20 J. White, *Rothschild Buildings* (London, 1980), pp. 11–14.
21 Ibid, pp. 16–19; J. Tarn, *Five Per Cent Philanthropy* (London, 1973), pp. 84,
    104–5; Wohl, op. cit., pp. 161, 169.
22 Queen to Gladstone, 30 October 1883, G. E. Buckle (ed.), *Letters of Queen
    Victoria*, second series (London, 1926), III, p. 452.
23 P. Magnus, *King Edward the Seventh* (London, 1964), pp. 179–80; Wohl,
    op. cit., pp. 237–49.
24 Ibid., p. 245, quoting from *Pall Mall Gazette*, 8 May 1885.

8 YEARS OF SENSATION

1   Samuel Barnett 'Sensationalism and Social Reform', *Nineteenth Century*,
    XIX, no. 2, February 1886.
2   Quoted in J. A. R. Pimlott, *Toynbee Hall: Fifty Years of Social Progress, 1883–
    1934* (London, 1935), p. 29. For the impact of *The Bitter Cry* see A. S.
    Wohl, *The Eternal Slum* (London, 1977), pp. 200–20.
3   *The Times*, 26 November 1883.

4   W. Besant, *All Sorts and Conditions of Men* (London 1882), II, p. 52; tennis, I, pp. 212–13, 282.

5   For an entertaining re-assessment of Besant's novel see S. T. Bindoff, 'East End Delight', *East London Papers*, III, no. 1 (April 1960), pp. 31–40. For the Drapers' Company charities, see K. R. Wing, *A History of Bancroft's School 1737–1987* (Woodford Wells, 1987), pp. 1–74.

6   Sims, quoted by Wohl, op. cit., p. 203; A. Mearns, *The Bitter Cry of Outcast London* (London, 1883), pp. 1, 7.

7   A. Briggs and A. Macartney, *Toynbee Hall: The First Hundred Years* (London, 1984), p. 6.

8   K. S. Inglis, *Churches and the Working Classes in Victorian England* (London, 1963), pp. 159–60, 165–6.

9   Briggs and Macartney, op. cit., pp. 76, 153.

10   References to both Lang and slumming, B. Tillett, *Memories and Reflections* (London, 1931), pp. 112–13.

11   *The Times*, 10 February 1886; Queen Victoria to Gladstone, 11 February 1886, Buckle (ed.), *Letters of Queen Victoria* (London, 1926), 3rd series, I, p. 52. See also H. M. Hyndman, *Record of an Adventurous Life* (London, 1911) pp. 400–7.

12   Inglis, op. cit., pp. 272–4. See also the discreetly written biography, F. G. Bettany, *Stewart Headlam* (London, 1926).

13   From Chapter 7 of W. Morris, *News from Nowhere* (London, 1941 edition), p. 60. See also E. P. Thompson, *William Morris: Romantic to Revolutionary* (London, 1955), pp. 568–88.

14   *The Times*, 19 December 1886. See also the report on the inquest of Linnell, *The Times*, 13 December 1886.

15   A. Besant, *An Autobiography* (London, 1893), p. 336.

16   See, *inter alia*: D. Farson, *Jack the Ripper* (London, 1972); S. Knight, *Jack the Ripper: The Final Solution* (London, 1976); R. Pearsall, *The Worm in the Bud* (Pelican edn., Harmondsworth, 1971) pp. 378–87.

17   D. Rumbelow, *The Complete Jack the Ripper* (London, 1975).

18   See Bernard Shaw's entertaining Foreword to Beatrice Webb, *My Autobiography* (Pelican edn., Harmondsworth, 1938), I, p. 10.

19   B. Webb's diary, Ibid, II, p. 349.

20   Champion cited in G. Stedman Jones, *Outcast London* (Oxford, 1971), p. 315. Passages cited as eyewitness accounts are from H. L. Smith and V. Nash, *The Story of the Dockers' Strike (1889)*, told by two East Londoners (London, 1889). See for the links with Thorne and others H. Pelling, *History of British Trade Unionism* (4th edn., Harmondsworth, 1987), pp. 87–90; and in general J. Lovell, *Stevedores and Dockers* (London, 1972), pp. 92–120.

21   Smith and Nash, op. cit., p. 172.

22   Ibid.

23   Tillett, op. cit., p. 134.

24   *Star*, cited by J. Pudney, *London's Docks* (London, 1975), p. 124. Chapter 13 of Pudney's book makes an entertaining narrative of these events.

25   For critical assessments of Tillett's role see J. Schneer, *Ben Tillett* (London,

1982), pp. 40–9 and for the reaction of the dock companies, Stedman Jones, op. cit., pp. 318–19.

9 Strange Exotics

1 W. J. Fishman, *East End Jewish Radicals 1875–1914* (London, 1975), p. 69.
2 V. D. Lipman, *Social History of the Jews in England, 1850–1950* (London, 1954), pp. 27–34 and 79–82; see also *Punch* (London, 1848), XV, p. 140.
3 L. P. Gartner, *The Jewish Immigrant in England, 1870–1914* (London, 1960), pp. 49–51; R. F. Leslie, 'The Background of Jewish Immigration', *East London Papers*, VI (1963), pp. 69–78.
4 Lipman, op. cit., pp. 90–101.
5 C. Booth (ed.), *Life and Labour of the People of London* (1892), I, p. 581.
6 Lipman, op. cit., citing Royal Commission on Alien Immigration, Report, 1903.
7 A. E. Wilson, *East End Entertainment* (London, 1954), pp. 83–92.
8 I. Zangwill, *Children of the Ghetto* (London, 1893), p. 112; Fashion Street reference, ibid., p. 9.
9 V. D. Lipman (ed.), *Three Centuries of Anglo-Jewish History* (London, 1961), p. 113, citing W. Evans Gordon, *The Alien Immigrant* (1903).
10 Fishman, op. cit., p. 77, citing B. Tillett, *The Dock Labourer's Bitter Cry* (1889); Pollard, loc. cit., pp. 81–2.
11 Gartner, op. cit., p. 130; Fishman, op. cit., pp. 183–4.
12 W. Wilkins, *The Alien Invasion* (London, 1892), p. 95.
13 C. Husbands, 'East End racism, 1900–1980: geographical continuities in vigilantist and extreme right wing political behaviour', *London Journal*, VIII (1983), no. 1, pp. 3–26; Paul Foot, *Immigration and Race in British Politics* (London, 1965), pp. 80–102.
14 W. Evans Gordon, 29 January 1902, Hansard, *Parliamentary Debates*, 4th Series, CI, p. 1279–81.
15 Lipman, op. cit., p. 75; K. Leech, 'The Role of Immigration in Recent East London History', *East London Papers*, IX (1967), no. 1, pp. 3–10; R. S. Churchill, *Winston S. Churchill* (London, 1967), II, pp. 81–5.
16 Leaflet cited by P. Foot, op. cit., p. 97.
17 L. Grade, *Dancing Steps* (London, 1987), pp. 19–27; D. Clutterbuck and M. Devine, *Clore: The Man and his Millions* (London, 1987), pp. 3–10.
18 Gartner, op. cit., pp. 231 and 280. See the biographies of Gertler by J. Woodeson (London, 1972) and of Rosenberg by Jean Liddiard (London, 1975).
19 B. Flanagan, *My Crazy Life* (London, 1961) p. 10.
20 C. Russell and H. S. Lewis, *The Jew in London* (London, 1900), p. 176; LCC report of March 1900, cited by A. S. Wohl, *The Eternal Slum* (London, 1977), p. 270; M. Rose, *The East End of London* (London, 1951), pp. 265–7; Zangwill, op. cit., p. 9.
21 Baedeker's *London and its Environs* (Leipzig and London, 1902 edn.), p. 141; H. V. Morton, *The Nights of London* (London, 1926), reprinted in H. V. Morton's *London* (London, 1940), pp. 389–91; K. Leech, loc. cit., pp. 6–7.

22   V. Berridge, 'East End Opium Dens and Narcotic Use in Britain', *London Journal*, IV (1978), no. 1., pp. 3–28; Everyman Library edn. of Rohmer's *The Mystery of Dr Fu Manchu* (London, 1985), with an introduction by D. J. Enright.

23   A. E. Wilson, op. cit., pp. 86 and 90.

24   *The Times*, 21 May 1900.

25   Lipman, op. cit., p. 94.

26   On Rocker, see Fishman, op. cit., pp. 214, 217, 220 and 229–308; his own memoirs of Britain have been published as R. Rocker, *The London Years* (London, 1956).

27   W. Fishman, *The Streets of East London* (London, 1979), p. 124.

28   *The Times*, 12 December 1910. On the Houndsditch Murders, see Colin Rogers, *The Battle of Stepney* (London, 1981), pp. 23–37, which amplifies the earlier material in D. Rumbelow *The Houndsditch Murders and the Siege of Sidney Street* (London 1973).

29   See for the events of 3 January 1911, ibid., pp. 85–120; R. S. Churchill, op. cit., pp. 409–10; Rocker, op. cit., pp. 206–12.

30   See J. P. Eddy, *The Mystery of Peter the Painter* (London, 1946).

31   *The Times*, 5 January 1911.

10 PEACE AND WAR

1   J. Schneer, *Ben Tillett* (London, 1982), p. 160; J. Lovell, *Stevedores and Dockers* (London, 1969), p. 27; A. Bullock, *The Life and Times of Ernest Bevin* (London, 1960), I, pp. 34–5.

2   P. W. Romero, *E. Sylvia Pankhurst: Portrait of a Radical* (New Haven and London, 1987), pp. 68–74.

3   P. S. Foner (ed.), *The Social Writings of Jack London* (Seacacus, N. J., 1964), p. 373, extract from *The People of the Abyss* (1903).

4   Baedeker's *London and its Environs* (Leipzig and London, 1902 edn.), p. 147; C. Poulsen, *Victoria Park* (London, 1976).

5   J. White, *Rothschild Buildings* (London, 1980), p. 85. E. S. Turner, *Dear Old Blighty* (London, 1984), is an evocative survey of this period; C. Lloyd, *Tower Hamlets at War* (London, 1985), pp. 10–11, is an interesting illustrated handbook, available from Tower Hamlets Central Library, Bancroft Road, E1.

6   *Illustrated London News*, 15 August 1914, p. 272.

7   H. Castle, *Fire over England* (London, 1984), pp. 59–60, for Linnartz impressions. This book is the fullest study of the bombing of Britain in the First World War, and has a valuable appendix, giving details of the main raids. See also K. Poolman, *Zeppelins over England* (London, 1960). Military reports on the air raids are in the Air Ministry files at the PRO in Kew.

8   See H. David Behr, 'The Mile End Air Election of 1916', *East London Record*, no. 4 (1981), pp. 2–12.

9   J. White, op. cit., pp. 177–8.

10   Castle, op. cit., pp. 182–5; Lloyd, op. cit., p. 14.

11   L. Grade, *Dancing Steps* (London, 1987), p. 22.

12 D. Lloyd George, *War Memoirs* (Compact edn., London, 1938), II, p. 1105.
13 Romero, op. cit., pp. 99–101; Turner, op. cit. p. 234.
14 'News in Brief' column, *The Times*, 4 September 1917.
15 Michael Paris, *Silvertown 1917* (London, 1986).
16 Inquest reports, *The Times*, 2 and 4 February 1918.
17 J. Pudney, *London's Docks* (London, 1975), p. 153.

11 THE LANSBURY YEARS

1 R. Postgate, *George Lansbury* (London, 1951), provides a biographical background but is reticent about Poplarism. That defect was remedied by Noreen Branson's *Poplarism 1919–1925: George Lansbury and the Councillors' Revolt* (London, 1979); see especially, pp. 32–81 and 232–8. *The Times*, 30 July 1921 and *Daily Herald*, same date, make an interesting contrast in reporting. For cabinet committee deliberations, PRO Cab. 23/26 of 28 July 1921 and Cab. 23/27 of 17 August 1921; cf. Cab. Index E1/14 (Poplar).
2 *Daily Herald*, 26 September 1921, cited by Branson, op. cit., p. 80.
3 Ibid. p. 102; PRO Cab. 24/28, CP 3371 15 October (?) 1921.
4 H. Pelling, *History of British Trade Unionism* (4th edn., London, 1987), pp. 158–69.
5 J. Thorne, *Handbook to the Environs of London* (reprint of 1876 edn., London, 1983), p. 133. For the Becontree estate, see T. Young, *Becontree and Dagenham* (London, 1934).
6 *East London Advertiser*, 6 May 1921, cited by Branson, op. cit., p. 13.
7 M. Rose, *The East End of London* (London, 1951), p. 263.
8 Joe Jacobs, *Out of the Ghetto* (London, 1978), p. 65.
9 Reminiscences of Les White in G. Weightman and S. Humphries, *The Making of Modern London, 1914–1939* (London, 1984), p. 75.
10 G. Jackson, *The History and Archaeology of Ports*, (Tadworth, 1983), pp. 145–7.
11 Ibid., p. 145; John Pudney, *London's Docks* (London, 1975) p. 157.
12 D. Hardey and C. Ward, *Arcadia for All* (London, 1984); Weightman and Humphries, op. cit., pp. 115–17.
13 Jacobs, op. cit., p. 60.
14 Colin Cross, *The Fascists in Britain* (London, 1961), pp. 49, 52, 103, 119; N. Nicolson (ed.), *Harold Nicolson, Diaries and Letters 1930–39* (London, 1966), pp. 87–9.
15 R. Thurlow, *Fascism in Britain* (Oxford, 1987), pp. 119–62.
16 C. Husbands, 'East End racism, 1900–1980; geographical continuities in vigilantist and extreme right wing political behaviour', *London Journal*, VIII (1983), no. 1, pp. 3–26; street analysis in R. Skidelsky's contribution to K. Lunn and R. C. Thurlow (eds.) *British Fascism: Essays on the Radical Right in Inter-War Britain* (London, 1980), p. 92.
17 N. Deakin, 'The Vitality of a Tradition' in C. Holmes (ed.), *Immigrants and Minorities in British Society* (London, 1978), pp. 158–85.
18 A. Boyle, *Trenchard* (London, 1962), pp. 652–3, citing HO144/20158:

Trenchard (1934) 107; Game (1936) 155–62; violence reports, Thurlow, op. cit., p. 110.

19 Cross, op. cit., p. 160; Thurlow, op. cit., pp. 110–12.

20 Cross, op. cit., p. 160. Several books wrongly give the date of the Battle of Cable Street as 5 October. For contemporary accounts see Jacobs, op. cit., pp. 254–6 and P. Piratin, *Our Flag Stays Red* (rev. edn. London, 1978), pp. 19–26; O. Mosley, *My Life* (London, 1968), ignores it.

21 Cross, op. cit., p. 161.

22 Ibid., pp. 166–7.

23 For Lansbury's peace mission and last years see Postgate, op. cit., pp. 311–26.

12 TARGET AREA A

1 L. Mosley, *Backs to the Wall* (London, 1971), pp. 17–18; Terence H. O'Brien, *Civil Defence* (London, 1955), pp. 281–2 for first air raid alerts and pp. 99–200 for the ARP Act and its consequences. Throughout this chapter I have also used my own recollections and occasional diary jottings.

2 R. M. Titmus, *Problems of Social Policy* (London, 1950), pp. 143–7. This splendid volume in the official History of the Second World War is a mine of information on the problems of the wartime social services.

3 Ibid., p. 357.

4 *The Times*, 24 February and 14 June 1940; R. Thurlow, *Fascism in Britain* (Oxford, 1987), p. 191.

5 Luftwaffe situation reports to OKM (High Command of the German Navy), 9 and 10 September 1940 cited in R. Wheatley, *Operation Sea Lion* (Oxford, 1958), p. 77. See also M. Gilbert, *Finest Hour: Winston S. Churchill 1939–1941*, p. 757.

6 O'Brien, op. cit., pp. 388–9; Mosley, op. cit., pp. 103–20; C. Fitzgibbon, *The Blitz* (London, 1957), pp. 44–78.

7 Reminiscences of Emily Golder, printed in Joanna Mack and Steve Humphries, *London at War* (London, 1985), p. 75.

8 Ibid., p. 50; Mosley, op. cit., pp. 129–30; Fitzgibbon, pp. 74–6.

9 O'Brien, op. cit., p. 392.

10 Titmuss, op. cit., p. 357.

11 P. Piratin, *Our Flag Stays Red* (rev. edn., London, 1978) pp. 73–5; Mosley, ibid., pp. 173–6; Fitzgibbon, ibid, pp. 108–11 (very hostile to Piratin); PRO Cab. 65/9/250 p. 66, N. Nicolson (ed.), *Harold Nicolson Diaries and Letters 1939–45* (London, 1967), p. 114.

12 PRO Infa/265; HO 203/4, Intelligence Reports, September 1940; Cab. 65/9/246 p. 46, 10 September 1940; Gilbert, op. cit. p. 774.

13 W. Shirer, *The Rise and Fall of the Third Reich* (London, 1960), p. 769.

14 John Pudney, *London's Docks* (London, 1975), pp. 167–8; G. Jackson, *History and Archaeology of Ports* (Tadworth, 1983), p. 157.

15 See the Mass Observation Reports cited by Philip Ziegler, *Crown and People* (London, 1978), p. 76.

16 O'Brien, op. cit., p. 419; Home Security War Diary, 11 May 1941, ibid, pp. 688–9; personal recollection.

17 Ibid, p. 677.

18 Titmus, op. cit., p. 281.

19 PRO Cab. 65/33/38 p. 150; report by Laurence Dunne, cited by M. Gilbert, *Winston Churchill* (London 1986), vol. VII, p. 354.

20 On flying bombs and rockets in general see David Johnson, *V for Vengeance* (London, 1981); PRO HO193/53; O'Brien, op. cit., pp. 653–7.

21 Ibid., p. 665; R. V. Jones, *Most Secret War* (London, 1978) pp. 458–9.

22 Angus Calder, *The People's War* (London, 1971), p. 649.

23 M. Gilbert, op. cit., vol. VII, p. 1219.

24 R. Glass and M. Frenkel 'How They Live at Bethnal Green', *Contact: Britain between West and East* (London, 1946), p. 43.

13 Labouring On

1 G. Jackson, *History and Archaeology of Ports* (Tadworth, 1983), p. 157. For a judicious assessment of the work of the Attlee administrations see H. Pelling, *The Labour Governments 1945–51* (London, 1984).

2 Paul Addison, *Now the War is Over* (London, 1985), pp. 76–9; LCC report, *East End Housing* (London, 1964); 'The Lansbury Story', *East London Papers*, III (1960), pp. 67–86.

3 F. J. Osborn and A. Whittick, *New Towns: Their Origins, Achievements and Progress* (London and Boston, 1977): pp. 165–79 for Harlow; pp. 203–19 for Basildon.

4 M. Young and P. Willmott, *Family and Kinship in East London* (Rev. edn. Harmondsworth, 1986), especially pp. 44–61.

5 Ibid., p. xx.

6 Ibid., p. 124.

7 John R. Short, *Housing in Britain; The Post-War Experience* (London, 1982), p. 109.

8 Ibid.

9 H. Goorney, *The Theatre Workshop Story* (London, 1981), pp. 72 ff.

10 *The Daily Telegraph*, 19 August 1963, cited by K. Leech 'The Decay of Spitalfields', *East London Papers*, VII (1964), p. 57.

11 For the Krays in general see John Pearson, *The Profession of Violence: The Rise and Fall of the Kray Twins* (London, 1972), with references to the Kentucky Club in 1962 on p. 103. For their services to charity see Charles Kray, *Me and My Brothers* (London, 1976), pp. 134–5.

12 The books by Pearson and Charles Kray mentioned above may be supplemented by Leslie Payne, *The Brotherhood* (London, 1973).

13 C. Husbands, 'East End racism, 1900–1980; geographical continuities in vigilantist and extreme right-wing political behaviour', *London Journal*, VIII (1983), no. 1, pp. 3–26, especially pp. 14–22 and on the *East London Blackshirt*, p. 25.

14 Husbands's article loc. cit., supplemented by J. Bartley and I. Gordon,

'London at the Polls: The 1981 GLC Election Results', ibid, pp. 39–59, with a National Front analysis on p. 51.

15 K. Leech, *Brick Lane 1978: The Events and Their Significance* (Birmingham, 1980); and Husbands's article, loc. cit.

16 G. Jackson, op. cit., pp. 151–6; John Pudney, *London's Docks* (London, 1975), pp. 175–6; R. Rees, 'The Port of London and Economic Change', *East London Papers*, X (1967), pp. 109–24.

17 See the reminiscences of Ivan Greeves, 'The Work of the Dock Engineer' in the North East London Polytechnic's survey, *Dockland* (London, 1986), pp. 47–57, especially, pp. 48–9.

18 Ibid., pp. 54–7.

19 Antony Hugill, *Sugar and All That: A History of Tate & Lyle* (London, 1978); S. Humphries and J. Taylor *The Making of Modern London, 1945–1985* (London, 1986), pp. 3, 15, 19.

20 Ibid., p. 20.

21 J. Pudney, op. cit., pp. 178–81; G. Jackson, op. cit., p. 159.

14 TRANSFORMATION SCENE?

1 Docklands Joint Committee, *London's Docklands: A Strategic Plan* (London, 1976), p. 29.

2 GLC Docklands *Progress Report* (London, 1978); see also Docklands Development Organisation, *The Largest Redevelopment Scheme in Europe*, (London, 1980).

3 G. Jackson, *The History and Archaeology of Ports* (Tadworth, 1983), p. 157; *Docklands News*, no. 6, August 1983.

4 M. Young, H. Young, E. Shuttleworth and W. Tucker, *Report from Hackney* (London, 1981).

5 A. Holme, *Housing and Young Families in East London* (London, 1985).

6 A. Briggs and A. Macartney, *Toynbee Hall: The First Hundred Years* (London, 1984) pp. 155–6.

7 *Church Times*, 20 May, 1988, p. 8.

8 David Sheppard, *Parson's Pitch* (London, 1966).

9 J. Groser, *Politics and Person* (London, 1944); K. Brill, *John Groser: East London Priest* (London, 1971); J. Williamson, *Father Joe* (London, 1961).

10 See the pamphlet by O. Hedley, *The Royal Foundation of Saint Katharine in Ratcliffe* (London, 1987).

11 Speech by E. Heath, 11 April 1984, Hansard, *Parliamentary Debates* (Sixth Series), vol. 58, p. 424.

12 *Docklands News*, no. 7, September 1983 and no. 8 October 1983.

13 Ibid., no. 10, December 1983.

14 Plans were outlined in *The Independent* on 30 March 1988. The fullest architectural survey and critical analysis for Canary Wharf and the whole of Docklands on both sides of the Thames is Elizabeth Williamson and Nikolaus Pevsner, with Malcolm Tucker, *London Docklands* (Penguin Books, 'The Building of England', London, 1998). Also of great interest is Alan Cox, *Docklands in the Making: The Redevelopment of the Isle of Dogs, 1981–95*

(London, 1995).

15 Bill Risebero, 'Architecture in East London', in Tim Butler and Michael
    Rustin, eds., *Rising in the East? The Regeneration of East London* (London,
    1996), p. 224. M. Hebbert, 'One "Planning Disaster" after Another:
    London Docklands 1970–1992', *London Journal*, vol. 17, no. 2 (1992), is
    also highly critical.
16 E. Williamson, op. cit., pp. 123–4. I have also found this book invaluable for
    the following paragraph.
17 *Docklands News*, no. 5, July 1983.
18 Ibid., no. 26, June 1985. *The Times*, 9 May 1998, Weekend Section, p. 10.
19 *Docklands News*, no. 50, August 1987, and *The Independent*, 27 July 1987,
    for the opening of the DLR. For later DLR and Jubilee Line development see
    E. Williamson, op. cit., pp. 40–1, 54, 100, 184, 253 and 259.
20 *Docklands News*, nos. 54, 55, 56, November and December 1987, January
    1988.
21 *Daily Telegraph*, 12 August 1987. For the following section (on the Wapping
    dispute), I used newspaper files for 1986 and early 1987.
22 On the vicissitudes of the Half Moon Theatre, Bill Risebero's contribution to
    Butler and Rustin, *Rising in the East*, is enlightening: see pp. 221 and
    228–9.
23 *Docklands News*, no. 1, March 1983.
24 N.K. Krupskaya, *Memories of Lenin* (London, 1970), p. 65. Disraeli first used
    the 'two nations' social distinction of 'the rich and the poor' in 1845 as a
    sub-title for *Sybil*, his High Tory novel of Chartist England.
25 Jane Cox, *London's East End: Life and Traditions* (Phoenix Illustrated edition,
    London, 1997), p. 131; a fascinating book, attractively produced.
26 *The Times*, 2 July 1987; Prince Charles in Limehouse, *East London
    Advertiser*, 11 December 1987.
27 *Hackney Gazette & North London Advertiser*, 11 May 1982.
28 Early comments on the Spitalfields proposals, *The Times*, 28 May 1986;
    special articles in *Sunday Times*, 5 July 1987, and *The Times*, 7 August
    1987. For City of London approval of development plans, see *The Times*, 24
    October 1987, and *Financial Times*, 24 October 1987.

Index